Malmesbury's Past, People and Places

by
Charles Vernon

Malmesbury Civic Trust

Published by
Malmesbury Civic Trust
Chalcourt, Dark Lane, Malmesbury, SN16 0BB

Printed by
CPI Antony Rowe
Bumper's Farm Industrial Estate, Chippenham, SN14 6LH

Front cover: The Market Cross decorated to commemorate Queen Victoria's Golden Jubilee in 1887. The Green Dragon Inn can be seen to its left and partly hidden on the right is the Prince and Princess. The building with the shuttered ground floor windows had been a Reading Room but since the opening of the one in Silver Street was in use as a Sunday School. Both of these would be demolished 10 years later to make way for the Cottage Hospital.

ISBN 978-0-9536692-4-0

Introduction and acknowledgments

This is my third general history book about the town of Malmesbury beginning with *Malmesbury Then and Now* in 1999, followed by *An Historical Guide to Malmesbury* of 2005. Unfortunately both of these contained errors and I hope this book contains less! It has been very long in preparation but should record changes up to the summer of 2014.

There are a number of works which describe our ancient and medieval history but the past two centuries are not so well covered so that is the period which forms the main theme here. For events which occurred from the early 19th until the end of the 20th Century researchers are able to consult the comprehensive and accurate material available in local newspapers. Since then the matters reported have changed and it is difficult to know how future historians will be able to obtain the same level of detail, the digital world being so ephemeral. So once again I am grateful for the past diligence of the reporters who worked for the Wilts and Gloucestershire Standard, Wiltshire Gazette, North Wilts Herald and the Wiltshire Gazette & Herald.

Photographs have been obtained not only from the extensive archive maintained by Malmesbury Civic Trust but also from those held by Athelstan Museum and many private collections. Recently the Malmesbury Chronicles have come to light. In the main this comprises a large collection of photographs taken in the mid 1980s by a team led by Tristan Forward. Unfortunately very few of the negatives have been printed and less than half have been indexed. It is now difficult to print black and white film so it would be beneficial to tranfer them into a digital format. This is a task which will take some time to complete.

It has been very difficult to choose which people, places and organisations to cover and to determine how much detail should be included. So, for example, only the High Street shops between the Market Cross and Kingswall are described and even for this relatively small number it has proved difficult to find full information.

A comprehensive index is provided but even there selection has been necessary. Readers are therefore urged to examine every page! There are many people who ought to be thanked for their help but the research process has stretched over such a long period and I am such a poor notetaker that I am unable to remember you all, but please accept my heart-felt thanks. I am deeply indebted to my wife Val for her meticulous proof-reading which has greatly improved the text.

Charles Vernon

Contents

Places of Worship

The establishment of the monastery marks the start of Malmesbury's written history. The monastery created many chapels but their location is unknown and no traces of them remain. Some of the dedications were to: St. Saviour; St. Mary, probably the predecessor of the present Church; St. Peter & St. Paul; St. Michael, remembered by St. Michael's House adjacent to the ruined Abbey tower; and St. Andrew, said to be the burial place of many Abbots. Outside the Abbey precincts there was a nunnery in Burnivale, closed amidst scandal in the 13th Century; All Saints chapel in the High Street; the Priory of St. John the Baptist near the Town Bridge; the Hospital of St. Mary Magdelen at Burton Hill; and a Carthusian friary at Whitchurch, amongst others.

After dissolution Malmesbury became a centre for many denominations of Nonconformists, a word first used following the Act of Uniformity 1662 meaning not conforming to the established Church of England. In the 19th and early 20th Century friction between the different denominations was exacerbated by the reintroduction of Roman Catholicism. Notwithstanding this, local well-to-do families provided financial support to churches other than those which they attended.

The Benedictine Monastery of Malmesbury

This institution was the source of the town's prosperity for 850 years. It is said that Maildulph, an Irish monk, around 637-642 established a hermitage near the fortification called Bladon, the remains of a previous settlement. There are over 30 ways of spelling his name ranging from Maildulph, sometimes without the 'l'. Old English offered different spellings and documents written in Norman French or Latin created further variants in translation. The hermitage is believed to have been in Burnivale below the fortification on top of the ridge. Maildulph started a school which developed a community around it to support the scholars. Thus the town grew and its name is thought to be derived from his.

Aldhelm (c639-709) was sent to Malmesbury to study under Maildulph, after initially being educated at Canterbury by Abbot Hadrian who had recently arrived in the country to spread the teachings of the Roman Church. Aldhelm was related to King Ine of Wessex and proved to be a great scholar, a remarkable preacher and renowned writer of riddles. He was appointed first Abbot of the Benedictine Monastery in 675. He travelled to Rome where his host, Pope Sergius, was rumoured to be the father of a new born baby. Aldhelm (no doubt anxious to please!) asked the infant in the Pope's presence if this allegation was true. The child, all but nine days old, replied in a clear voice that Sergius was holy and undefiled. This miracle established Aldhelm's reputation but was only one of many attributed to him. For example when returning from Rome he brought back a slab of marble. En route the animal carrying it, probably a camel, fell, injuring itself and breaking the slab. After a prayer the animal was healed and the marble repaired although there was a vein in the stone where the break had been. Whilst on his travels Aldhelm was given and also bought many holy relics which he brought back to Malmesbury. He corresponded with the foremost centres of learning of the time in Bonn, Cologne, Paris and Pisa. Journeys to these places were formidable undertakings and must have taken a considerable time, so the correspondence must have been of some importance. Due to his royal connections and the fact that the town stood near the border of Wessex and Mercia, the monastery estates were vastly expanded mainly through gifts from the rival kings. It became the most important Abbey in southern England. When Aldhelm died in 709, although by then the Bishop of Sherborne, he was brought back from Doulting, Somerset for burial in Malmesbury. The town then became a centre for pilgrimage with many more miracles said to have occurred both at his shrine and at the places where his body had rested along the route from where he died. After Archbishop Lanfranc, a sceptical Norman, heard of the miraculous cure of a crippled boy named Folkwine in

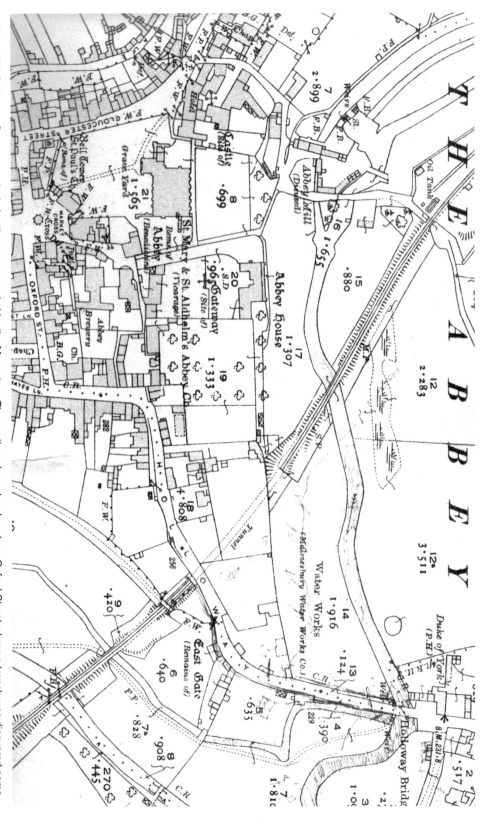

This 1921 Ordnance Survey map includes the area occupied by the Monastery. The southern boundary lay along Oxford Street where a trench was discovered some years ago during the installation of a new gas pipe. Abbot Colerne gave the area around the Market Cross to the townsfolk after the townsfolk had encroached upon it.

Malmesbury, Aldhelm was declared a Saint in 1080.

Lullus (c710-786) was one of Malmesbury's early monks who went on a pilgrimage to Rome in 737. There he met St. Boniface and was persuaded to become a missionary in northern Germany. He became Archbishop of Mainz around 754 and re-established the monastery at Bad Hersfeld in 769 which had been founded 30 years before. St. Lullus (he was canonised in 852) is regarded as being that town's founder and a week-long festival is held there in his honour every October.

During King Alfred's reign between 871 and 901 John Scotus, (probably Irish but at this period Irishmen were often referred to as Scots) a man of clear understanding and amazing eloquence, came to teach at the monastery. He came from the Court of King Charles the Bald of France and William of Malmesbury tells a tale about his time there: *He was seated one day opposite the king at another part of the table. As the cup went round and the dishes disappeared Charles, whose face was a little flushed with wine, seeing John do something which might offend French fastidiousness, chaffingly said, 'What is it that stands between a Sot and a Scot?' John threw back the insinuation on to its author by replying, 'The matter of a table only!'* He suffered a curious death when he was fatally stabbed by his students with their styli (pens).

Around 1010 a monk named Eilmer (c984-c1066) is said to have made the first flight. William of Malmesbury's *Gesta Regnum Anglorum* (The Deeds of the English Kings) translated by Professor Lynn White described it thus; *He had by some means, I scarcely know what, fastened wings to his hands and feet so that, mistaking fable for truth, he might fly like Daedalus and, collecting the breeze on the summit of a tower, he flew for more than the distance of a furlong. But, agitated by the violence of the wind and the swirling of the air, as well as by awareness of his rashness, he fell, broke his legs and was lame ever after. He himself used to say that the cause of his failure was his forgetting to put a tail on his back part.* However the Abbot forbade him from trying again and he lived to be an old man.

Little is known about William of Malmesbury (c1095-c1143). Most information comes from casual references to his own experiences in his writing. He certainly spent his early life in the town. His father was probably Norman and wealthy enough to afford books which assisted William's education. At an early age William entered the monastery and was soon helping Godfrey of Jumièges (Abbot from 1081 to 1106) to improve the library. It was not long before he started writing his own works. Queen Mathilda, widow of William the Conqueror, charged Malmesbury monastery with the production of a history of the Kings of England. This became William's *Gesta Regnum Anglorum*, which was researched by him travelling the kingdom and was first published in 1125. The first edition of *Gesta Pontificum Anglorum*, the story of various Bishops, the fifth book of which covered the life of St. Aldhelm, was completed the same year. William was particularly well-read being familiar with over 400 works written by 200 authors, so no doubt the Library was well stocked when he became Librarian. Around 1129 he visited Glastonbury and wrote about local saints which he followed with the *Antiquity of Glastonbury*. In that same year he produced a summary of Roman imperial history. He revised *Gesta Regnum* after 1135 and then worked on its continuation, the *Historia Novella*. Although he was a prolific author few of his works still exist as the monastery library was largely destroyed at Dissolution. Towards the end of his life he became Precentor (the official in charge of music) of the Abbey, apparently having turned down the Abbacy. It is not known when he died but it is believed to have been shortly after the last recorded event (1142) in his writings.

Abbey Church of Saint Mary and Saint Aldhelm, Church of England
The great builder, Bishop Roger of Sarum (d1139) probably planned the present building, the third Abbey Church, which was begun in the first half of the 12th Century and consecrated in 1180. At that time the estates of the Abbey were huge and as such demanded a magnificent

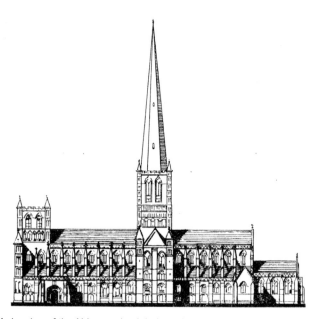

A drawing of the Abbey as it might have been in the 14th Century by R. E. Woodman.

headquarters. Its architecture is typical of the late Norman period with large circular pillars, rounded archways over the windows and doors with pointed arches, a newer style, between the pillars of the nave. The porch entrance is particularly fine, although showing the ravages of time. The outer archway is about 18 feet wide. The lower outer parts depict Virtues conquering Vices, with what are believed to be signs of the Zodiac and Labours of the Months shown on the inner two lower columns. Thirty-eight scenes from the Old and New Testaments adorn the upper semicircles of the arch. They begin at the innermost left arch with the Creation of Adam and end with Pentecost on the outer right arch. Inside the porch there is a vision of the Lord in Majesty over the doorway and carvings of six Apostles on each side. The work was carried out by a band of Norman masons and very similar work has been identified in Yorkshire.

Further work was completed during the 14th Century including the raising of the roof to replace the wooden timbers with stone vaulting, new windows and the addition of a spire. At the end of that century a square tower was built over the two western bays of the nave and shortly afterwards the parvise was added above the south porch. The building was very much bigger than at present. The central spire, approximately 430 feet tall and higher than Salisbury's, had a wooden framework covered with lead. This spectacularly fell towards the end of the 15th Century (although the 20th Century architect Brakspear believed it was around 1535). The cause is unknown but one theory is that it was struck by lightning and the discharge of energy in wet stonework at its base might have been similar to an explosion. The fall effectively demolished the eastern end and provided a local source of building stone – many carved decorative stones can be seen all around the town. As a result more than half of the Church was lost. Nothing was done to rebuild the lost parts other than to erect a wall at the eastern end of the nave.

After the Dissolution in 1539, William Stumpe (c1490-1552) bought the Abbey and outbuildings for £1516 15s. 2½d., a huge sum in those days. He was born at North Nibley (near Wotton under Edge) where his father was a weaver who became a clothier and parish clerk. William started out as a weaver and it is not clear how he earned his fortune but by 1524 he was one of the four richest men in Malmesbury. His eldest son James married Bridget, daughter of Sir Edward Baynton. Baynton took over the Abbey in December 1539 on behalf of the King. William Stumpe acted as his deputy dealing with those properties which he subsequently bought! Leland, Henry VIII's clerk of property, reported that *every corner of the vaste Houses of Office that belonged to T'Abbay be fulle of lumbes to weve clooth yn and this Stumpe entendith to make a strete or two for clothiers in the bak vacant ground of the Abbay that is within the towne Waulles.* This development never took place. Leland also said that the town was producing 3,000 cloths per year. By this time St. Paul's, the parish church, was in a very poor state and Stumpe gave the Abbey church to the town The licence to use it as a parish church was issued in 1541. St. Paul's steeple is now used as the Abbey's bell-tower. Stumpe was a very important man in Wiltshire being one of perhaps a dozen gentlemen chosen to govern the county. On his death he owned a vast estate of properties from Tewkesbury in the north to Warminster in the south.

It is not known when the west Tower of the Abbey collapsed but it was probably unstable when built as the nave had not been designed to accommodate it. The addition of bells hung from it following the fall of the main spire would have not helped. This second calamity seems to have occurred in the first quarter of the 17th Century (although Brakspear thought it was some 50 years earlier). No attempt was made to repair it, instead the nave was shortened by two bays and another new wall erected, leaving just one third of the original building. Part of the remains of the central Tower fell in 1660. 4 arches are shown on the 1648 Bird's Eye map. John Aubrey (1626-97, an antiquarian brought up at Easton Piercy) noted that during celebrations to celebrate the King's restoration *were so many and so great vollies of shot, by the inhabitants of the Hundred, that the noise so shook the pillars of the Tower, that one pillar and the two parts above fell that night.* Improvements started in 1822 including a new Gothic window in the west end, the floor being raised to cover the square bases of the pillars, the triforium arcade repaired and the high pews removed. Walter Powell MP paid for gas lighting to be installed in 1875. More work was carried out at the beginning of the 20th Century, as parts of the structure were dangerous. The Bishop of Bristol, Forrest Brown, took it upon himself to raise the necessary funds. Two ruined bays at the west end, threatening the porch, were rebuilt and the roof continued over them. The ruined south western turret was completed and the walkway on the roof made accessible. Begun in 1899 and completed in 1912 this work cost £4,850 and was overseen by Harold Brakspear (1870-1934). This was the first project he had carried out on a major building and established his reputation.

In July 1927 the Abbey was closed to allow further renovation, again supervised by Mr. Brakspear. The gas lighting had blackened the stonework and scaffolding was erected inside the Abbey so

The west end of the Abbey just before the rebuilding started. The base of the gas lamp is still in place today.

The interior of the Abbey, 1864.

that this could be scrubbed clean. Two large coal fired cauldrons either side of the nave which consumed ½ ton of coal each Sunday (but seemed to make little difference to the temperature) were removed. The organ was moved from the west end to its present position. The floor was lowered and the pews replaced with seats. Major General Richard Luce (1867-1952) broadcast an appeal for funds on the wireless, the very first time that this had been done. A £7,000 bequest, which enabled repairs to start, ran out (£14,000 was spent in all) and a Carnival in 1928 was devoted to the restoration fund. A service was held on 6th December 1928 to re-hallow the Abbey. Repairs to the roof had to be started after a piece of plaster fell down in March 1934. Sir Harold (he was knighted after work at Windsor Castle in 1931) prepared the initial report but he died on 20 November 1934 and his son Oswald took over. The work including the restoration of the original colours on some of the roof bosses was completed by November 1935. Many repairs and improvements have been carried out since such as a new organ in the 1980s costing £71,000 followed by £40,000 spent on a new heating system.

Having been blessed with another large legacy, further works have been undertaken including the complete renewal of the internal and external lighting in 2003. A major project to remodel the west end to provide a place for meetings, a facility for refreshments and toilets was considered for some years but the cost of around £3 million proved an obstacle too great to overcome. Maintenance of this ancient building is continuous and expensive so donations are gratefully received. Further information about the Abbey can be obtained from the Stewards in the Abbey and the guidebooks available there.

On the death of King Athelstan (c895-939) in line with his wishes, his body was brought to the town for burial. Grandson of Alfred and eldest son of Edward the Elder, Athelstan became the first King of England. On his father's death he took the crown of Mercia. Within a fortnight his half-brother died allowing him to take over Wessex and in 927 he conquered the Viking kingdom of York. Coins minted in Malmesbury proclaimed that Athelstan was ruler of all England. He generously donated more gifts to our Monastery (details are given in Sir Richard Luce's book, *The History of the Abbey and Town of Malmesbury*) and held court in Malmesbury. He had a residence here although its location is not known so the town might lay claim to be the first capital of England. The tomb in the Abbey is believed to be medieval and it is unlikely it ever contained his body.

St. Helen's Chapel, 23 Bristol Road

In the 10th or early 11th Century this was a small single cell chapel and is probably the oldest building in the town. It was set high on a natural stone platform close to the north of the Saxon Kingway, a road connecting Royal properties, which came up Harpers Lane from a ford across the river. The large original corner stones can be seen together with the mass dial to the right of the door. It was substantially rebuilt in the 17th Century into a cottage and further additions have been made in the past 50 years.

Saint Paul's Church, Birdcage Walk

It appears there was a church on this site during the late Saxon period but the last building here probably dated from the late 12th or 13th Centuries. The tower was probably added in the 14th Century during refurbishment.

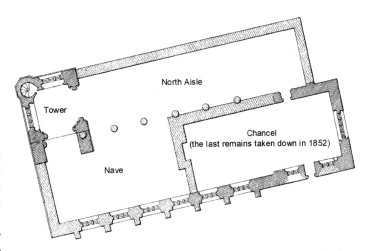

The plan of St. Paul's Church. The darker shaded areas of wall still exist.

However by the time of the Dissolution the fabric was falling into disrepair and the nave was badly damaged. The Chancel at the east end was used as civic offices whilst the tower was part of a private house. Later the area of the main body of the building, now called Birdcage Walk, was used as a lumber yard until all was finally demolished in 1852. The Chancel's south wall was reused as the back wall of buildings on the north side of Gloucester Street, the outlines of windows and doorways are still visible.

The tower is now used as the Abbey's belfry. Curiously when the Abbey was a separate parish, the bells of St. Paul's called its parishioners to worship in another! There are eight bells, the oldest of which is the treble inscribed *Sancte Georgei ora pro nobis* (Saint George, pray for us), however its exact age is unknown but may be earlier than the 16th Century. Two others date from the following century. Whitechapel Bell Foundry carried out a major restoration in 1910. Malmesbury is fortunate in having an enthusiastic group of bellringers who raised a large sum of money in 1951 to purchase 3 new bells and retune the rest. The clock was made by Henry Weight in 1858 in his premises in what is now called Griffin Alley. A modern electric mechanism was added in 1952.

St. Mary's Hall, Westport

John Aubrey described the original as *a prettie church, where there were very good windows and a fair steeple, higher than the other* (St. Paul's – the present belfry) *which much adorned the toune of Malmesbury; in it were five tuneable bells, which Sir Wm. Waller melted into Ordnance or rather sold; and the church was pilled down that the enemie might not shelter themselves against the garrison of Malmesbury. The church was dedicated to St. Mary. Here were three aisles, which took the whole area. It is reported to have been more ancient than the Abbey. In the windows, which were very good, were inscriptions which declared as much*. His description of the replacement in 1680 was *now is here rebuilt a church like a stable*.

The southern aisle was added in 1840. 70 years later the floor was renewed with the pews and a three-decker pulpit removed. At the reopening the vicar remarked there had been a danger the congregation might have been *precipitated some three feet below to continue their worship*! The church was closed in 1946 and soon after the perimeter stone wall was lowered to improve visibility at the junction. It was used as a grammar school classroom during the late 1940s and became the Church Hall in 1977. The graveyard for St. Mary's Church was in Burnham Road but was deconsecrated when Hudson Road was developed. In 2003 the 1st Malmesbury (King Athelstan) Scouts bought the building and it has since been used as a community hall.

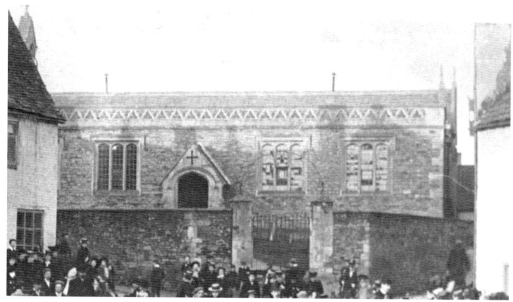

St. Mary's Church in 1901 showing the high walls, lowered in 1948.

United Reformed Church (Westport Congregational Church), St. Mary's Street,

The Rev. S. Gawen, vicar of St. Paul's, felt the Act of Uniformity 1662, intended to compel all clergymen to give their assent to the Book of Common Prayer, was unjust and along with 2,000 other ministers gave up his living. If he did not found the Westport Congregational Church he was its first minister but died in 1671. It is thought the first chapel was built soon after 1689. This building stood near the site of the present building in St. Mary's Street and was reached through an archway above which stood two cottages. The original chapel was rebuilt in 1788 and enlarged in 1828. The church was Presbyterian from its formation until 1811 when most English Presbyterian Churches were renamed Congregational. The present building with a large schoolroom was erected in 1867 for £1,933. During the 1930s the church sent missions to a daughter chapel in Corston. Unfortunately that chapel closed in July 1943. During the 1950s members of the cast of the Archers BBC radio serial attended annual church fetes including Chris Gittings who played Walter Gabriel in 1957. The church was closed for several weeks in 1959 to allow redecoration and extensive alterations to be carried out including enlarging the vestibule and creating a children's corner. In 1963 the choir were given permission to wear robes becoming one of the few in their denomination to do so. The Congregational Church merged with the Presbyterians from 5th October 1972 to form the United Reformed Church. In the following January Malmesbury's first female minister, Stella Beare, was appointed. During 1992 further major alterations costing £80,000 were made to the interior of the church, particularly on the ground floor. At the same time the spire, which had been struck by lightning during the war, was repaired.

Unusually for a Nonconformist Church the building features a number of stained glass windows. High on the eastern wall is the Rose Window gifted by Charles Jupe, the main financier of the 1867 rebuilding. Below this is a triptych made by Swaine Bourne, an evangelical craftsman of the Arts & Crafts movement and installed here early in the 20th Century. A memorial window to the Adye family is in the south wall with the Clark and Ponting families commemorated in the north wall together with a window commemorating four men of the congregation who died in the Second World War which has recently been repaired.

In 1869 two cottages between the Church and St. Mary's Street were demolished. One of these is believed to have been the home of Thomas Hobbes (1588-1679). Hobbes was born prematurely on Good Friday when the Armada threatened the country. Neither of his parents was distinguished; his father (also Thomas) was curate of Brokenborough. He was practically illiterate and a drunkard but a great card player. Such was his enthusiasm that he often fell asleep in church and had to be roused by his Clerk. There were also complaints that he failed to attend services. Unfortunately one day he struck and nearly killed the vicar of Foxley who apparently simply wanted to talk about his son's education. He was forced to flee to London where he died in obscurity years later.

After attending a church school for two years, the younger Hobbes attended a grammar school in the Sheepfair, now the Triangle. The master, Robert Latimer was described by Aubrey as

The United Reformed Church showing the stained glass windows in the east wall.

'a good Grecian', who being a Bachelor (of Arts), not above 19, taught him and two or three ingeniose laddes after supper till 9, at his own house in Westport, where the broad place is, next door north from the Smyth's shop opposite the Three Cuppes, as I take it; by whom he so well profited that at 14 years old he went, a good scholar, to Magdalene Hall in Oxford and before he went did translate Euripidis Medea out of Greek into Latin iambiques. Hobbes did not think much of Oxford but in 1607 obtained a Bachelor's degree. After that he became tutor to the teenaged (and married) William Cavendish and served three generations of the earls of Devonshire.

He travelled extensively throughout Europe with his aristocratic patrons and met Galileo in 1630. Hobbes was a vigorous proponent of scientific materialism and it was his regret that he was considered to be a philosopher rather than a scientist. He maintained a lively correspondence with other great men like Francis Bacon, Descartes, Fermat and Ben Jonson. *Leviathan* (1651) was his greatest work in which it is argued that as people are inherently selfish they need to be ruled by an absolute civil power to enforce public order. However his works often contained anti-monarchist sentiment and it is fortunate that he tutored the future Charles II in maths whilst in exile in France. The King later granted him a pension of £100 per annum and hung Hobbes' portrait in the Royal Closet. Hobbes was proud of his birthplace and always used the style Thomas Hobbes of Malmesbury in his books. He died in 1679 and is buried in Ault Hucknall Church, Derbyshire.

Baptist Chapel, 23 Abbey Row
This congregation was formed about 1688. They quickly established the practice of baptism in the river near to Mill Lane which drew many onlookers. Rev. Jenkins described one such

The Abbey Row Baptist Chapel. The cottage on the left was demolished c1955. The wall plaque showing the date of building and modification was defaced in 2013.

occasion; *Throngs of people had gathered together to witness the ceremony, the hill forming a splendid vantage ground giving most of the onlookers a view of the minister. There were also present several young men of "the baser sort," who, to all appearances, were bent on turning the proceedings into sport. The minister hearing their rude laughter and anticipating their mischievous designs cried out to them loud enough for all to hear, "There will be no laughing in hell!" and with this unexpected rebuke the young men ceased their jestings and upon the whole assembly there rested a felt silence.* The Baptists originally met in a small building in Abbey Row later used for stabling. The present building was put up in 1802, enlarged by adding galleries in 1814, the north end lengthened in 1816 and the whole refurbished in 1910. After the death of the long serving pastor, George King in 1981, the congregation drifted away, some travelling to worship in Chippenham. Prospective plans for an art gallery foundered until it was bought by the King's Church in 1997 and once again has a vibrant congregation. There are a number of graves around the chapel with others in a graveyard on the north side of Burnham Road. The stone gate piers, railings and the gravestone of Mary and Giles Carter who died in 1823 and 1829 respectively are listed.

The King's Church is a Pentecostal church. The modern Pentecostal movement began in Los Angeles in 1906 with some extraordinary spiritual manifestations. The Reverend A. A. Boddy, an Anglican priest, introduced it shortly afterwards to Britain. The Assemblies of God were constituted in 1924, adopting a congregational form of governance. The origins of Malmesbury's church date back to 1948 when Mrs. Rowe of Swindon had a vision telling her to come here. Going down the hill from the Triangle she walked past St. Mary's Lane but was guided back to the Toc H Hall next to St. Mary's Church (now the small house called Westport Studio). Here the first meetings of the Assemblies of God Pentecostal were held. In 1956 they moved into the Food

Office in Market Lane which had closed when rationing ended. In 1986 their first minister, David Skelton, was appointed. The following year they purchased the Parish Rooms in Silver Street (now King's Church Nursery).

The Silver Street premises were built as Free Reading Rooms by Walter Powell MP (1842-1881) in 1870. Walter was the youngest of the three sons of Thomas Powell who owned coalmines near Newport and had interests in railways and shipping. Walter attended Rugby School between 1858 and 1861. His father died in 1863 and the businesses were sold. However the company Powell Duffryn stills bears his name. In 1867 Walter moved to North Wiltshire with his mother and rented Dauntsey House. There he made friends with the rector of Little Somerford, Rev. Arthur Evans. Evans was chairman of the Conservative Association and in December 1868 Walter was chosen as the Tory candidate for the Malmesbury constituency. Early the following year he was elected as MP by 607 votes to 310 and ended 35 years of Liberal domination of the seat. A grand celebration was held for his supporters in the George Hotel in February 1869.

Tragedy struck his family that year when his eldest brother Thomas together with his wife and son were killed by outlaws whilst travelling in Abyssinia. Walter went to Egypt to deal with the formalities. On his return he started a number of works to benefit Malmesbury and the surrounding district. The first was the gift of these Reading Rooms. James Thomas Bird (1843-1898, a printer who lived in Abbey Row) in his 1876 *History of the Town of Malmesbury* described this as *a splendid building* (it would be cynical to suggest that his opinion might have been influenced just because Walter was his major financier!) and explained; *The first room is set apart for the use of the upper classes, and tradesmen, who choose to avail themselves of the privilege, and the inner room is provided for the lower classes. There is a large and capital Library, and a good supply of London and Provincial Newspapers, and Periodicals; all supplied gratis by the munificent donor of the building. The rooms are decorated with a fine collection of Buck and other horns, skins &c. Various games, such as Drafts, Dominoes, &c. are allowed to be played, the necessaries being also supplied by Mr. Powell.* The partition between the rooms could be removed to make a larger area for meetings. Four years later a games room and soup kitchen were added.

Powell generously supported local social events and provided 50 tons of coal every winter for the aged poor of the town as well as giving tea and sugar. Residents of the Somerfords and Corston also benefited from similar gifts. He was an active supporter of the railway branch-line and provided gas lighting for the Abbey in 1875. Then he developed an interest in ballooning. In 1880 he met Henry Coxwell who took him on a flight. He was so taken with the pastime that he spent a lot of time pursuing it and in October of that year had to send a telegram to apologise when he was unable to propose the

The Eclipse balloon lifting off from Cross Hayes, June 1881.

election of a new coroner. In June 1881 he wished to give a demonstration to his constituents. Thomas Wright brought his balloon, Eclipse, to Cross Hayes. This was inflated from a specially laid gas pipeline joined to a 4½" main in the High Street. The balloon apparently took 20 hours to fill and the town was without gas for the night! The day of the flight was treated as a local holiday with the Town Band and another from Didmarton playing. The flight itself was over within an hour, the balloon having travelled west over Lea and Somerford. Walter rented a field next to the gas works in Bath so that it was easy to make regular flights.

Walter became friendly with Captain James Templar of the balloon department at Woolwich. They had a spherical balloon of Lyons silk made up at the Silk Factory in Malmesbury and completed at Powell's home in Somerford. The car was fitted with the latest improvements including cork seats and life belts. Unfortunately this was not used when Walter Powell made his last flight on 9th December 1881. He, Templar and Mr. A. Agg-Gardiner took off from Bath at 1.55pm in the Government balloon Saladin to make observations for the Meteorological Office. By 4.40pm they could see the sea near Bridport, Dorset and sought to land. Part of Templar's report reads; *I opened the valve and descended about 150 yards short of the cliff. The balloon, on touching the ground, dragged a few feet and I rolled out of the car with the valve line in my hand. This caused the balloon to ascend about 8 ft. when Mr. Gardiner dropped off and unfortunately broke his leg. I found that the rope was being pulled through my hands, and I called to Mr. Powell, who was standing in the car, to come down the line. He took hold of the line and in a few seconds it was torn through my hands. The balloon rose rapidly. Mr. Powell waved his hand to me. I took a compass bearing.* It was thought the balloon had fallen into the sea and with a reward on offer boats searched for several days. But it was not until 27th January 1883 that the Penny Illustrated reported the balloon and car had been discovered in the mountains of the Sierra del Pedroso in northern Spain. Walter's body was never found and Malmesbury lost one of its greatest benefactors. Henry Coxwell wrote that he had not allowed Walter to borrow one of his balloons to attempt a new altitude record of seven miles and he was concerned Walter had a fixation about making a Channel crossing, so this may have been a rash attempt to achieve that ambition.

On 17th August 1882 4 Silver Street and other properties were auctioned by Walter's Executors and the Borough Council bought it for use as the Council Chamber. The particulars read; *All that substantial and well-built Messuage and Premises, Situate at Silver-street, Malmesbury, lately used as Reading Rooms, having a frontage of 24 feet, and running the total length of 170 feet to the rear of the premises. The rooms are lofty and well-ventilated, and divided by a pair of folding doors; gas and water laid on; has an excellent coal cellar, and underground passages. At the rear thereof is a capital Sitting-room, Kitchen with cooking range and offices. There is an excellent light and airy Bedroom above, and Water Closet on landing. The whole of the grates, chandeliers and other gas and water fittings will be included in the purchase.* Whilst owned by the Borough the premises were used as the Technical School from its opening in 1892 to 1902. When the Council moved to the Town Hall the Bristol Diocesan Trust bought it for £500 in 1921 to use it as Parish Rooms. It became a schoolroom during World War II and in 1951 was sold to the Catholic Church.

After the Kings Church took over the building the Minister moved into the cottage behind which was originally the home of the caretaker. The Church later formed the Kings Nursery which has proved so successful that the church decided to move to Abbey Row

Ebenezer Chapel, Silver Street
Ebenezer Chapels are found throughout the world and the name comes from the Bible; *And the men of Israel went out of Mizpeh, and pursued the Philistines, and smote them, until they came under Bethcar. Then Samuel took a stone, and set it between Mizpeh and Shen, and called the name of it Ebenezer, saying, hitherto hath the LORD helped us.* (1 Samuel, 7: 11-12)

The Independent Church in Malmesbury was formed in 1796 when services were held in a cottage in Berry's Entry, High Street (now No. 41). The premises were too small and two cottages for sale in Silver Street were converted into a Meeting House. The church united with Westport Presbyterians during the pastorage of Rev. Edwards who took up his post in 1812. The Chapel was sold and used for trade. In 1814 and again in 1825 Primitive Methodists from Sherston hired the building for a short time. This group received rough treatment from the locals who regarded them as 'ranters' who had no right to be treated with civility. Soon afterwards some Baptists unhappy with the Abbey Row pastor moved in and held services here for over 10 years.

The Independent's union with the Presbyterians, although flourishing at first, failed to prosper as not all the congregation had consented to it. In 1841 Friends of the Old Independent took over the building. The premises were enlarged in 1848. More work was carried out in 1885 including the removal of the old pews and the installation of bench seating for 300 at a cost of £300. An adjacent cottage to the south was converted into two classrooms. In 1914 there was no settled minister and it was again proposed to reunite with Westport Congregationalists. The deacons resisted this and it would seem that the church prospered as the building was refurbished during the late 1920s. At this time Sidney Adye, a High Street grocer, was the treasurer. It was not until December 1952 that finally the two churches permanently united. The reasons were that this Church had not had a minister for 25 years and the congregation had dwindled. For a while services continued to be held at Silver Street on two Sundays a month. The building has been used as the Masonic Lodge since 1958.

Moravian Church, Oxford Street

This denomination, the correct name of which is Unitas Fratum or Unity of Brethren, is the oldest free church in north Europe being founded in 1457. It was started by followers of the Bohemian priest John Hus who was martyred in 1415. After years of persecution some of its members sought refuge in neighbouring countries, particularly Saxony though having come from Moravia that was the name by which they became known. In the 18th Century they became a Missionary Church concentrating on slaves in the West Indies.

John Cennick (1718-1755), who had been a Wesleyan evangelist and a follower of George Whitfield, started a religious society in Malmesbury during 1742. He invited the Moravian Brethren to take charge of congregations in North Wiltshire including Malmesbury in 1745. The Malmesbury society became a separate congregation in 1748. Cennick also began churches allied to the Plymouth Brethren and Baptists. However all of the

The west front of the Moravian Church. In recent years access has been blocked into the graveyard.

North Wiltshire Moravian churches other than Malmesbury faded away after his death. The chapel in Lower Oxford Street was built in 1770 and a schoolroom in 1860. The congregation dwindled to around 15 and the church was put up for sale in 1991. Services were held in the old schoolroom until 2008 when that building was also sold and converted into a residence. The Church was renovated but after carrying out unauthorised work on the Manse (a Listed Building) work came to a halt. For 10 years this important building has been deteriorating and although enforcement action began, that was put into abeyance when it became unclear who owned the building. **The building is now for sale.**

Primitive Methodist Chapel, Bristol Street

The Primitives broke away from the main Methodist movement in 1812. The group from Sherston came here in 1825 but withdrew after a short time. In 1854 the Brinkworth circuit, then a major centre of evangelism sending missions all over Southern England and Wales, sought to 'Mission Malmesbury'. They sang hymns and preached in the open air in Burnivale. An overzealous Church of England curate, believing they had no right to preach other than in his Church, harangued the 'wicked' congregation and sought to have them banned, without success. One of the missionaries, Rev. S. Turner, described Malmesbury as *a dark, dead place*. The Primitives also used the open spaces of Horsefair and Cow Fair (Cross Hayes). The first building they used was a barn in St. Mary's Lane. The foundation stone of the Bristol Street chapel was laid on 18th April 1856 and the building cost £350. Once established the church flourished and by 1859 was the basis of the Malmesbury Circuit. The congregation outgrew this small site and a new chapel was built in the Triangle in 1899.

The old 'commodious building' was bought for £144 by Henry and Frederick Poole, Myriorama Proprietors, for use as a studio and storerooms. In 1905 Henry guaranteed a loan that Fred had taken out with the Wilts & Dorset Bank of up to £500. Fred died on 17 January 1907 and Henry had to pay £447 12s 7d, as the estate was otherwise insolvent. The Myriorama shows were coming to an end with the development of cinemas and so in 1909 James A. Jones, Ironmonger & Cycle Agent, bought the premises to be used as a motor garage & workshop. He ran a fleet of hire cars and this was their base. James' son Montague managed the business but died in 1918. E. S. T. Cole, who was married to James' niece, took over. Jackie Hulse (1896-1961) ran Malmesbury Coachworks here from around 1933 but later traded as Hulse's Private Hire Service until the Second World War.

The Bristol Street Primitive Methodist Chapel in 1964.

Later it became a warehouse until the 1960s for Coopers of Bristol, suppliers of ladies underwear and corsetry. The Kings Church considered buying it in 1966. Two years later Max Woosnam, a local personality and author of a booklet on Eilmer, bought the building and lived in a caravan inside until 1998 when it was converted into a three-storey house.

Cross Hayes House, 28 Cross Hayes

This town house was built in 1728 with a foundation stone on the south west corner inscribed WC 1728. It has a T plan with a projecting rear wing. In the late 18th Century an extension was added at the rear to the southeast. Charles Goddard Dewell (1834-99) inherited his uncle Dr. Timothy Dewell's estate comprising a number of properties in the town. Charles was a Captain in the army and became ill whilst serving in Greece during 1856 with 91st Regiment. He went to convalesce in Italy and in his hotel met Father Marshall, a Church of England cleric who had converted to Catholicism. Charles was similarly converted. On being posted to India he met Father Larive, a Frenchman, of the Order of St Francis de Sales. Charles had an ambition to reintroduce Roman Catholicism to Malmesbury (why is not clear – he was brought up in Corsham) and asked Father Larive to start a mission. Charles resigned his commission and the pair arrived in Malmesbury in May 1861. They intended to move into Cross Hayes House but his agent, an ardent Protestant, had let it on a lease which did not expire for five years. Father Larive left to start a mission in Devizes whilst Charles became a Jesuit brother. Although discouraged by the Bishop of Clifton and his Superior at Annecy, Father Larive took possession of the house and in the parlour was able to celebrate the first Mass in Malmesbury since the Reformation on Palm Sunday, 14th April 1867. A congregation of 22 from local towns and villages was present. Later the house became a convent first for Sisters of Mercy from Bristol who taught at the school from 1870 to 1884. Then the Order of St. Joseph of Annecy took charge of the school. The nuns had intended that this would be their first residence in Britain but due to the problems with the lease had opened a house in Devizes instead. The convent closed in 1990 but two years later three nuns of the Sisters of St. Clare were in residence for three years before they left for Norway. Although the house remained in the Church's ownership until 2008 it is now privately owned.

St Aldhelm's Roman Catholic Church, Cross Hayes

The original church was built in 1867 abutting the pavement of Cross Hayes to the north of Cross Hayes House of which only the southern part remains. Within a short time the congregation had grown and larger premises were needed. Funds were short and Father Larive travelled to France and Italy seeking more. He was granted an audience by Pope Pius IX who gave him 4,000 lire. The present building was completed in 1875 and seats 120.

Hostility with some locals arose after the opening of St. Joseph's School in the old church and Father Larive was injured by a stone thrown

The interior of St. Aldhelm's Church prior to the First World War.

at him. This tension led to him being recalled to Annecy having laid strong foundations for the faith. A reminder of him can be found in the Lady Chapel – a statue of Our Lady of Salette which he brought from France in 1866. He was succeeded by Father Decompoix who was priest for more than forty years. The numbers attending the church remained small until Father Morrin became the new priest in 1912. Energetically he became involved in the life of the community and made the doctrine of the church more widely known.

Father Morrin also raised money to improve the church. Just before the First World War a new sanctuary was built, heavy roman arches were replaced by slender gothic ones. Central heating and electric lighting were installed. The arrival of Father Grorod in 1925 heralded further work including a new altar and pulpit and the installation of three stained glass windows. These depict the Sacred Heart of Jesus, St. Mary and St. Aldhelm and were donated by the Bishop, having been removed from Bristol Pro Cathedral prior to its demolition. Father Grorod had served as an ordinary soldier in the French Foreign Legion during World War I. While saying his prayers in the barrack room he was interrupted by the rude remarks of his colleagues. Excusing himself to God he went and thumped the one making the loudest noise which enabled him henceforward to pray in peace. After World War II the sacristy was built and the old school demolished. In the mid 1960s rose beds in front of the church were replaced by tarmac for parking and railings put on top of the wall next to the pavement.

In 1965 Father George O'Sullivan became parish priest. Although he spent two years between 1984-86 in Yeovil he was greatly loved by his congregation and made a large impression on the whole community. He died in post in 2013.

Wesleyan Chapel, 11 Oxford Street
John Wesley preached in the town three or four times between 1739 and 1741 but the Wesleyan Methodists first arrived in Malmesbury on Good Friday 1882 when they held an open-air service at the Market Cross. They sent a three-month mission which met in the Town Hall and services were held there until 1886 when the chapel was built. On the ground floor there was a schoolroom & vestry with the chapel above. The total cost was £1,542. The Urban Sanitary Authority in one of its last meetings discussed the desirability of moving the building to widen the street but as work had started it was deemed to be too expensive. By the third anniversary of the chapel's completion this was described as *a flourishing denomination* with the building *scarcely large enough*. However this popularity did not last. In 1916 due to the shortage of ministers after many had gone off to war the chapel closed. It then became an extra ward for the Red Cross Hospital. 25 beds on the first floor were provided for *men well advanced on their way to recovery, it being difficult in this detached building to provide night as well as day attendance.* On the ground floor was a recreation room, sitting room for nurses, kitchen and bathroom. After the war's end the premises were taken over by the Young Men's Christian Association (YMCA).

The YMCA first had a clubhouse in 1886 at 7-9 Gloucester Street, having started the year before with meetings in the Friendly Sabbath schoolroom at Market Cross. In 1897 Colonel Charles Luce enabled the Society to move into Cranmore (now renamed Abbeyfield) House, Market Cross after the Hospital moved to new premises. During the First World War the YMCA building was used as a ward for the Red Cross Hospital from 1916. In 1920 the hospital was short of accommodation and these premises became the maternity wing. So the YMCA moved again, this time to the old Wesleyan Chapel. Extensive building works were carried out and in October 1920 Princess Helena Victoria opened the new premises. Snooker and billiards could be played on the ground floor with the upper floor being available for hire. The staircase was to the left of the doorway into the Club Room from Market Lane. The subscription was 10s. per year in the 1930s unless you lived more than 2 miles from Malmesbury when it was 4s. Presumably you were not expected to use the facilities so often if you lived out of town! The premises were extended in 1927 through the acquisition from Stroud Brewery of half of the Malting House along Market Lane. These were rented out as offices. Lack of support and financial difficulties led to the closure of the YMCA at the end of 1966. Four years later the building was sold to the Borough Council which incorporated it into the Town Hall.

The Triangle Primitive Methodist Chapel shortly after its opening.

Primitive Methodist Chapel, The Triangle

Having grown out of their Bristol Street premises, this chapel was built in 1899 at a cost of £1,400. Donors were able to lay memorial stones with their names engraved, which are still in place. Seating was provided for 350 although in 1904 they were described as *a small body, enthusiastic and enterprising*. By the end of the First World War the debt arising from construction had been paid off. The Church, like many other organisations, ran a Benefit Society which was wound up in 1929 after 70 years existence. In 1932 the Primitives joined with the Wesleyan Methodists, who had been without a chapel since 1919 when their Oxford Street chapel had been sold, to become part of the Methodist Church. Around 1970 there was a Methodist Malmesbury Circuit comprising 13 chapels in this area. It was latterly part of the Chippenham Circuit but the congregation became so small that it closed in the summer of 2004 for conversion into a private house.

Burton Hill School Chapel

In 1955 the School started raising funds to build a chapel for the girls as it was difficult for those using wheelchairs to attend churches in the town. Work began in 1957 but it took two years to raise all of the £5,000 needed. It was built on the site of former stables and was inter-denominational. The service of dedication

The Burton Hill School Chapel, 1964.

took place in September 1960. In 1990 The King Athelstan Boy Scouts Troop found a temporary home here when it was described as the 'old' chapel so it seems to have had a short use.

Military Connections

The hilltop has been fortified since at least 500BC. When carrying out repairs to the Town Wall archaeologists discovered the foundations of a stone wall of that date together with other evidence suggesting prior occupation – could Malmesbury possibly be the oldest continuously occupied English settlement? The defences were sited on top of the escarpment on the western, northern and eastern sides but due to the necessity to make the total length suit the number of likely defenders the southern wall originally ran roughly in line with Ingram Street. This was later moved further down the hill between the South Gate (marked in Lower High Street) and the Little Gate, at Back Hill steps. The area outside the wall but north of the river was known as Netherwall. The approach from the west along Abbey Row is the only one unprotected by a water barrier on level ground. Thus on this level ground the castle was built.

During Saxon times Malmesbury was on the northern border of Wessex and therefore needed strong defences. Despite this the Vikings sacked the town three times between 872 and 877 before King Alfred recaptured it in 880 when he allegedly made it a borough or fortified town. When the Danes returned in 1016 it is said one of the party sought to demolish King Athelstan's shrine but fell down dead whereupon his compatriots fled. Bishop Roger of Salisbury after his seizure of the monastery in 1118 started constructing a castle *scarcely a stone's throw from the principal church*. However this did not prevent Robert Fitz-Hubert taking the town by surprise in 1139 during the 'Anarchy' (the Civil War between King Stephen and the Empress Matilda). The King put him to flight within a fortnight. Duke Henry of Anjou took up his mother's claim and after landing on the south coast in 1153 made straight for Malmesbury. Henry of Huntingdon gave this account;

But the energetic youth (Henry) gathering his people together, both those whom he found en route and those whom he had brought with him, greatly hating delay, laid siege to the castle and after an assault took it. But though the town was taken, the main tower, which was held by Jordan for the King, remained unsubdued. Jordan, with the utmost speed, sent a messenger to the King to inform him of what had happened. When the King learned the bad news from the messenger, the usual dignity of his countenance became overcast with frowning sorrow. Nevertheless without delay he gathered all his forces together and fixed his camp not far from Malmesbury.
The day after his arrival he set his forces in array, replete with chosen knights and carefully instructed in the plan of battle.
The army was indeed immense, well provided with leaders, bristling with golden ensigns, terrible, and exceedingly beautiful.
But God, in whom alone is safety, had withdrawn his countenance from them. The floods of heaven were opened with such torrents of rain and persistence of cold biting blasts of wind, that God himself seemed to have taken the Duke's side. For the storm was behind the Duke and his men and in the face of the King and his men, so that these latter were neither able to hold their arms nor handle their lances, streaming as they were with the rain.
And because God had ordained that he would hand over the land that was his to his boy without effusion of blood, since neither of them was able to cross the river and the King was not sufficiently strong to reach his goal through such floods, he broke off his operations and, consumed with vexation, marched back to London.

Before leaving the area Stephen agreed to demolish the castle but Jordan surrendered it to Henry. With such a loss of face it was not long before he signed a treaty whereby he would retain the crown for his lifetime then it would pass to Henry who became King Henry II. With that war at an end the monks became more concerned about the proximity of the castle to their religious house and the rude behaviour of its occupants. The Abbot obtained the Pope's authority to excommunicate offenders. In 1216 King John was persuaded to sell the lordship of the Manor to the monastery and allowed the castle to be demolished.

During the civil war of 1642-46 Malmesbury was strategically placed between the parliamentary stronghold in Bristol and the King's base at Oxford. In February 1643 Prince Rupert took the town from its parliamentary garrison. Within 2 months General Waller retook the town after a short siege during which it is said that houses along Abbey Row were blown up. The town changed hands another 4 times with Colonel Massey finally seizing it for the Parliament in May 1644 after another violent assault. Once the war was ended the town's defences were ordered to be slighted, or totally removed. Due to the lie of the land the wall can still be traced on the north, east and south sides but research has not been able to firmly identify where the wall stood to the west.

The maintenance of armed forces is expensive and in medieval times there was no permanent army. In order to be prepared, militia organised by the County's Lord Lieutenant began in 1757. One Company was raised in Malmesbury. Lists of eligible men were drawn up and members picked by ballot. The unit was administered at meetings held in the White Lion Inn. In the Crimean War (1853-1856) about 30 Malmesbury men were called up for garrison service in the Mediterranean. During the Cardwell Army reforms of the 1880s the militia were reorganised and 3rd (Militia) Battalion Duke of Edinburgh's Wiltshire Regiment was formed. It seems that enlistment became voluntary and recruits were required to attend annual training camps. During the Boer War (1899-1902) the town's men either served with 2nd Battalion on active service or 3rd Battalion which guarded prisoners on the island of St. Helena. Further Army reforms in 1908 saw the disbandment of the Militia and the introduction of the Special Reserve.

Another local unit of volunteers was formed in the war against France when there was a threat of invasion in 1794. The Wiltshire Yeomanry cavalry raised a troop in Malmesbury comprised of three officers, six non-commissioned officers, a trumpeter and 57 gentlemen or yeomen. The Yeomanry were not obliged to serve overseas and dealt with riots in various places across the county before the establishment of the Police force. During the First World War they served on the Western Front and in the Second the Middle East, North Africa and Italy. The Malmesbury Troop was reformed in 1926 but it does not seem to have been part of the reconstituted Territorial Army in 1947.

In 1859 another fear of invasion by the French caused the War Office to ask Lord Lieutenants to form new Rifle Volunteers. Malmesbury was the second town in Wiltshire to heed this call to arms, raising a Company, later called A Company 2nd Volunteer Battalion Wiltshire Regiment. 16 men volunteered for service in South Africa in 1899 and were enlisted in Malmesbury by Colour Sergeant William Perry, the Volunteer Company's Regular Army Instructor and attested by the Mayor, Henry Garlick on 15 January 1900. They signed on to serve the Colours for one year, or until the war was over. The contingent was discharged

The Volunteers are greeted on their return from South Africa outside the Town Hall in 1901.

on 30 April 1901 at the Regimental Depot, Devizes. Two of them died, Private Montague Baker (Crudwell) from enteric fever on 11 June 1900 at Bloemfontein and Lieutenant Walter Cecil Luce from the same cause on 11 February 1901 at Springfontein. After their return each veteran was presented with a silver English half-hunter watch supplied by Henry Barton, High Street jeweller, engraved with *Malmesbury's thanks to ...., 2ⁿᵈ V.B. Wilts Regiment, for active service in the South African Campaign, 1901.* A tablet was erected by subscription to commemorate the loyalty and patriotism of these men which unfortunately is now kept in storage in the Town Hall. Haldane's 1908 Army reorganisation led to this unit being disbanded on the formation of the Territorial Force.

3ʳᵈ Wessex Brigade Royal Field Artillery Ammunition Column was raised as part of the Territorial Force and had its headquarters in this town. Within a year they had 60 recruits. During the First World War the unit did not see active service but most of the pre-war members transferred to take an active part. After the war the Ammunition Column was not reformed. It was not until 1937 that a platoon of 4ᵗʰ Battalion Wiltshire Regiment was raised here. Just prior to the war the Territorial Army was doubled in size and the platoon became part of 5ᵗʰ Battalion. In 1947 5ᵗʰ Wiltshire was reconstituted as 651 Regiment Light Anti Aircraft Regiment Royal Artillery and a detachment of their Q Battery was based in the town. Very little was reported about it in newspapers except for a Bofors 40mm gun appearing at an Ekco sports day. The Regiment was disbanded in 1955. In 1960 a detachment of C Company 4ᵗʰ Wiltshire Regiment was reformed in Malmesbury but the battalion disappeared in the Territorial Army reorganisation of 1967.

A number of part-time defence units were formed during both World Wars. In WW1 the Volunteer Training Corps provided local defence and pre-conscription training, in WW2 the principal one was 2ⁿᵈ Battalion Wiltshire Home Guard. The stories of these units are told in the author's *Our Glorious Dead* and *Malmesbury versus Hitler*. In April 1954 an exhibition of weapons including a Vickers machine gun, Sten sub machine gun and PIAT anti-tank 'rifle' was held in an unnamed ironmonger's shop window with the intention of reforming A Company Home Guard but nothing more was reported about the idea.

In March 1941 25 boys of the Grammar School were formed into the Malmesbury Secondary School Flight, Air Training Corps. At the end of the war it was renamed 992 Squadron. Although initially based at the school, in the late 1940s it moved to the Youth Centre in Ingram Street. Due to difficulty attracting recruits and adult helpers it was suspended for a short while until being reformed in 1952. During the mid 1960s a lack of cadets led to disbandment being considered but the crisis passed. The unit moved to the Tetbury Hill drill hall before 1974 and after the first

admission of girls in 1987 it has prospered becoming one of the most successful squadrons of the Dorset & Wiltshire Wing.

Shortly after the formation of the Army Cadet Force in February 1942 a Company was formed, sharing its headquarters with the Home Guard at Abbey House's squash court (now the Parish Office in Holloway). It later moved into the Drill Hall. Unfortunately the ACF seemed to shun publicity and the last newspaper report was dated June 1989 when a new commander was appointed. Presumably the unit was disbanded soon afterwards.

Army Cadets at the Market Cross c1960.

723 Company Girls' Training Corps was raised in August 1942, initially at St. Joseph's School but quickly moved to the Grammar School. After the war it was based at the Youth Centre, Ingram Street. In 1964 the name changed to the Girls' Venture Corps. Although the Malmesbury girls often won trophies the unit found it difficult to attract new recruits and when the number dropped to 8 it closed in 1969. Their leader, Mrs. Betty Nolan, said the movement had not kept up with the times and *there is far too much red tape and silly restrictions*.

Girls' Venture Corps arriving for a Remembrance Service
(S. Nolan)

The town's many War Memorials and further details of the military are fully described in the books referred to above.

It has been difficult to ascertain the location of all the Drill Halls in Malmesbury. The Rifle Volunteers at first were based somewhere in Cross Hayes, probably in a room at the rear of the George Hotel. Later a wooden building near the water tower at Abbey House was built for them. This was used for enlistments in 1914 but was demolished afterwards. Another was built and opened on 4th January 1912 on the western side of Bremilham Road close to the junction with Bristol Road, now houses called Holford Rise. This was used by the Ammunition Column but in 1923 was bought by Alfred Ernest Adye (1869-1943) who turned it into a motor garage. In 1930 he passed it on to his sons Reginald Victor (1901-1962) and Norman Ernest (1905-1983) who entered into a partnership. Reg ran the garage whilst Norman opened a Radio Shop at 6 High Street. The motor dealership was expanded in 1932 when the Gig House, Oxford Street was bought – these premises were sold in 1948. The garage was sold in 1982 and the drill hall demolished soon after. A basement in a building behind 32 Cross Hayes was used by the Yeomanry and for the Wiltshire Regiment platoon in the 1930s. Both units moved to a new building on Tetbury Hill in 1939 which is still owned by the Ministry of Defence and used by the Air Training Corps.

The Ammunition Column's Drill Hall after it became Adye's garage workshop. (M. Adye).

R.A.F. Hullavington was granted the Freedom of the Borough in 1970 and regularly exercised its privileges until 1992 when the R.A.F. were running down their usage of the site. That same year 9 Supply Regiment, Royal Logistic Corps, took up residence and they were granted the Freedom in 2010. On that occasion and in 2013 parades were held in the town to welcome the Regiment back home from tours in Afghanistan. The base has been renamed Buckley Barracks and the unit is now known as 9 Theatre Logistic Regiment.

Local Government

The Warden and Freemen of Malmesbury

The Old Courthouse, St. John's Street is the meeting place of the Warden and Freemen of Malmesbury otherwise known as the Old Corporation. The building probably dates from the 14th Century and is thought to be a remnant of the Hospital of St. John the Baptist. The origins of the freemen come from Anglo-Saxon times when King Edward the Elder (c875-924) confirmed the town's status as a Borough. The freemen of the town were granted five hides of land (about 600 acres – still known as King's Heath) by King Athelstan as a reward for their help in defeating the Danes at Brunanburh in 937. This reputed Charter reads:

I Athelstan, King of the English, on behalf of myself and my successors grant to my Burgesses and to their successors of the burg of Meldufu that they may have and hold always all their tributes and free customs, as they held them in the time of King Edward my father, fully and in honour.

And I enjoin on all beneath my rule that they do no wrong to these Burgesses, and I order that they be free from claims and from payment of scot.

And I give and grant to them that royal heath-land of five hides of land near my vill of Norton, on account of their assistance in my struggle against the Danes.

The Charter of this grant has been confirmed by my seal by the witnessing of Edmund, by brother, and by the advice of master Wolsin my chancellor and Odo my treasurer and Godwyn.

Godwyn, who bears the King's standard, obtained this on behalf of the Burgesses.

Prior to the Dissolution of the Monasteries responsibility for the administration of the town was shared between the Abbey and the Freemen. However in 1635 Charles I, having made an investigation into the governing bodies of boroughs, granted a further Charter which formerly recognised the Corporation of the Alderman, 12 Capital Burgesses and 24 Assistant Burgesses with a High Steward as advisor and man of law to be the body to administer local government here. These officials, other than the High Steward, were drawn from the freemen or commoners of the Borough. The commoners have four 'ranks' – commoner, landholder, Assistant Burgess and Capital Burgess. In modern times until the summer of 2000 membership was restricted to men who fulfilled the following requirements: he was a son or son-in-law of a commoner, was married and lived within 1½ miles of the centre of the Market Cross. On admission a new commoner is entered into the list of one of the six 'hundreds' – Taylors, Fishers, Glovers, Coxfoot, David's Loynes and Thornhill. Each of these has 31 members. The initiation ceremony, which used to take

The Old Courthouse where the Warden & Freemen meet, 1964.

place at Kings Heath entailed firstly digging a shallow hole in the turf. Into this the prospective commoner would put a silver coin and the following would be said to him: *Turf and twig I give to thee, as King Athelstan gave to me, a good brother thou shalt be.* Then the initiate would be struck across the back three times with a twig. When a vacancy occurs in the hierarchy through death or discommoning (normally due to moving away from the town) the most senior commoner is promoted to the ranks of the landholders. Advancement above this is by election, an Assistant Burgess being elected by all the Burgesses and a Capital Burgess by the remaining survivors.

Until the start of the 18th Century any male inhabitant could be a commoner provided that he was married and occupied an ancient tenement in town. In 1727 new rules were introduced restricting commoners to those outlined above together with their apprentices (this last was removed in 1821). In the early 19th Century the commoners felt that they were not getting the full advantage from

The initiation of a commoner. (Athelstan Museum)

Kings Heath which was largely overgrown. An Act of Parliament was obtained in 1821 to allow the Heath to be split into allotments to allow each commoner to share in the cultivation of it. This Enclosure Act fixed the number of commoners at the number existing then, 280, each allocated around 1½ acres (those closest to town were smaller, the furthest ones larger). Unfortunately modern lifestyles have reduced the numbers that could meet the criteria and in 2000 there were only 216 commoners. Therefore the rules have been changed to include women and unmarried people who can show that they are descended from a commoner and live within the 1½ mile radius. This has filled the ranks once more.

Richard Jefferies had the following to say in 1867; *It is even said that the true Malmesbury population are all more or less intimately related – one great family. This is one advantage of a corporation – it makes men perhaps greater friends, more attached to their native place; and imbues them with what is called esprit de corps. At the same time it debars progress. Some even stigmatise the corporation as the ruin and bane of Malmesbury, asserting that there is not a single tradesman in the place who is really a Malmesbury man in proof of this statement. Such may now be the case, but it is evident that of yore the corporation has been of the greatest service to this town.*

The Freemen meet at four Courts which are held on Trinity Tuesday, King Athelstan's feast day (the following Tuesday), Michaelmas (29th September) and New Year's Eve. The land to which this body owes its origins, Kings Heath, still belongs to the Old Corporation 11 centuries after it was given to them. Due to the need to maximise food production, Kings Heath was taken over by the War Agricultural Committee in 1940 and the allotments disappeared. It was not until 1951 that control returned to the Old Corporation but with the proviso that it was to be farmed as a single entity.

The Alderman and Capital Burgesses were also responsible for electing Members of Parliament. Malmesbury was one of the true rotten boroughs – two MPs elected by thirteen voters. Before the Reform Bill Malmesbury's MPs were Tories and none of the later members were associated with the town. Sir Charles Forbesse (as reported in 1832) refused to pay as much to be the town's MP as previously, a sum supposed to have been £12,000. The Reform Bill of 1831 was hotly debated in the town. Under the Bill the borough stood to lose both MPs but a subsequent amendment reinstated one for a new constituency which included several nearby villages. Malmesbury was the only place where this happened. Ironically most of the old 13 electors were disenfranchised as they did not own their own property! A grand celebration to celebrate the passing of the Great Reform Act was planned near St. John's Bridge on Tuesday 21st August 1832 but many hours of rain caused it to be postponed despite 13 extensive tables having been erected and four hogsheads of beer delivered. It was described thus: *The morning of Wednesday opened with every appearance of the weather clearing up. The bands of music played throughout the streets, whilst crowds of people in their holiday attire were pouring in from the adjacent parts, presenting a scene of the most animating description. The principal shops being closed, at 2 o'clock a procession of professional gentlemen and tradesmen paraded the different streets of the town arm-in arm, preceded by bands of music, and thirty handsome flags and banners. On the approach of the Procession to the entrance of the field the number of persons congregated was so dense as to render it almost impossible to stir. The gates, at which Officers were stationed, being opened, those who possessed tickets, amounting to nearly 2,000, were admitted to the tables. At a cross table at either extremity of the field was a baron of roast beef of enormous dimensions, each surmounted by a small dark-blue flag, bearing the inscription, "The Roast Beef of Old England." Just previous to the sitting down to dinner, at the sound of the bugle, the Band struck up the tune "God save the King" which the assembled multitude joined in singing the following lines written for the occasion as a Grace - no Clergyman being present to engage in so important a duty.*

> *TUNE,—" God save the King."*
> *Author of ev'ry good,*
> *Bless to our use this food*
> *What Thou dost give;*
> *Grant we may always see,*
> *That blessings flow from Thee,*
> *Now, let us thankful be,*
> *And while we live.*

At the conclusion of the dinner, which was of the most inviting nature, and during the evening, the usual loyal and patriotic toasts were given and heartily responded to. The aggregate quantity of viands amounted to 2 oxen, 4 sheep, about 600 half-quartern loaves, and upwards of 80 plum-puddings, besides 8 hogs-heads of strong beer. On the following day the remains were distributed to nearly 100 poor families.

Such an assemblage was never before witnessed in the town; it being computed that there were at one time not less than four thousand persons in the field; every commanding position outside the gates being thronged. The evening concluded with a grand display of Fireworks.

The town was excluded from the provisions of the Municipal Reform Act 1835 which abolished many other old corporations. Peregrine Bingham, the Commissioner who came to investigate the Corporation in September 1833 reported; ... *the defective state of its municipal institutions is said to deter respectable persons from resorting to the town, while the singular distribution of the town lands, the share assigned to the select body of the corporation, and the mode in which the select body is perpetuated, seem to have a striking tendency to unsettle industrious habits, and deprave the morals of the place.* Notwithstanding this damning indictment the Corporation survived; probably because Malmesbury was already benefiting from many of the measures to improve public health the Act was intended to encourage. These are described in the Public Utilities section. Although the Old Corporation nominally continued to hold political control of the borough until 1886 the administrative functions were exercised by the three Parish Vestries (forerunners of Parochial Church Councils) – the Abbey, St. Paul's & St. Mary's and other statutory bodies which are described in the later sections. Another round of reform after the Municipal Corporations Act 1883 caused much consternation and the Deputy High Steward, Thomas Henry Chubb (1824-1888) went to discuss the position with the Minister, Sir Charles Dilke. Once again it was agreed that Malmesbury was a unique case this time due to Athelstan's Charter. The Alderman & commoners were renamed Warden & Freemen and although they lost their political and judicial powers, they kept their land and property. Much of the present activity of the Old Corporation concerns the ownership and maintenance of these properties. In 1998 Nos. 39/41 Bristol Street were rebuilt and the cottage next to St Johns Bridge was refurbished in 2002 to banish the damp, although it has been flooded since. Plaques showing the Old Corporation's seal now mark the buildings that they own.

The Old Corporation has been associated with some famous people amongst whom are:

Lord Thomas Wharton (1648-1715) was High Steward of the Corporation from 1690 to 1699 and obtained the Charter of 1696, returning to the same post in 1705 for another 10 years. He was a fierce leading opponent of King James and supporter of William of Orange. He wrote the catchy ballad *Lilliburlero* (music by Purcell) telling of the Irish succeeding against the English, a tune which is still used by the BBC World Service. He rebelled against his strict Presbyterian upbringing such that Lord Macaulay wrote that *to the end of his long life the wives and daughters of his nearest friends were not safe from his licentious plots. Of all liars of his time he was the most deliberate, the most inventive and the most circumstantial.*

Joseph Addison (1672-1719) became one of our MPs in 1709 on the recommendation of Thomas, Lord Wharton, whose secretary he became when the latter was appointed Lord Lieutenant of Ireland. Addison represented Malmesbury until his death. Before this he had established a reputation in literary circles having been commissioned in 1705 to write *The Campaign* to celebrate the victory at Blenheim. He contributed to the *Tatler* and in 1711 co-founded the *Spectator* for which he wrote essays that were noted for their clarity, wit and elegance. However there is no record that he had any personal associations with the town.

Sir Thomas Wharton by Anthony van Dyck.

Charles James Fox (1749-1806) was the second son of the Right Honourable Henry Fox (created Baron Holland of Foxley in 1763) who owned Norton Manor. Henry was High Steward from 1750 until 1762 as well as being a Privy Councillor and Secretary of State for War. At this time the town's MPs came from great Whig families who were rarely directly associated with Malmesbury. Charles was High Steward from 1769 to 1775 and was one of the town's MPs elected in 1774, having previously represented another rotten borough, Midhurst, at the tender age of 19. He resigned his Malmesbury seat after only a year in protest at the Government's treatment of the American colonies. He later became a supporter of Parliamentary Reform particularly advocating disenfranchising rotten and pocket boroughs to redistribute those seats to the growing industrial towns.

Joseph Pitt (1759-1842). When Thomas Estcourt gave up as High Steward in 1812 the Earl of Peterborough again tried to gain election but was defeated by Joseph Pitt, 10 votes to 2. Joseph was a self-made man, born to yeoman parents in Little Witcombe (near Birdlip). His early career was described by Lord Campbell, later Lord Chief Justice, in 1812 thus; *Pitt used to hold gentlemen's horses for a penny when, appearing a sharp lad, an attorney at Cirencester took a fancy to him and bred him to his own business. He soon scraped together a little money by his practice in the law and by degrees entered into speculation ... Everything has thriven with him. He has now a clear landed estate of £20,000 a year ...* He became a solicitor in 1780 and by 1800 he was rich enough to purchase a large amount of land in Cheltenham where he planned to build a new town to rival that spa town. Between 1825 and 1830 he completed the first part of this project, the Pittville Pump Room. Unfortunately this failed to prosper and after his death was sold to the local council. He also bought much property including Eastcourt House as well as many of the houses in Cricklade, becoming one of that pocket borough's MPs due to his property ownership. As High Steward of our Corporation he became the 'borough monger' and thus controlled the representation not only of Malmesbury and Cricklade but also Wootton Bassett. In Wootton Bassett he had to pay between 20 and 45 guineas each to purchase the votes of the 309 electors. Pitt steered through the reorganisation of the Corporation in 1820. The Alderman and Burgesses were known as Pitt Pensioners because of the annuities paid to them. He was associated with the bank of Pitt & Co that had branches in Bristol, Cheltenham and Cirencester. Unfortunately he backed a number of unsuccessful businesses and had to sell Eastcourt House along with other properties. He died in 1842 aged 83 and is buried in All Saints Church, Crudwell where there is a memorial in the north east corner of the church. On his death he owed £150,000 and his estate was administered by the Court of Chancery. In 1826 he was succeeded as High Steward by his son also named Joseph who held the post until 1842. Another son, Charles (1800-1874), became vicar of the Abbey from 1829 until his death. Charles and his wife Theresa Elizabeth (1812-1888) had 8 children, one of whom, Charles Wightwick Pitt (1843-1914), played a prominent role as a surgeon in Malmesbury.

Malmesbury Town Council

Malmesbury Town Council is the successor to centuries of municipal governance but has little of the power formerly exercised. The town is proud to boast it is England's oldest Borough although regrettably there is no substantive evidence to support this. King Alfred is supposed to have given the town its first Charter in 880 but this is based on the 1381 Charter which purports to recite earlier Saxon documents now believed by scholars to exaggerate the town's historical importance. The Old Corporation was replaced by a democratic Borough Council in 1886 with C. R. Luce (1829-1926) appointed as the first Mayor. The Council's area was larger than that controlled by the Old Corporation as it used the Urban Sanitary Authority's boundaries and took over its functions making it responsible for roads, street lighting and public health. It is likely the extensions to the Borough took place to keep pace with new development. In the south and east the rivers formed the boundary (with a small pocket north of the river at Baskerville), from the Duke of York it followed the warditch on top of the Worthies, from Reed's Farm up Tetbury Hill as far as the cemetery, back to the river & west for 100 yards, to Park Road, south to Bristol Road adjacent to the Workhouse and on to rejoin the river west of Trucklebridge.

One of the street nameplates presented by Joseph Poole. There are about a dozen remaining.

The Borough was extended again, first in 1934, then in 1956 and in 1984 the large area out to the bypass, Filands and Park Lane being included. Burton Hill, Cowbridge, Foxley & Common Roads are still not officially part of the town.

Joseph Poole (1847-1906) was elected Mayor in 1890. On relinquishing office he donated street nameplates, starting a tradition of retiring Mayors presenting something for public benefit. The Council comprised the Mayor and four Aldermen elected by Councillors for one and six years respectively and 12 Councillors elected by voters for three years. The Borough Council was the most important arm of local government until 1974 when most of its powers were passed to North Wiltshire District Council. The present Town Council has 16 members elected every four years and has the powers of a Parish Council. As had become normal on Local Government reorganisation, Malmesbury led the fight to be known as a Town rather than Parish Council. The Town Council now is responsible for a number of recreations grounds, administers the cemetery which is jointly owned with Malmesbury St. Paul Without Parish, owns the Town Hall, the Market Cross and War Memorials, as well as providing information services for tourists and the general public from our larger hinterland.

The Borough Council first met in the old Reading Room in Silver Street. In 1921 they moved into the Town Hall. When facing this building in the Cross Hayes the portion on the right was built by the Malmesbury Market House Company in 1846/7. Rented out to auctioneers by the end of the century the lessees were Fielder and Rich. This firm was founded in 1795 and its successor, Fielder and Jones, still have offices at 10 Oxford Street. The Town Hall was described in *The Builder* of 29th July 1848 as follows; *Its chief front which faces the old cattle market in Cross Hayes consists of three arches with gates opening on to an area for pitching corn and cheese; behind are*

The Town Hall in 1964 before the Fire Station moved out and two years after the one-way system was introduced.

butter and poultry and other market places. Above is a large assembly room, roofed with timber, besides two smaller apartments. The front of the building is faced with carved freestone.

It was called the Town Hall long before the Borough Council bought it in 1920 for £1,250 with £100 legal costs. A new hot water system and repairs came to an additional £903 18s. 11d. Councillor James Jones was largely instrumental in arranging this purchase and the 1927 enlargement of the premises. This was achieved by buying part of the adjoining building (on the left) in 1926 and rebuilding it. Originally a wool warehouse, in the 19th Century it became the malthouse of Smith's Brewery taken over by Thomas Luce in 1821 and then bought by Esau Duck in 1889. Bought for £300 the rebuilding amounted to another £2,598. Further expansion was completed in 1970 when the old chapel on Oxford Street and offices on the Market Lane frontage were bought and a service core added to join the three separate buildings. On the reorganisation of local government, North Wiltshire District Council took over the complex in 1974. In 2005 it was handed back to Malmesbury Town Council which spent £1.3M refurbishing the property including making better connections between the various components of the complex and attempting to reduce the number of different floor levels, there had been nine at ground level!

The Mayor appealed in the Wiltshire Gazette of 19th February 1931 for exhibits for a new collection to be called the Athelstan Museum. At first housed in the Town Hall, in 1973 it moved to 20 Gloucester Street but the floor could not bear the weight of the proposed displays. On 24th April 1975 it reopened in the Town Hall. For more than 30 years it was the responsibility of North Wiltshire District Council but in 2006/7 it was transferred to the ownership of Friends of Athelstan Museum. With the help of grants they modernised the displays and provided a new impetus.

Malmesbury Rural District Council
Under the Public Health Act 1872 a Rural Sanitary Authority was created which took over some responsibilities from the parishes. The Highway Act 1879 made it also the Highway Authority. The Local Government Act 1894 created district and parish councils leading to the conversion of the Rural Sanitary Authority into Malmesbury Rural District Council, which took over many more functions of the parish. The Council comprised 20 Councillors, one for each parish with a Chairman. The District encompassed a large area, from Luckington in the west, Crudwell in the north, to Dauntsey and Hullavington but excluded the town which was controlled by the Borough Council. There were three times as many people in this area than in the town. The Council originally met in the Guardians Board Room at the workhouse. They moved to offices at 10 High Street from 1927. Many officers served both the Borough Council and the Rural District Council. For example in 1900 the two authorities had Montague Henry Chubb, solicitor, as Clerk, Dr. Charles Wightwick Pitt as Medical Officer and Henry Hewer, manager of the Capital & Counties Bank, as Treasurer. The Mayor of the Borough Council and the Chairman of the R.D.C. both sat as magistrates in the Town Hall.

Emergency Services & Healthcare

Police

Constables were appointed by magistrates at quarter sessions with the first record in Malmesbury dating back to 1642. They were unpaid, untrained and usually unwilling to undertake a sustained investigation unless they had a personal interest. Between 1729 and 1741 two constables each were appointed at borough sessions for Malmesbury and Westport. From 1753 another constable was added for the Abbey parish. The agricultural and Chartist riots put an intolerable strain on this system. During November 1830 there were major agricultural disturbances throughout the Southwest in protest against poor wages and food price rises. Much damage was caused and machinery destroyed. The Wiltshire Yeomanry were called upon to assist on a number of occasions and were rewarded with the accolade of being made a Royal regiment. The Municipal Corporations Act 1835 gave Boroughs the power to set up Police forces. A letter to the Wilts and Gloucester Standard in November 1837 complained of door knockers being stolen and windows broken, stating that Constable Panting had *about two hundred ruffians to deal with* and urged the town's magistrates to establish a Police force. However Malmesbury Borough did not do so. Some historians have asserted it did but this confusion may have resulted from the magistrates' court being called the Borough Police Court. Counties pressed for similar powers which led to the County Police Act 1839. Wiltshire set up their force in the same year, the first outside London, appointing its Chief Constable that November. It was to comprise not less than 200 constables. Despite the inadequacy of the previous system there was great local resentment about the new Constabulary and in April 1840 two county officers were jailed by Malmesbury justices after being convicted of assault.

The Police of Malmesbury Division c1900 with one Constable mssing. They are standing in front of the stable block in the yard at Burnham Road, since demolished.

The police station at 1 Burnham Road (at that time called Horse Fair Road, Brokenborough parish) was built in 1853 and remained in use until 1955. A sergeant lived in the station house, with cottages for other members of the force next door plus cells and stables at the rear. At the turn of the 20th Century Malmesbury formed one of nine Divisions of the Wiltshire Constabulary. There were subdivisions at Kemble (now in Gloucestershire) and Sherston with eight other stations. The establishment of the town's contingent was one superintendent, three sergeants and eleven constables. The Superintendent was also the Inspector of Contagious Diseases (Animals). In 1920 it was decided the Divisions ought to cover the same area as that covered by the Petty Sessions. In consequence Malmesbury was incorporated into the Chippenham Division.

A new station opened at Burton Hill in 1955 when that in Burnham Road was vacated. This is now the base for the Malmesbury Neighbourhood Policing Team, responsible for an area of over 110 square miles, comprising one Sergeant and three Beat teams of a Constable and a Police Community Support Officer (PCSO). The beats cover Malmesbury Town, Malmesbury Rural and Ashton Keynes with Minety. The force is divided into Sectors with Malmesbury being part of the Royal Wootton Bassett Sector. The Inspector in charge and emergency response officers are based there. Proposals are being discussed to close the Burton Hill station and for accommodation to be provided in the town centre.

Fire Brigade

The town has had a Fire Engine for a long time (one built around 1700 and last used in 1845 at Burton Hill House is in the care of the Museum). The Police Superintendent was reported directing operations at a fire in Market Cross in 1845. However it was not until 1851 that the Fire Brigade was established. At the outset it seems to have been financed by public subscription. It started off with a 5 inch pump with 80 feet of hose to draw water from the river or wells and 12 paid part time staff. In the early years about two fires were attended annually and charges were made for their services. On 16 January 1868 responsibility for the Fire Brigade was passed to the Vestries of the parishes of the Abbey, St. Pauls and Westport. The cost of fighting fires within the parishes would be borne by the poor rates whilst fires elsewhere would be charged to the property owner or his insurers. $^{29}/_{40}$ of the costs were paid by St. Paul, $^{10}/_{40}$ by Westport and $^{1}/_{40}$ by the Abbey. Repairs to the engine in 1884 were carried out by the manufacturers, Shand and Mason and it was kept in the Tolsey Gate which was no longer used as a lock up.

As soon as the Borough Council was set up it agreed to take over the Fire Brigade from the Vestries. The engine was removed to the Hurdle Store owned by Mr. Hanks in Cross Hayes which was less damp than the Tolsey. The scale of charges for fires outside the town was: hire of the engine excluding horses £2 2s., Superintendent (Borough Surveyor) £1 1s., Engineman 1s. 6d. per hour and 10 Firemen 1s. per hour each. Kelly's Directory of 1895 states the fire station

The manual fire engine c1895. The lessees of the Town Hall, Fielder, Rich & Son have their sign on the wall.

was in Ingram Street but in 1898 to 1903 the address given is Bristol Street. It is likely this was the Stoneyard, Katifer Lane with the engine kept in an old cottage later converted into a carpenter's workshop. Uniforms were first provided in 1897. In 1909 the Council rented part of the Town Hall in Cross Hayes for storing the market hurdles where there was also space for the fire engine. There was difficulty in obtaining horses to take the engine outside the Borough as there was no formal contract with the Kings Arms which had previously provided them. It took some time to deal with a fire at Thornhill Farm and Councillors were concerned that the town was left without cover. It was therefore proposed to buy a second fire engine.

Great changes took place in 1910 – a Merryweather Gem steam pump was delivered (given the name Alexandra in honour of the newly crowned Queen) and the old brigade members were discharged. The new personnel appointed were Captain, Lieutenant, 1st & 2nd Engineers with eight Firemen. Malmesbury Rural District Council agreed to contribute £25 per annum towards the cost of the Brigade. After Harry Jones of the Kings Arms died in 1911 the Earl of Suffolk provided two horses. Monty Duck and Maurice Clark were paid to look after them. Later it was decided to use them for the collection of rubbish and watering the streets. Sometimes when the alarm sounded someone had to run and catch the horses loose in a meadow by the river in Holloway.

By the end of the First World War only four of the pre-war firemen remained, two having been killed in the war. The establishment was cut from ten to eight. On 10th October 1925 another step forward was taken with the purchase of a petrol driven Dennis 35hp, 250/300 gallon light turbine with ladder, christened King Athelstan. The purchase price of £1,050 was raised by public subscription, as for all appliances then. The Rural District Council

Herbert Storey who handed over a cheque for £800 and then asked Mrs. Scott Mackirdy to name the new Dennis fire engine.

increased their annual contribution to £75. In March 1926 the Brigade was embarrassed by a major fire at Sopworth that got out of control. A defective flue in the nursery of Sopworth House caught light during the night. The owners, Colonel and Mrs. Stanley tried to raise the alarm by telephone but were unable to get any response. Eventually a Police Constable in Luckington saw the glow of the fire on the horizon. He got a lift to the Police Station in Sherston. From there he was able to phone the Police in Malmesbury who called Edgar Basevi, the town's photographer, who lived at 32 Gloucester Street. Basevi woke his neighbour Bill Paginton, a fireman whose job was to alert the Fire Captain, Egbert Edwards (1879-1945) who lived at 27 Holloway. The fire engine was on its way within 6 minutes and arrived in Sopworth 18 minutes later. By the time it arrived the fire had been burning for at least 2½ hours and the Chippenham Brigade was already there. Councillors at the Borough Council meeting on 2 April called on the Postmaster General to carry out a full enquiry. It seems the telephonist on duty at Malmesbury's exchange (Reg Wakefield) was asleep.

Shortly afterwards Capt. Scott Mackirdy (1881-1938) promoted a mutual aid scheme between a number of communities bounded by Tetbury and Corsham in the west, Marlborough in the east and Trowbridge and Devizes in the south with Chippenham at the centre housing the control room. Between them they could call upon 10 motor pumps, two trailer pumps and many other appliances. Malmesbury was part of the West Midlands District of the National Fire Brigades Association and entered their competitions each year. The District comprised 61 authorities and the brigade was pleased to win a trophy in July 1927 at Banbury. During 1928 a new electric alarm system with a bell in each fireman's home was installed. It took an average of 4½ minutes to call out the crew. Malmesbury was justifiably proud of its firemen and installed a prominent sign on each of their houses.

The Fire Brigades Act 1938 prepared the service for war although little changed locally. The Rural District Council should have become the local Fire Authority but they did not disturb the arrangement whereby the Borough Council administered the Brigade, with both Councils contributing to the cost and sometimes complaining about their share. A small trailer pump was acquired which was towed by the Chief Officer's car.

At the end of the war the King Athelstan appliance was worn out. It was replaced by an Austin Hose Reel Tender (HRT) with trailer pump, a type commonly used during the war and this lasted until 1964. It was joined by a similar auxiliary towing vehicle (ATV) that could tow the pump and carry other equipment such as extra hose reels. These were the two appliances when, following the Fire Services Act 1947, the Brigade became the responsibility of Wiltshire County Council.

The Fire Station in the Town Hall caused problems due to the limited width of both entrance and exit. The engine had to drive through from the yard behind which was also used for exercises. In 1964 a narrow Dennis F8 appliance built in 1953 with a Rolls Royce engine moved here from Calne. This vehicle remained until the Station moved to its present building in the Old Station Yard in 1969.

Since then there have been regular changes of equipment, for example, in 1969 a Bedford tender, 1979 a Dodge tender, and so on. The fire engine in 2004 was the prototype Dennis

The last appliance to use the Town Hall, a Dennis F8. This vehicle, registration number JMW 424 is preserved in the Atwell Wilson Museum in Calne. (T. Thomas).

Sabre Water Tender Ladder Rescue Appliance. This was designed by a consortium of five brigades and extra equipment including an exhaust brake, winch, cutting and lifting gear. A change in policy led to a brand new Scania Crew-cab appliance being delivered in April 2013. Retained (part-time) fire fighters are wholly responsible for Malmesbury station. They are summoned by the alarm which is raised by a signal from the control room in their Headquarters at Potterne, Devizes. In 2013 Wiltshire Fire & Rescue Service moved out of the tri-service control room in Devizes. The Ambulance Service had moved out three months previously leaving the Police as the sole occupants of the pioneering facility which opened in 2003. A merger is intended with Dorset Fire and Rescue within two years to save money following the reduction in Government grants.

Ambulance Service

Councillor Scott Mackirdy presented a Studebaker ambulance to the Borough Fire Brigade on 20th November 1927. However in 1931 this vehicle required repair but the parts were not available so it was replaced with a Buick. Before World War II it cost users 10d. per mile with a minimum of 5s., Riddick's Directories stating *which charge merely represents the actual cost of running*. This motor ambulance was taken over by the National Fire Service in 1941. The following year the NFS wanted more room for firemen in the Town Hall so the ambulance moved to a garage at the back of the George Hotel in Cross Hayes. The Buick ambulance expired the same year. A requisitioned Rolls Royce was converted but was returned to its owner when the war ended. A Ford V8 was used for a short while until an ex Army Austin with an open front was obtained. Wiltshire County Council took responsibility for this from 1948 but arranged for it to be run by the Red Cross. They provided one driver on call with seven other voluntary members and the ambulance was still garaged behind the George Hotel.

In 1958 Malmesbury received a new Austin Princess four berth ambulance. Although by this time paid staff were employed, in the mid 1960s it was decided the station would be closed between 5pm and 8am – during that time Chippenham's ambulance had to cover the areas which were dealt with by Calne & Malmesbury during the day. After the fire engine was relocated from the Town Hall a 5 year lease was signed by the Ambulance Service in 1970 for the old Fire Station there.

The Ambulance station at the rear of the George Hotel, 1964. Roper's Fish & Chips is next door with Stan Hudson's garage the other side of Griffin Alley.

In 1974 management of the service changed from Wiltshire County Council to the Wiltshire Area Health Authority, part of the NHS. They wanted to improve the service and four years later a purpose built Station was built next to the Fire Station in Station Yard. During the 1980s the garage seemed

The garage in Station Yard with a full complement of ambulances in 1985. (Malmesbury Chronicles)

to have three ambulances but the number soon dropped. Further structural changes took place with the formation of the Wiltshire Ambulance Trust in 1996, the Great Western Ambulance Trust in 2006 and the South Western Ambulance Service in 2013. Malmesbury's station is expected to close to save costs.

General Practitioners

At the beginning of the 20th Century the General Practitioners in town were R. Kinneir (1842-1922) of Tower House, P. H. Nutting LRCP of Mundens, Abbey Row and C. W. Pitt MRCS (1843-1914, son of Revd. Charles – vicar of the Abbey 1829-1874) at 10 Gloucester Street. The much loved Dr. Bernulf Hodge (1901-1978) joined Dr. Pitt in Gloucester Street in 1929 and continued to practise for another 41 years. On joining Dr. Hodge was apparently obliged to take his meals in the house but only after Dr. Pitt and his family had eaten! The surgery at Mundens combined with that of Gloucester Street in the 1920s and eventually moved to Prospect House, Olivers Lane. The practice in Tower House continued until Dr. Michael Pym (1926-1984) moved it into Laystalls, Cross Hayes in 1978. Approval was given in 1975 to build a Health Centre at the Hospital in Burton Hill but public opinion was so strong against the proposal, it was scrapped.

By the late 1980s both surgeries were overcrowded and the two practices agreed to move into Gable House, 46 High Street. The project was made possible by Doctors David Charles, Nigel Pickering and Kate Badcock from Laystalls practice combining with Doctors Barrie Crane, Michael Brummit, Chris Townsend and Heather Greenwood of Prospect House. Premises at the rear were used by other Health professionals. The new practice opened in 1988 with eight doctors, four nurses and up to 20 administrative staff. The Family Health Centre, run by the Kennet & North Wiltshire Primary Care Trust, had District Nurses, Health Visitors, a School Nurse and many other specialists either based there or regular visitors. Surgeries previously held in the villages of Oaksey, Great Somerford and Hullavington ended in 1997 although villagers could preferentially book appointments on Tuesday and Wednesday afternoons at Gable House.

In June 2008 all of these health care facilities moved to the new Primary Care Centre at Burton Hill on the site of the old hospital. The doctors at the practice in 2014 were David Charles, Nigel Pickering, John Pettit, Jackie Neale, John Harrison, Anna Le, Victoria Couchman, Tom Estcourt, Laura Haynes, Chris Philips and Thomas Winwood. There are three nurses as well as administrative and support staff. Other healthcare professionals share the same building including an NHS dental surgery, neighbourhood teams, health visitors, physiotherapists, community midwives and podiatrists. There are 14,600 registered patients. The boundary of the area covered runs through Kemble, Minety, Brinkworth, Seagry, Stanton St. Quintin, Grittleton, Sherston and Tetbury with some patients just outside this 'contracted' area.

Compared with today when home visits are usually reserved for those with limited mobility, local doctors used to have 'Round Days' when they would drive around different areas on different days. If you wanted the doctor to call, a red flag or red cloth left in the hedgerow alerted him to your need. Woe betide a doctor who ignored this summons. Even during the heavy snow of January 1963 Dr. Hugh Penman used skis to visit patients in Minety. In the days before the 'Patients' Charter', the doctor was supposed to be omniscient. About a hundred years ago a friend of Harry Jones, landlord of the Kings Arms, sent for his Doctor. On arrival Dr. Pitt said "I believe he is dead". The friend immediately retorted "I beant dead", whereupon his wife said "Be quiet Oliver, the Doctor knows better than you". Later a prominent solicitor in the town telephoned Dr. Willie Winch to say that a man had died in his office. The reply was: "Did you present him with the bill?"!

Malmesbury Community Hospital

In November 1889 a meeting of the town's leading ladies with the three general practitioners led to lady collectors being appointed to raise funds for a nursing institute. The Countess of Suffolk chaired the Administrative Committee and early in 1891 she reported on the first year's work: the Monthly Nurse (the contemporary term for midwife) attended 13 successful cases. She also assisted the District Nurse who had dealt with 26 patients, many of whom were extremely poor. Richer people had to pay a fee. There was also a Nurse for private patients. It was hoped to open a small ward for which subscriptions were solicited. A year later it was reported that Charles Luce was constructing a building to house the nurses and to contain two or three beds for *patients when poverty, accident, or special ailment may qualify for admission.* These premises were on the site of Bird's printing offices plus the house next door near the Market Cross – now known as Abbeyfield (Cranmore) House which has a date stone for 1892. The new building was valued at £1,200, had five beds and was formally opened in May 1893. The demand for medical services quickly grew and larger premises were required. Again a site was provided by Colonel Luce, the Prince & Princess pub and the Friendly Sabbath School on the corner north of the Market Cross – together with £500 towards re-building. John Alexander was in charge of fundraising and obtained substantial contributions from his acquaintances in the United States. The new facility opened in October 1897. It was described in the Wilts & Gloucester Standard thus;

On the ground floor, the entrance from the side street leads into a large hall, 30 feet by 10 feet, giving direct access to matron's sitting room, nurse's day room, nurse's bed room, and a single ward for paying patients, the kitchen and domestic offices being arranged at the north end of the hall, with a separate entrance for the tradespeople from the side street. The mortuary, having direct cross ventilation and a top light, is placed in the yard at the north end of the hospital, and is also entered from the side street. The first floor, approached from the hall by a wide

The new Hospital being rebuilt in 1897.

staircase, contains two wards, one for male, the other for female patients. Each ward measures 28 feet by 14 feet, giving accommodation for four or five beds in each. The matron's bedroom is conveniently placed between the two wards, and has direct access to both. Each ward is provided with separate well isolated lavatory accommodation, and one bath room, with a plentiful supply of hot and cold water, serves both wards. A single ward is also arranged on this floor for paying patients, and an operating room with a north top light. There is also a separate bedroom for the use of servants. This new building cost over £2,000 and in the first year 47 patients were treated. The YMCA moved into the old premises across the street.

The town's General Practitioners always ran the hospital with specialists being called in when necessary. The local landed gentry subscribed to the running of the hospital and could provide a 'letter of introduction' for any employee who needed treatment to exempt them from charges. In 1910 the Board of Guardians of the Workhouse were charged 7s. 6d. per week when one of their inmates had

The Market Cross and Hospital c1910. Note the gas light on No. 1 High St.

to be admitted to the Cottage Hospital. Rule 2 stated that "Patients of unsound mind, epilepsy, enteric, infectious and contagious or incurable disease shall NOT be admitted."

By the end of the First World War the hospital was too small. The YMCA hall in Abbeyfield House was purchased and turned into an annexe containing seven beds in 1920. Lady Suffolk bought the XXX Inn (St. Michaels House) for use as the maternity home but the adaptation was held in abeyance. Larger premises were still needed, more room was required for patients and since only the Matron could be accommodated, houses had to be rented for the other nurses. The trustees explored the possibility of extending the Market Cross premises but the cost, £7,000, and other problems such as the noise of motor traffic (even though straw was often laid on nearby roads to deaden the sound) caused them to abandon this idea.

Joe Moore, the Chairman of Managers of the Malmesbury Cottage Hospital, bought the Manor House on the Chippenham Road, Burton Hill in July 1925 for £8,000. The old hospital was closed on 12th December 1925 and subsequently sold for £4,870. The new premises were opened on 16th January 1926, having cost a further £2,414 15s. 4d. to adapt. Here there was an operating theatre, 30 beds, five private wards and six maternity beds, as well as accommodation for staff and an on-site laundry. The staff comprised a matron, two sisters, two staff nurses, five probationers and a sister midwife. The Countess of Suffolk donated £1,000, the income from which went towards the running costs. At this time there was a weekly report in the local papers recording those who had made gifts to the hospital which usually comprised vegetables, flowers, cakes, meat or papers. Up until the National Health Service Act 1946 the Carnival continued to contribute funds to the hospital.

The services offered by the hospital expanded over the years - an Ear, Nose and Throat Clinic was added in 1930, a Heart Clinic in 1931 and a Speech Therapist after 1947. Later the hospital came under review for a considerable time and the facilities gradually diminished. Around 1990 the operating theatre closed but a few years later a day surgical unit for minor procedures was opened. The activity at the hospital was probably the highest it had ever been. Each year over 100 babies were delivered, 7,500 casualties treated and 1,500 X-rays taken. There were three wards & two single bed rooms for 300 patients a year, a day hospital, physiotherapy & occupational therapy treating 3,000 patients, clinics provided by 15 consultants from Bath, as well as twilight community nursing and district nursing services. The hospital specialised in nursing of the elderly, convalescence and terminal care. From this peak services started to diminish.

Until the end of the 1990s the Minor Injuries Unit offered 24-hour cover but then only opened during the day. Plans were announced in 2003 for a new type of hospital which would be a flagship for community healthcare. But facilities began to close – X-rays in 2004 followed by the Maternity Unit, despite being lauded in Parliament as a centre of excellence. At the end of 2006 the last patients were moved to Chippenham and demolition began.

The purpose built Primary Care Centre is next to the main road with a 28 apartment close care facility, Townsend Court, alongside and the 80 bed care home, Athelstan House, at the rear. There are six intermediate care beds provided for the NHS and ten short stay beds for people undergoing rehabilitation before returning home. These are run by the Order of St. John Care Trust. Athelstan House specialises in dementia and mental health conditions. It provides long term nursing and residential care as well as offering short term rehabilitation or respite care.

Dentists

The first evidence of dentists working in the town comes from Kelly's 1903 Directory when Sutton Gardiner, High Street, Walter Perry, High Street and Collier W. Pridham LDS, 20 Gloucester Street were in practice. Mr. Perry is listed in 1907 and Mr. Pridham continued to be listed until 1915. However in the 1911 census William Lintern, the Rural District Highway Surveyor, occupied 20 Gloucester Street so Mr. Pridham must have just run a surgery there.

After the Great War until 1931 H. E. Connell Cole had a daily dental surgery at Mrs. Willsdon's, High Street, 9am to 7pm. At the same time Alfred Daniel Soar took up residence at 20 Gloucester Street and his advertisements stated; *Hours 10am to 6pm Fees moderate, painless extraction, re-modelling and repairs a speciality. All work guaranteed.* He also had a surgery in Tetbury during the 1920s, retiring in 1943. During the late 1930s John Isaac Dudley Griffiths ran a clinic at 44 Gloucester Street on Fridays.

Between 1943 and 1959 Leonard Gardiner was the resident dentist at 20 Gloucester Street, acting as Burton Hill School's dentist for the 12 years leading up to his retirement. In 1958 a partnership led by Leslie Barker-Tufft and Charles Brown bought Avon House, Abbey Row, moving their practice from 30-32 High Street which was to be developed. This was a large concern with surgeries in Chippenham, Calne, Corsham, Melksham and Wootton Bassett. The surgery was run by an Associate who paid the partnership 50% of his earnings in return for the premises and hardware but also had to pay rent for living accommodation. A number of other dentists worked for this partnership until in April 1974 the practice was sold to Michael Lewis and Christopher Dixey. They moved the surgery to 27a Abbey Row which had been used by Dr. Sillars and ten years later moved to 21 St. Mary's Street which was renamed the Barley Mow Dental Surgery. This practice has expanded over the years and one of the associates, Michael Bassett-Cross set up his own practice at Eastgate House, Oxford Street in 1996. Michael Lewis left the practice in 1997 when the practitioners were Christopher Dixey, Bruce Morden and Rory McNulty. Christopher Dixey retired in 2002 and was replaced by Nikki Ford.

In the early 1970s there was a dental clinic for school-children at 22 Cross Hayes, as inspection and treatment for them was required by the Education Act 1944. This later this moved to Gable House in the High Street. There is now an NHS practice located in the Primary Care Centre.

Malmesbury League of Friends

This society was founded in 1960 with the object of helping the matron, staff and patients of the hospital by buying amenities not provided by the state. The first items purchased were six garden chairs, 30 wooden fruit bowls & fruit knives and a door for the mortuary! The original Chairman was Edward A. Hider (1906-1977). Their projects soon became more ambitious. They raised £1,500 for a sluice room, completed in 1963. Immediately fundraising began again for a new

Sister's office. More minor projects quickly followed, for example portable telephones for the use of patients in 1966. The following year the first large scheme was tackled, new out-patients and X-ray departments with modern equipment provided by the authority then in charge, the Mid-Wilts Hospital Management Committee. The original budget was £6,000, Linolite pledged £200 per annum for 7 years, Carnival gave £750 in 1967, £800 in 1969 & £1,000 in 1970 and South Cotswold Rotary £500.

The early 1970s saw the construction of a Day room completed in 1975 for just under £6,000 and it was reported that £23,000 had been raised in 10 years. Legacies, flag days and social events continued and with secure funds, projects could be completed quicker. In 1977 a £4,700 side ward was completed. The League did not approve the Regional Board's first tender for the work and £1,000 was saved.

Not only did the League provide facilities for the comfort and convenience of staff and patients they also ensured the best medical equipment was available. In 1980 they provided an advanced shortwave diathermy machine not available at Bath or Swindon for use in the Physiotherapy Department. A Slit lamp for the Opthalmic specialist, a photo-therapy unit for jaundiced babies and a new foetal heart monitor were amongst other items provided. New beds were installed throughout the hospital with the help of Carnival and South Cotswold Rotary Club. Finances were reported to be healthy with the receipt of two substantial legacies and an anonymous donation which paid for another new side ward. A Day surgery unit was planned for 1985/86 and the League were asked to contribute £30,000 of the £330,000 total cost and this was raised in less than a year. The work was completed on time in October 1987 but there was great frustration when the unit remained unused because of the unaffordable running costs. Part of it opened in May 1988 but it was not completely open for another two years. At the end of the decade £6,000 was contributed towards £20,000 for an ultra-sound scanner in Chippenham to be used by expectant mothers from that town, Devizes and Malmesbury.

Optimism was high about the hospital's future after the publication of a leaflet entitled *Health Services in Malmesbury The 1990s.* which outlined plans for substantial investment. However within a year there was an NHS reorganisation and management passed to a new Trust. Fire Regulations required new wider electronically controlled doors, flooring, carpet, curtains, bathroom fittings & redecoration and the League provided nearly one third of the £100,000 cost. By 1993 £200,000 had been spent by the Friends over 20 years. Thereafter the threat of cuts and closures increased which the League did its best to prevent and the Carnival pledged money to assist this aim. In 1995, after another two legacies had been received, £50,000 was spent on the Minor Surgery unit with the Health Care Trust only having to add £10,000. Two years later the Day Surgery Suite was enhanced with a further grant of £19,000. Shortly afterwards a Birthing pool was added to the Maternity ward.

As facilities closed in the Community Hospital the emphasis of the League changed. In 2003 money was given to the Alzheimer's Society to provide care at home for sufferers following the closure of the Day Care Centre. In 2011 £25,000 was pledged towards a mobile chemotherapy unit which will visit the Primary Care Centre and obviate the need to travel to Oxford. Further grants of £12,000 have been made to the Air Ambulance, which in 2014 announced it would run its own helicopter after the contract to share Wiltshire's Police machine comes to an end.

Public Utilities

Water

Malmesbury owes its existence to ready access to water on the hilltop. For centuries the town relied upon wells, many communal, and springs. For example several families along Bristol Street used a spring whose water was (and still is) piped through the stone wall opposite the old Plough Inn, 12 Foxley Road. As part of the town's efforts to improve public health in the middle of the 19th Century a reliable water source was required. A good spring was found in Conygre Mead on meadow land owned by the Manor. The name Conygre Mead means rabbit field and this had provided a source of meat for the monks of the Abbey. The Malmesbury Waterworks Company Limited was formed on 9th September 1864 with the object of providing a water supply to the town. Lord Northwick gave the Company a perpetual right to take this spring water which was piped to a pumping station in Holloway (now a small public garden) from whence it was pumped to the tower near Abbey House. This tank gave much trouble in later years. The pump was driven originally by a gas engine, later electric. Every morning and evening it was switched on to top up the tank. During the day men from Wessex Electricity would keep an eye on the marker on the tower to ensure that the tank did not completely empty. There was concern over the purity of the water supplied by the Company and the lack of pressure, particularly on Sundays. After an outbreak of typhoid in 1899 the Borough Council wanted to buy out the Company and after arbitration over the price, £6,540, was able to do so in 1902. At that time the maximum output was 220,000 gallons per day.

The quality and reliability of the supply from Conygre Mead had been in question for some time and a new source of water was needed. As the borehole at the old milk factory in Park Road was suitable, the Borough Council bought it in 1940. This site was used by the military as a laundry during the war, the soldiers being billeted in Stainsbridge Mill. It then became a Council Depot which in 1986 was converted into

The Holloway pumping station, centre foreground, with the water tower on the horizon.

the present small industrial estate. Before the end of the war discussions about water supply began between the Borough and Rural District Council. As demand increased, the existing tank's capacity of 55,000 gallons was inadequate and it was at the end of its useful life. In 1950 a scheme for a new concrete tower at Whychurch with two compartments, one holding 200,000 gallons for the Borough, the other 100,000 for the Rural District areas of Cowbridge, Burton Hill, Milbourne and Filands. This was completed in 1953 by Sir Lindsay Parkinson & Co. Ltd., whose tender of just over £50,000 was the lowest received.

In 1962 the North West Wiltshire Water Board took over responsibility for water supply from the Borough Councils of Calne, Chippenham, Devizes and Malmesbury and the Rural District Councils of Bradford & Melksham, Cricklade & Wootton Bassett, Calne & Chippenham, Devizes and Malmesbury. The water tower developed serious leaks in 1973 and although repairs were made a new tower was built in 1983 at a cost of almost £500,000. It is smaller, only holding 132,000 gallons, but an underground reservoir increases the total capacity to 396,000 gallons.

The 1798 Improvement Act allowed the laying of drains, the first of which ran from the Postern Gate along Oxford Street to Cross Hayes Lane in 1799. These sewers were made of stone and known as 'drock' drains which discharged directly into the rivers. After the formation of the Borough Council, 12" pipes were substituted for these *large square drains along which a man might have wheeled a barrow.* The Council put forward a scheme in 1904 for a sewage works to be constructed outside the borough which the Rural District opposed. The Medical Officer reported that no illness had been caused by river pollution and through natural action *the water became as pure as it was before.* Despite pressure from the County Council this scheme went no further.

It was not until after the Second World War that the issue was revisited. A comprehensive scheme was agreed in 1951 but progress was slow due to the Government placing restrictions on capital expenditure. The 3.9 acre site for the sewage works north of the railway near Cowbridge and adjacent to the Malmesbury-Lea footpath was bought in 1953 but it was not until 1961 that work started. The final cost was £120,369 12s. 9d. Further extensions and improvements have been made since, including in 2007 the installation of a large new sewer over the Wortheys serving northern and western parts of the town with improved treatment facilities. Land has been acquired to cope with future increased demand.

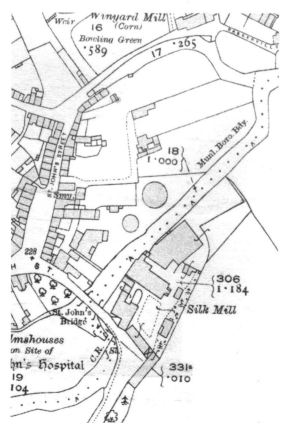

The gasworks are in the centre of this map, the coke ovens to the south west of the site.

The areas next to the rivers have always been subject to flooding but the issue has become more important as the economic losses have increased due to fitted furniture & carpets and the contents of a modern home being more prone to damage. A severe flood in July 1968 with more the following May led the Bristol Avon River Authority to carry out some flood alleviation work in 1971. Seven years later the hatches which had controlled water levels but required to be manually raised and lowered began to be replaced but it was not until 1985 when the last were removed. This system worked well until tightened budgets reduced river maintenance to a minimum leading to flood damage in January 1999, October 2000, October 2002, January 2007, November 2012 and December 2013. The Environment Agency is preparing a new scheme.

Gas Supply

The gasworks was one of the benefits that resulted from the 1798 *Act for Paving the Footways, and for Cleansing, Lighting, and Regulating the Streets, and other public passages and places within the Borough of Malmesbury, in the County of Wilts; and* the *Avenues leading into the same; and for Removing and Preventing Nuisances, Annoyances, and Obstructions therein*, sponsored by the Corporation. The Act named 26 individuals plus the Alderman, High Steward and Vicar of St. Pauls as Improvement Commissioners. Any vacancy would be filled by the remaining Commissioners' nominees who had to reside within five miles of the Borough and with a few exceptions had to earn £10 per year in rent or profit from property. 'Poor Law Rates' of 6d. in the pound were collected from all householders in the Borough together with Sunday tolls at the turnpike gates levied on animals coming to and from the town except for those taking people to church. They started a drainage network, arranged for cleansing of the streets and laid pavements. One interesting Clause in the Act reads; *That all Persons inhabiting within the said Borough, shall, from and after the passing of this Act, sweep, scrape, and clean the Footways before their respective Houses, Buildings, Walls, and Premises ... on every Saturday* ... Perhaps this needs to be re-enacted!

In 1836 the Commissioners encouraged the formation of the Malmesbury Gas & Coke Company and began to erect gas streetlights, often outside Commissioner's premises! The public supply of gas had begun 25 years before in London with the first provincial scheme beginning in 1816. In 1894 a second gasholder was built with a diameter of 51 feet 6 inches, capable of holding 31,000 cubic feet, giving a total capacity of 55,000 cubic feet. Latterly there were three coke ovens to produce the gas which was stored in the two gasometers. Pressure was maintained by placing lead weights on top of a small tank in the meter room, greater weight being needed when the gasometers were low. The Company was taken over by the South Western Gas Corporation on 1st November 1934. But the industry was nationalised in 1948 becoming South Western Gas Board. In 1949 Malmesbury's gas production ceased with town gas being piped from Stroud. The discovery of natural gas in the North Sea led to conversion of the town's 627 gas customers from town gas in July 1971. Shortly afterwards the gasometers were demolished.

Following the demolition of the larger gasholder the small one remains.

Postal Services

At the end of the 15th Century the King's messages were sent by horsemen known as Posts who would each cover about 20 miles of road. A public service started in 1635 and as early as 1689 post for the area was sent from London via Highworth three times a week. The universal Penny Post introduced in 1840 led to an expansion of the network. The first Victorian postmaster in Malmesbury seems to have been a watchmaker, Henry Garlick Hanks (1789-1879) of 31 High Street. He was succeeded by his son John Hook Hanks (1829-1876) whose widow Emma (1839-1886) carried on for a few years. Albert Pugh and then Miss Ruth Bartlett continued the service from No. 31 until 1902.

At this time mails arrived and were delivered three times a day Monday to Saturday and once on Sundays. There were wall letterboxes at the Triangle, the Railway Station and Burton Hill. Each had five collections a day with one on Sundays except for Burton Hill. Money orders were issued and paid between 8am and 8pm each weekday. Mail-carts ran from Chippenham through the town to Tetbury with connections to other towns.

J. E. Ponting bought the tenements at Berry's Entry at the end of the 19th Century, constructing a new building there in 1902, the address being 41 High Street. This was leased to the Post Office until they bought the freehold many years later.

From 1902-1990 all the services were located here; telegraph, sorting and counter with the telephone exchange on the first floor from 1907 until 1946. In 1960 the entrance from the High Street to the sorting office at the rear of the premises was widened to allow small vans to enter. Post Office Counters moved their operation into the Circle-K (now Co-operative) Supermarket at 8 High Street in 1990.

Although the premises were now larger than required, little effort was made to locate somewhere more suitable. In August 1999 the Post Office announced that it was hoping to relocate the Sorting Office to the outskirts of the town but in June 2012 the operation was moved to Royal Wootton Bassett. The building is now occupied by Mindvision.

The Post Office is in the centre with a sign reading Post Office Public Telephone hanging outside.

Telephone

The telegraph system preceded the development of telephones. Before Malmesbury had its own telegraph office, telegrams for the town were sent to the railway station at Minety and then conveyed by a Post Office employee on horseback. This cost 1s. per mile, or 7s. for the whole journey. In 1868 the High Street Post Office was connected to the system by a cable from Minety. The cost of sending a telegram dropped to 1s. for 20 words. It was not until 1890 that a wire was laid to Easton Grey and by 1902 Joseph Poole, owner of the Myriorama travelling shows, reported receiving and dispatching over 100 telegrams a week. His request for a telegraph at the Westport sub-post office was denied.

Towards the end of the 19th Century the Borough Council was approached by the National Telephone Company for permission to provide a service in the town. This was refused on the grounds that it was bad policy to hand over a monopoly to a private company. In 1903 the Council asked the GPO to provide the service for which 25 customers had to be found. Only Alfred Long, the High Street grocer, came forward although five Councillors also indicated they wished to be subscribers. It was not until the summer of 1906 that sufficient people had applied and the new exchange opened on 7 August 1907. This manual exchange, type CBS1, on the first floor of the Post Office, was manned at night by the caretaker who lived on the top floor. This flat was still occupied by a Post Office engineer in the 1960s. The number of lines served increased from 50 in 1922 to 193 by 1939 covering an area from Shipton Moyne in the west to the Somerfords in the east. A new automatic exchange, type UAX 14, was built in Lower High Street before the start of the Second World War but not commissioned until 1946. Dialling 999 for emergency calls was introduced in 1950. In 1970 Subscriber Trunk Dialling brought to an end the necessity for long distance calls to be connected by operators in Chippenham. Digital technology led to an exchange being built at Burton Hill in 1987. The old exchange was sold in 1990 and two years later converted into the Town Forge.

The Forge was run by Andrew Poynton, Fellow of the Worshipful Company of Farriers, who specialises in remedial work with interests ranging from orthopaedic, young stock and management of subtle lameness in competition horses. He also works with severe laminitic cases, for which his innovative thermoplastic Imprint support shoes were first designed. Andrew handles referral work from veterinary practices throughout the UK. As little hot metalwork is now required the building was converted into a house in 2014.

Electricity

Cowbridge House was among the first houses in the area to have an electricity supply which was generated from their mill. J. E. Ponting in the High Street had its own generators but it was not until 1922 that a public supply was first contemplated. Capt. E. M. Scott Mackirdy encouraged the Western Electric Distributing Corporation Ltd. to obtain a Special Order in August 1923 *To supply electrical energy ... within the Borough of Malmesbury and so much of the parishes of Brokenborough, Charlton, Lea and Cleverton, and Saint Paul Without ... as lies within a radius of one mile from the north-western corner of the Abbey Building.* The Borough Council wanted no overhead wires.

LOCAL TELEPHONE EXCHANGE DIRECTORY.

1	Call Office	Post Office
17	Adye & Hinwood, Ltd., Bacon Curers ...	Malmesbury
4	Adye & Son, Provision Merchants	High street
5	Alexander W., Coal and Corn Merchant ...	Gloucester road
6	Bartlett Bros., Tailors & Breeches Makers ...	High street
8	Bower & Son, Drapers and Outfitters ...	High street
9	Clements H. C., Butcher	High street
10	Duck & Reed, Brewers	Malmesbury
11	Emery I., Baker and Confectioner ...	High street
2	Farrant H., Licensed Grocery, Provisions ...	High street
12	Garlick H., Butcher	High street
13	Hindle T. W. W., Veterinary Surgeon ...	Sunnyside
14	Jones H., Posting Master ...	"King's Arms" Hotel
20	Jones & Son, Cycle and Motor Dealers ...	High street
16	Lockstone W. & E., Grocers, &c. ...	Oxford street
3	Long A. E., Grocer & Provision Merchant ...	High street
18	Millen Dr. S. A., Physician	Milverton
19	Moore J., Posting Master	"Bell" Hotel
15	Ponting J. E. & Sons, Ironmongers, &c. ...	High street
21	Ratcliffe H. N., Chemist	High street
22	Ratcliffe & Son, Engineers, &c. ...	Westport Works
23	Rich T., Fishmonger and Butcher ...	High street
24	Rich Wm., Posting Master	Gloucester road
25	Suffolk & Berkshire, Earl of	Charlton Park
25a	Ditto ditto	Estate Office
25b	Ditto ditto	The Cottage
26	Woodman W., Baker and Grocer ...	The Triangle
27	Yorkshire Insurance Co. (J. D. Curtis, Insp.)	Malmesbury
28	Great Western Railway	Malmesbury

The first telephone directory contained in the 1906 Riddick's Malmesbury Almanack.

However Councillors immediately made complaints about the number of broken paving stones when cables were laid. The Malmesbury Electric Supply Company Ltd. was registered on 16 October 1923 and Capt. Mackirdy became Chairman.

A generating station was constructed in the Postern Mill, no longer used by the Stroud Brewery. It was hoped that a water turbine would supply sufficient power for the network but the flow was unreliable and a petrol engine from an army tank was provided on standby. A bank of glass-sided batteries supplied direct current at 240 volts. The system expanded, an overhead cable was installed in Bristol Street followed by wires to Stainsbridge & Tetbury Hill by 1926. The following year a contract was agreed to electrically power the water supply pumps. In 1929 cables connected Horsefair to Foundry & Burnham Roads. Arrangements were made during the Truckle Bridge rebuilding to maintain the head of water for the turbine generator and the town's network was linked to Chippenham. An overhead wire was completed to Charlton Park.

In 1932 the changeover was made from Direct Current to Alternating Current. As a result the town's generating station was redundant. One wonders if any contributions were made by the supplier towards the cost of new appliances required by customers. Probably this change led to smaller generating costs and reduced charges were introduced the next year. In the next few years the expansion continued. In 1934 Lea was connected but it was not economic to include isolated parts north of the Filands road. The YMCA switched to electric lighting in 1935 and St. Johns Street, Burnivale and Foxley Road joined the network. However when four new council houses were built in Brokenborough in 1954 there was no electricity in the village until February 1955.

The Law

Much of the dispensing of justice was administered by the Corporation. Borough Sessions, presided over by the Alderman or his Deputy, were held in the town's Courthouse from at least the beginning of the 18th Century. These courts dealt with the repair of roads and bridges, apprenticeships, the setting of poor rates and other administrative matters as well as criminal hearings. Petty Sessions for the Malmesbury hundred were heard in the town from the first half of the 19th Century. The parliamentary committee on Municipal Corporations in 1833 reported that:

The alderman and twelve capital burgesses ... form the Ruling Body of the corporation: a body, which has long ceased to answer any municipal purposes, and has exercised no function but that of returning to parliament the nominees of the patron of the borough.

From the foregoing statement, it appears that this body is self-elected, irresponsible to the inhabitants of the town, and composed chiefly of labourers without education, and of the least instructed class of retail tradesmen.

The present alderman, a pig-killer and chief magistrate of the town, is scarcely able to write his name.

The alderman-elect, Simon Pike, chief magistrate for the ensuing year, is a labouring plasterer and tiler; and can neither read or write.

Richard Neate, and Christopher Aaron, successively chief magistrates, were both of them unable to write, and had no other substance or calling than keeping a few cows.

It may be supposed that such persons, however irreproachable in their private capacity, would scarcely be competent to discharge the function of chief magistrate in a considerable town. But, whether it be owing to the singular distribution of certain town lands which prevails in Malmesbury, or to any other cause, the morals of the labouring class in that town appear to be below the standard of the neighbouring country; and among those who have served the office of chief magistrate some are not exempt from the reproach of frequent intoxication, even during their year of office.

No doubt there was some special pleading for the town because although the report of the Royal Commission in 1835 stated that; *At Malmesbury, the magistrates are often unable to write or read*, the Borough Sessions continued until 1886 when the Old Corporation lost its political power and a new panel of magistrates was formed. Prominent local citizens together with the Mayor of the Borough Council and later the Chairman of the Rural District Council became magistrates, dealing with criminal cases and licensing applications.

For many years the Town Hall housed the local law courts. The magistrates probably started using it after 1886. Before the last war sittings of magistrates were held on the first and third Wednesday of the month. From 1st April 1977 the Malmesbury magistrates ceased to be a separate Division but fortnightly hearings continued in the Town Hall until 1991. The hearings were held in the Wesleyan or Assembly Rooms. Although some local worthies continued as magistrates their administrative base was in Chippenham.

The County Court, serving 43 parishes including Tetbury, also sat in the Town Hall from at least 1859. A century later Malmesbury had become part of the Swindon County Court, but hearings were still held here monthly. In 1919 the following was reported;

THE JUDGE ON THE STAGE. – At Tuesday's County Court his Honour Judge Elliott transacted the business of his court from a seat on the platform, around which heavy maroon drapery belonging to a travelling theatrical company was suspended. A narrow opening in the drapery just gave a view of his Honour. At the foot was a piano and other stage accessories, while two of the large windows had the light entirely excluded by heavy curtains, closely drawn. What the learned Judge thought of his extraordinary surroundings must be a matter for surmise.

Forrester and Forrester acted as Clerks to the County Court and in 1927-8 when the Town Hall was closed during construction of the extension hearings were held in their office. During the 1970s these hearings came to an end.

Forrester Sylvester Mackett, 59 High Street

This firm has been practising in the town since at least the early 1790s under a variety of names. Henry Gale, the first of the antecedents, sold his practice to William Stephen Jones (1817-1898) in 1857 after taking holy orders. Jones, a native of Malmesbury and articled to Thomas Chubb, had opened an office in Cross Hayes in 1847 and five years later moved to 59 High Street, premises still occupied by the practice. William Forrester (1833-1902) was admitted as a solicitor in 1855 and entered into the partnership of Jones & Forrester in 1858. Charles Forbes Moir (1861-1928) came to the town in 1886, joined as a partner and the practice became Forrester & Moir. William Forrester married twice and had six sons, two of whom became solicitors but only the second, Arthur Livesey (1870-1936), after a short career in engineering, joined the firm in 1902. His father died that year during his third term as Mayor. Reginald Arthur

William Forrester wearing the Mayor's chain. It now has a double row of links as each Mayor used to donate one.

Collingwood Forrester (1907-1999), Arthur's son, became a solicitor in 1932. Moir too had a son who was a solicitor but he chose to work in London. The firm changed its name to Forrester and Forrester.

In 1935 Reginald opened an office in Chippenham and two years later took over Chubb & Son of Malmesbury. Unfortunately Arthur was killed the following year having fallen from the first floor at the Old Bell. Reginald remained the sole partner for the next 10 years. After the war Derek Williamson (1902-1959) joined him to run the Malmesbury branch. After he died James Toogood was persuaded to join the firm from Robbins Olivey who acted as London agents for Forrester & Forrester. For many years articled clerks spent six months in London with Robbins Olivey to widen their experience. In 1961 Toogood and John Burridge, who had been articled to Reginald, became partners. The Chippenham office expanded through acquisition, notably Keary, Stokes & White in 1962, a large Chippenham practice started in the 18th Century which had an office at Corsham. Another office was opened in Tetbury in 1974, but both it and the one at Corsham were closed in 1990. Reginald retired in 1977 but his daughter did not maintain the family connection. In 2012 Forresters merged with Sylvester Mackett and the combined practice has offices in Chippenham, Trowbridge, Warminster and Malmesbury.

Chubb & Son

Thomas Chubb (1793-1869) began work as a solicitor in town during 1819. He became the Corporation's Deputy High Steward and dealt with the municipal reform of the 1830s and served as the County Court's Registrar. His son Thomas Henry Chubb (1824-1888) held the same posts and secured important concessions in the municipal reform of 1883-86. Thomas Henry had four sons, the second of whom, Montague Henry Chubb (1855-1942) and fourth Alfred William Chubb (1861-1957) continued the business. Montague Chubb carried out many public functions being appointed Town Clerk and Clerk to the Magistrates in 1874. He became first Clerk to the Joint Burial Board in 1882, first Clerk to the 'new' Corporation in 1886, Deputy High Steward 1888 and High Steward in 1918, as well as being Clerk to the Rural District Council and holding many other posts in surrounding villages. He was given the Freedom of the Borough in 1935 on his 80th birthday after 50 years service to the Borough Council. Chubb's practice at 36 Cross Hayes closed in 1937 shortly after Alfred left the district. The clients were transferred to Forrester and Forrester.

Montague Chubb, a pencil sketch by H. Collier.

Clark & Smith

Frederick Ernest Smith (1844-1939), although born in Worthing came to Malmesbury in 1870 to take articles with John Alexander Handy (1827-1890). Walter Trevelyan Clark (1856-1916), son of Samuel (also a solicitor), was articled to Frederick Blake and admitted as a solicitor in 1879. Soon afterwards Smith and Clark who lived close to each other in Gloucester Road, entered into partnership and bought Blake's practice. Their office was at 1 Market Cross, now occupied by a travel agent. Clark's son, also Walter Trevelyan (1890-1960), went to work in London but returned to join the partnership on his father's death. Frederick retired in 1930 and moved back to Worthing seven years later. The practice continued to be run by Walter's family until his grandsons Donald Trevelyan (1916-1984) and Godfrey Trevelyan (1920-1978) broke up the business in 1961, trading separately for several years. Godfrey had offices at 52 Gloucester Street and retired in 1975 when Donald (who had been in practice in Tetbury) opened an office in Oxford Street, later moving to St. Michael's House, Market Cross. On Donald's retirement the practice was sold to Blakemore's of Tetbury who shut the Malmesbury office sometime after 1985.

Jeary & Lewis

John Treasure of Gloucester opened an office in Olivers Lane in 1975. At some stage Robert Clarkson took over. In 1984 Michael Jeary and Jill Canvin bought the practice, still trading as Robert Clarkson, but their partnership broke down. The following year David Lewis left North Wiltshire District Council and replaced Jill. David entered into a partnership and the practice was renamed Jeary & Lewis. In 1988 they opened an office at 46 Market Place, Chippenham and in 1991 closed the Malmesbury office.

Transport

Highways

The road layout within the town centre is virtually unchanged since Saxon times. Also the road connections with other settlements are ancient. Alfred's Kingway led from Royal estates in Foxley through Malmesbury and south through Corston (thus the 20th Century Kingway railway bridge) to Chippenham. The Oxford to Bristol route through the town was of strategic importance until the Great West Road through Reading, Newbury, Marlborough, Chippenham and Bath gained prominence. As more goods and people travelled between towns, the weight of wagons and coaches increased causing damage to road surfaces. A measure to counter this was the introduction of turnpikes to levy charges on wheeled vehicles. They were introduced on the Cirencester via Tetbury, Chippenham, Cricklade and Sherston roads in 1756. A direct turnpike route to Cirencester through Hankerton was opened in 1778. It was not until 1809 that turnpikes were made on the road to Wootton Bassett and Swindon. The Chippenham, Cirencester and Tetbury roads were dis-turnpiked in 1874 with the others following two years later.

Parish vestries had the responsibility to maintain roads after the reign of Henry VIII. The Highways Act 1835 obliged each parish to appoint a surveyor and gave them the power to collect a rate to cover the costs. A further Act in 1862 made a radical change by enabling the County Justices of the Peace to divide the County into Highway Districts which grouped parishes together. The Malmesbury District covered: Alderton; Ashley; Bremilham; Brinkworth; Brokenborough; Charlton; Crudwell; Dauntsey; Easton Grey; Foxley; Garsdon; Hankerton; Hullavington; Kemble; Lea & Cleverton; Long Newnton; Luckington; Malmesbury St. Paul; Minety; Norton; Oaksey; Poole; Sherston Magna; Sherston Parva; Somerford Magna; Somerford Parva; Sopworth; Westport. Excluded were those parts of Malmesbury St. Paul and Westport which lay within the Borough boundary. Each of these parishes elected a waywarden except Brinkworth and Sherston which had two each. These officials formed the Highways Board which appointed a clerk, treasurer and district surveyor. The cost of administration was spread over the whole district although the repair costs were still charged to individual parishes. Malmesbury's Board first met in April 1864 and elected the Earl of Suffolk as Chairman.

Within the Borough the Improvement Commissioners were responsible for maintaining, lighting & cleaning the streets and paving footways. In 1862 this body became the Urban Sanitary Authority which was succeeded by the democratic Borough Council in 1886. Responsibility for all roads was vested in Wiltshire County Council on its formation in 1889 but the Borough continued to maintain roads within the town for another 30 years.

The roads were maintained with stone often obtained from fields closeby. Considerable money was spent during dry weather employing men and equipment to spray water to minimise dust. However just before the First World War a great change took place – tarspraying. It seems the first area given this treatment was Burton Hill, carried out by the County Council. This was followed by the Borough in May 1914 spraying High Street (although surfaced in 1906 with a mixture of black rock and tar, fresh stone had to be laid in 1909), the north side of Burnham Road and westwards from Tower House in Oxford Street to the Triangle. In 1916 The Council bought their own machine after experiencing difficulty in finding a contractor to carry out the work when required. After the war further roads were surfaced – for example St. Johns and Ingram Streets in 1921. The Rural District Council reported that increased traffic required more roads to be treated with tar to lower the maintenance cost. They sought Government grants for the purpose but had to increase the Rate from 3s. 2d. to 5s. 2d. in 1925. The Council's Surveyor regularly reported progress as more of the road network was tarred until 1932 when it can be assumed all had been done.

As all roads into the town, except from Sherston, have to cross a river there are five major bridges, St. John's or the Town Bridge from Chippenham, Cowbridge from Swindon, St. Leonard's or Holloway Bridge from Cirencester, Stainsbridge from Tetbury and Truckle or Turtle Bridge from Foxley with two minor ones, Goosebridge and Abbey Mill Bridge. In the early 19th Century St. John's Bridge was in fact two, a single arch over the stream leading to the mill and two arches across the river. A new structure was erected, the mill leat being restricted to a culvert with the main bridge comprising three arches. However this proved inadequate and the bridge was rebuilt in 1884 with its road width increased from 14' 6" to 20' 8". The only later improvement was the installation of a separate footbridge in 1964. Holloway Bridge was rebuilt in 1822 as its three arches were too small for flood water. It was reconstructed in 1888. During the 20th Century strengthening work was needed – Truckle Bridge (where unusually there was a temporary bridge for light traffic) and Cowbridge were rebuilt in 1930 and Holloway Bridge in 1935. However it was not until 1962 that Staines Bridge was widened from a single track by a prefabricated concrete span being placed on top of the old structure. Cowbridge proved to be incapable of carrying 44 tonne vehicles and was replaced in 2007.

Staines Bridge in 1960 looking north. Athelstan Garage is on the left with an Athelstan coach on the forecourt. The market is behind the advertising hoarding with the Railway Hotel hidden behind trees in the centre.

Improvements have been necessary to deal with changing traffic patterns. St. Mary's Church wall was rebuilt to widen Gloucester Road in 1908 and 40 years later the walls were lowered to improve visibility at the St. Mary's Street junction. St. Dennis Lane was widened in 1936 when half of 34 High Street was demolished. It was proposed to improve Cross Hayes Lane in 1938 when the Borough Council purchased 11 Oxford Street and the buildings to the south of it but the work was not carried out until 1957. The following year a scheme to widen Foxley Road at its junction with Bristol Road which had been proposed for 30 years was implemented. No. 4 Bristol Road was demolished in 1974 to make the junction with Burnivale safer. Burnham Road was widened in 1964 when the outhouses of Nos. 18-26 were removed. The Town Centre one way system up the High Street, along Oxford Street, down Cross Hayes Lane and around Cross Hayes was introduced in 1962. The bypass was built in 1974. Silver Street was made one-way c2005.

The narrow streets of the town have contributed to many accidents. One of the earliest occurred in 1915 when a car struck a pedestrian in Abbey Row. The injured lady pedestrian sued the car driver but lost the case. *The defendant did not act with reasonable caution and prudence by going too fast over a tarred road. ... the actual cause of the accident was not due to the defendant's negligence but to the*

The dangerous junction of the Swindon and Chippenham roads next to the Priory and opposite the Black Horse. This was not improved until the bypass opened.

plaintiff being so deaf. There must be judgment for the defendant with the usual costs. The first fatal motor accident occurred on 8 March 1921. The scaffolding was being removed from the War Memorial at the Triangle whilst a number of children played nearby. Beatrice Fry, 10 years old, suddenly jumped into the path of a lorry full of pigs on its way to Adye & Hinwood's bacon factory. The Inquest jury attributed no blame to the driver. Four years later Cecil Peglar was riding a motorcycle down Gloucester Road but collided with a horse drawn milk float at the junction with Park Road. He died after his head struck a lamp-post. In 1933 Elizabeth Gleed, aged 4, ran away from her 11 year-old sister outside a Fun Fair in the field behind the Railway Hotel and was struck by a Western National bus which had just crossed Stainsbridge on its way to Stroud. This was the scene for another fatality in 1946 when Mrs. Phyllis Rogers was knocked down by a car. Sunset Hill on the Tetbury Road was the location for a motorcycle accident in 1940 when Ronald Porter was killed and 11 years later Cyril Bond and John Curtis died when the utility van in which they were passengers collided head on with a milk tanker at the same place. Another motorcycle accident occurred near the Town Bridge in 1947 when John Beverstock took the corner too wide and collided with a lorry. Abbey Row is another blackspot – William Blake was crushed by a lorry when he was blown off his bicycle in 1959 and David Dawkins, 2 years old, was struck by a lorry when his mother was distracted three years later. Carol Vizor was killed by a lorry on Keene's Hill, Bristol Street near the junction with Foxley Road whilst cycling to work at Linolite. Reginald Price who worked for Ekco was hit by a lorry and killed in 1966 after he got out of a van which was collecting chairs from the Catholic Church in Cross Hayes for a children's party. A freak accident led to the death of Bertram Gardner when timber fell off a trailer at Burton Hill in 1990. Richard and Denise Rugg died in 2002

The toilet block of nos. 18-26 Burnham Road in 1964.

after their car collided with a van near the Dyson factory on Tetbury Hill. The owner of a burger van, Gordon Woodward, was killed after being struck by a motorcycle on the bypass in 2012.

To reduce accidents in the town centre a detailed survey was carried out by the County Council in the late 1990s. One proposal accepted was to introduce a central zone with speed limited to 20 mph. The zone's boundaries are just south of the Town Bridge, the Triangle and the bastion in Holloway. Within this area there are a number of speed cushions which are designed to allow buses and emergency vehicles to pass over them without hindrance. The idea of extending the zone along Gloucester Road and Bristol Street has been discussed but no action has yet been taken.

Car parking in the town centre has been a problem for a long time. It was first reported in the 1920s that farmers had difficulty finding a place to park on market days and there were complaints about parking in side streets. The Borough Council was urged to provide places where cars might be left. In 1924 parking was prohibited in Market Cross outside the hospital after 8pm but after the hospital moved this was rescinded. In 1926 parking places were designated in the following areas: Horsefair, 12; outside the Old Bell, 4; Cross Hayes, 75; Market Cross, 11; St. Johns Street, 14. In 1929 it was decided that lights were not required on cars parked at the Market Cross. An area for 16 cars marked out with white lines and lit by four street lights was also provided in Cross Hayes in 1932 where overnight parking without lights was permitted. Waiting in the High Street was limited to 20 minutes in 1954 but this was increased to one hour in 1971. Parking in Cross Hayes was restricted to two hours from 1969 when the first Traffic Warden, Mrs. Audrey Poole, was appointed but she resigned after a few months. The Borough Council opened the Old Station Yard as a car park in 1970 but it was poorly used at first as it was surfaced with gravel. It was not tarmacademed for another 13 years. The yard at the old Police Station in Burnham Road became a car park in 1979. Another derelict site, the old gas works, was made into private parking by the Warden & Freemen in 1994 followed two years later by the Old Orchard in St. Johns Street.

For more than 40 years further sites for parking have been sought including an area at the top of Holloway, in the grounds of Abbey House, the old Girls' School in Cross Hayes and the "four & twenty steps" field behind the Silk Mills, now a supermarket. In an effort to improve the turnover of cars, parking charges were introduced in Cross Hayes (25p per hour) in 1996 accompanied by the employment of a full time Traffic Warden. Tariffs have risen since – Cross Hayes increased to 50p per hour in 2006 but is now 40p for one hour, £1.20 for two. Station Yard was free until a daily charge of £4 was introduced in September 2006. This was reduced to £1 that December only to be increased to £5.60 for the whole day in April 2011. By 1998 Station Yard was overflowing and in 2005 a temporary extension for an extra 30 cars was provided. However the present high level of charges has reduced normal usage to about a quarter of the 145 spaces.

Railway
Malmesbury was ignored by the early pioneers of the railway age. The first scheme seems to have been the Wilts & Gloucester Junction Railway of 1845. This would have connected Stonehouse with Chippenham via Tetbury and Malmesbury. Although some surveying was done it failed in the face of opposition from landowners. A number of other ideas were floated but few got very far until the Wilts & Gloucestershire Railway considered putting a line from Christian Malford to Stroud. A great party was held on 1st July 1865 in a field near the Duke of York pub when the Countess of Suffolk cut the first sod. A very ornate spade and wheelbarrow used at this event is in the Athelstan Museum. The jollification was premature. The problems faced by this Company could not be overcome and it was wound up in 1871.

The worthies of Malmesbury were not put off by this expensive failure and began discussions to join the intended branch line of the Malmesbury Railway Company with the Great Western

The Railway Station in the early 20th Century. The Engine Shed to the left is the only building remaining.

Railway. In October 1871 a meeting was held in the Town Hall chaired by Colonel Charles Miles of Burton Hill House. Opened by Mr. W. S. Jones of Jones & Forrester, solicitors, it was attended by Walter Powell MP along with many other gentlemen and traders of the town. The proposal was to run a branch line to join the main line at Dauntsey, just over 6 miles away and estimated to cost £60,000. It was hoped to boost trade and improve the town's market, providing cheaper coal as well as enabling goods to be easily transported to and from the town. The station was to be sited on the largest area of flat land available to the north of the Abbey. Many troubles had to be overcome before the grand opening on 17th December 1877 and the full story is told in Mike Fenton's book, *The Malmesbury Branch*.

Changes occurred quickly in the local community and economy. Henry Long (1830-1902) who ran a daily omnibus from the Greyhound (now called the Smoking Dog), which he owned, to Chippenham (journey time 1½ hours) sold his transport equipment within a month of the railway opening. House prices rose. Malmesbury's market held on the 3rd Wednesday of the month prospered and February 1878 saw its best attendance for over 30 years. However enthusiasm did not endure and by 1900 the market was not so brisk. But trade for the Silk factory as well as for Adye and Hinwood's bacon factory in Park Road improved. Railway excursions were a feature with extra trains run for the Flower Show held at Burton Hill House. The other main items conveyed were coal and agricultural goods inwards with farm produce and milk traffic outwards. Stan Hudson remembered milk carts driven by farmers' sons racing neck and neck either to get to the station first or just to catch the milk train. Notwithstanding this activity, receipts did not cover the running costs and the company was taken over by the Great Western Railway on 1st July 1880.

The start of the First World War led to increased traffic on the branch with troops mobilising, military stores moving, Belgian refugees arriving to stay at Charlton Park and war casualties coming to the military hospital there. Towards the end of the war services had to be scaled down due mainly to the shortage of men, rolling stock and coal. With the war over things returned to normal with tourists coming on special excursion trains.

The GWR began local delivery of goods from the station in 1923 using a horse and cart later replaced with motor vehicles. However competition for passengers increased with more motor buses and coaches. The milk traffic diminished and by 1938 had been lost completely to road transport. Cost cutting measures had to be introduced and in 1933 the branch was connected to the South Wales main line, which had opened in 1903, at Little Somerford. The stretch to Dauntsey was largely taken up. This reduced the length of track to 3½ miles.

1st September 1939 saw the first train of evacuees arrive in Malmesbury carrying 900 children from London. About 200 of them stayed in the town with the remainder sent to nearby villages. On the outbreak of war the timetable was immediately revised with fewer services. However traffic increased as RAF personnel moving to and from the airfield at Long Newnton used the branch, as did medical staff after a military hospital was established at Charlton Park. Linolite received and despatched the goods associated with their production of de-icing hose clips. Later in the war prisoners-of-war arrived for the camp at Easton Grey.

The Labour Government nationalised the railways on 1st January 1948. Despite this, closure of the branch was considered but there was strong opposition from local businesses including Linolite, Ekco and A. B. Blanch & Co. which started manufacturing agricultural machinery at Crudwell in 1950. However passenger services were doomed and the last train ran on 8th September 1951. Goods traffic continued until 1962 and the track was lifted the following year. The station site was sold to the Borough Council in 1967 and developed into the light industrial estate and car park of today. The only reminders left are the old engine shed, used by Kwik-Fit as a workshop (displaying a commemorative sign provided by Malmesbury Civic Trust), the bridge abutments two hundred yards from Mill Lane and the tunnel under Holloway which can be seen from the River Walk during the winter months after the trees have lost their leaves.

Bus Services

The number of Malmesbury's coaching inns (the Unicorn, Bear, White Swan, George, King's Arms and White Lion) suggests the town was an important stopping place. In the early 19th Century Royal Mail coaches ran from Devizes calling at the King's Arms before carrying on to Gloucester. In 1837 the Brighton mail suffered an accident close to the steeple when a horse shied and the guard was thrown from his seat. After the railway network expanded, mail coaches were replaced by mail carts to and from Chippenham and Tetbury.

There were many local carriers to convey goods and passengers to London, Bath, Bristol, Chippenham, Cirencester and other towns. Henry Long, the publican of the Green Dragon in 1865 ran a daily omnibus to Chippenham with the return trip in the afternoon. He had also ran a two-horse omnibus to the Tetbury Road (Kemble) railway station and Cirencester on Mondays and Fridays for a year but discontinued it as the number of passengers did not cover the increased cost of the newly introduced 'to and fro' turnpike toll. Two years later he had moved to the

Greyhound from where he drove the 'Volunteer' omnibus to Chippenham. He was often accompanied by two lurchers which, when alerted by Harry's whistle, would go in the direction pointed by his whip to run down some game. Whilst this service ceased with the arrival of the branch line, Harry Jones, the landlord of the King's Arms, arranged for an omnibus to meet every train with a fare of 2½d. to the town centre. This service continued until the First World War.

Harry Jones standing next to his bus.

On 1 October 1921 Bristol Tramways introduced motor buses to the town with their no. 31 service, linking Malmesbury to Bristol via Badminton, Chipping Sodbury and Yate. The following year (Alfred) Claude Norton (1895-1968) started a service between Cirencester and Malmesbury using a 20 seater with solid tyres going via Crudwell, Oaksey and Somerford Keynes. Shortly afterwards Bristol Tramways began route no. 73 from Swindon to Brinkworth and Malmesbury. In 1928 an evening bus to Swindon ran out of petrol causing a considerable delay. The return trip *was done in greyhound racing style*! The Swindon service was infrequent with no buses between 8am and 1.15pm. Western National's route 223 served Stroud, Tetbury, Malmesbury, Chippenham and Trowbridge from the time of their formation in 1929. Bristol Greyhound ran an express coach service from London to Bristol through the town but this was withdrawn in 1930. Red Bus Services of Stroud started a route numbered 70 between Stroud and Malmesbury via Tetbury. After being taken over by Red & White, discussions between competitors led to coordination of this service with Western National's. Just before the outbreak of war a new Bristol Tramways service no. 126 was introduced from Chippenham through Sutton Benger to Malmesbury.

After the war the villagers of Foxley and Norton were anxious for a bus service. In 1950 it was reported to the Rural District Council that this could not be arranged *without causing serious difficulty to travellers in other areas*. These discussions continued for nine years until it was finally decided that a service was not feasible. It is curious that the Bristol Tramways route map showed route no. 126 extended from Malmesbury to Norton! At the same time Athelstan Coaches sought to introduce competition on the Malmesbury to Cirencester route and obtained a licence despite the objections of Norton's Coaches which resulted in the latter improving their service. The following year a complaint arose as Western National's last bus from Chippenham, a fully laden double-decker, was driven into a side street where it awaited the bus from Malmesbury and the passengers had to change buses to complete their journey – this was soon rectified by the changeover taking place in Cross Hayes. After an industry reorganisation in 1950 the Stroud-Trowbridge service was shared between Western National and Bristol Tramways while the Red & White service was transferred to Bristol, being renumbered 470. This led to Bristol changing their route number to 423 and Western National restricting their service to Trowbridge-Malmesbury in 1957 and then just Chippenham-Malmesbury (no. 295) three years later. In anticipation of the closure of the railway Bristol extended service 31 to Swindon and ended the no. 73.

During the 1950s double-deckers were in use and when a single-decker was reintroduced for a 2pm Saturday service to Swindon it could not cope with demand. A new fare of 2d. was introduced between Corn Gastons & Cross Hayes on services 31 and 470. During the Suez crisis petrol rationing reduced services. At the end of the decade Bristol Omnibus started no. 67, an express service to Bath hospital on Wednesday & Saturday to suit visiting times. Unfortunately it was shortlived due to lack of passengers.

Passengers complained that waiting in Cross Hayes was unpleasant. The Borough Council bought the old Brewery Tap at 34 Cross Hayes in 1954 but it took another five years until it came into use as the bus shelter. Two years later the Council decided it would be better if the buses stopped in the centre of the square. This caused controversy, a public enquiry was held which found in favour of the move. Argument continued until the buses returned to their original stops

One of Athelstan Coaches' buses in the centre of Cross Hayes.

on the east and south in 1975. This led to objections from the Police and complaints from bus drivers that it was unsafe as to dismount from their cabs they had to step into the flow of traffic. Eventually in 1995 new shelters were erected close to the two bus stops.

Athelstan Coaches began rapidly expanding, taking over Dauntsey Vale Coaches in August 1959, Fry's Coaches, Minety in January 1960, followed by Claude Norton's operation including the bus service to Cirencester which he had run for 38 years. Jack Grimes (1915-1968) of Athelstan Coaches pledged to safeguard the Minety service and wanted the village to be connected to Cirencester. At the 1962 Public Enquiry into the relocation of Cross Hayes bus stops it was said that three companies ran 231 buses each day with 13 on Sundays. There were still 17 buses every day between Hullavington and Chippenham even though a large part of RAF Hullavington had closed. However the services from Tetbury & Long Newnton were poor, allowing either three minutes or three hours in town. Fares began to increase but even so the Western National said 65% of services ran at a loss, there being heavy fuel tax. Jack Grimes thought coordination was poor, the 'Surgery Bus' arriving at 6.40pm did not allow time for a visit to Doctor and the chemist – a slight improvement of a 37 minute interval was introduced, but Dr Hodge suggested 1½ hours would be more appropriate. Services began to reduce particularly Bristol Omnibus and Athelstan's service to Swindon on Tuesdays and Fridays no longer went through Charlton. Another fare increase followed in 1965, the Chippenham fare rose by 2d. to 2s. 11d. single but the route still used double-deckers. The following year the price to Chippenham became 3s. 3d., but in contrast the Bristol Omnibus fare to Swindon was only 2s. 10d. after a 4d. rise. Athelstan reduced the Cirencester service and increased fares from 3s. to 3s. 6d. return, their first increase since 1961. Further cuts followed – Bristol withdrew an early morning bus from Swindon, Western National reduced the number of Chippenham buses calling at the railway station. The spiral of decline continued with more fare increases. The 423 route (Stroud-Malmesbury via Tetbury) had no passengers over a six week period on Sundays and Bank Holidays so those services were withdrawn. The 1960s drew to an end with further closures including the Chippenham to Great Somerford service.

All of Western National's Wiltshire operations transferred to Bristol Omnibus from 1 January 1970 but locally this only involved the Chippenham service. The following year bus companies threatened to withdraw all rural services as losses could no longer be sustained. As a result Wiltshire County Council suggested subsidies, half from them and half from other Councils. Malmesbury Rural District Council agreed to pay £943 towards the £3,773 loss on four services; 290/1 Chippenham-Malmesbury-Sherston, 295 Chippenham-Malmesbury, 423/4 Stroud-Malmesbury & 428 Stroud-Malmesbury. However Tetbury Rural District Council initially refused to fund 423/4. The Borough Council was only required to make a small contribution (no doubt due to the short lengths of route inside their boundary) of £38 in 1971 rising to £75 two years later. Athelstan Coaches stopped their once a day service from Malmesbury to Swindon via Crudwell, Oaksey & Minety after the subsidy paid by British Railways since the branch closure ended. 1973 saw the introduction of single-decker buses operated by one man. Bristol Omnibus disclosed they lost £258,512 on rural buses and North Wiltshire District Council agreed to pay £20,000 towards all of the services in their area. In 1977 there were swingeing service reductions; 290 Chippenham-Malmesbury via Christian Malford & the Somerfords was withdrawn, 295 Chippenham-Malmesbury halved, 490 Swindon-Malmesbury-Bristol evening service ended and Sundays buses cut from five to two. The following year there was no Sunday Swindon service at all.

1980 began optimistically with a new Bristol service 291 to Malmesbury from Chippenham via Dauntsey Vale but this had to be heavily subsidised by the District Council. However the following year Bristol Omnibus axed the Tetbury-Malmesbury route and no longer ran through to Bristol although a limited stop service had been tried for a short time. It was no longer the main operator; Athelstan Coaches ran services to Cirencester and Swindon; Fosseway Coaches, only founded by John Pickford in 1979 at Grittleton, served Yate, Bristol and Tetbury; Hatts Coaches, of Foxham founded in 1928, served Chippenham; Cheltenham & Gloucester began an express service from Cirencester to Bath in 1983. Bus deregulation in 1985 meant operators had to register services which did not require subsidy – only the Fosseway service to Yate was registered. Athelstan Coaches changed their name to Overland & Counties after Tony Nielson took over and improved services. In 1987 the company opened a new route to Cirencester and Gloucester which left at 9.10am, with the return starting at 2pm. They also took the Chippenham route from Hatts & improved it, as well as reopening the office at Market Cross. The Swindon route had been changed to go through Milbourne & Lea which isolated Cowbridge – in response Fosseway began a morning service from there. Overland & Counties continued to expand taking over Wayfarers Coaches, Limpley Stoke, buying two new buses costing £75,000 and announcing a move from Park Road, Malmesbury to Bumpers Farm, Chippenham. Tony Nielson complained that a 350% increase in excise duty took a swipe at the dying bus industry and sold 18 surplus vehicles at auction. For five days in 1989 a trial Town Bus service was run using a minibus serving Cross Hayes, Abbey Row, St. Mary's Street, Burnham Rd, Corn Gastons, Parklands, White Lion Park, Park Road, Reeds Farm, Gateway supermarket and the Station Yard carpark.

The 1990s began with the shock of Overland and Counties going into receivership, an ambitious plan for a West Country Pullman coach to London failed to attract sufficient passengers. Thamesdown Transport, Swindon Council's bus company, took over the Swindon route and Anton Travel of Minety owned by Angus Hutton operated the Cirencester, Malmesbury, Chippenham route. Flint's Coaches of Nettleton near Chippenham, which became Coachstyle in 1995, had run the Bath service since 1978. The bus shelter at 34 Cross Hayes was shut and sold in 1994. Within a short time Andy James Coaches of Sherston, a company founded in 1982 with a fleet of 18 vehicles, became the main operator in the area. Andy James followed his father Derek who had run school buses from a base in Easton Grey for many years. In 1998 Andybus bought eight new Mercedes 30 seater buses. Until 31 March 2014 the following services operated around the town:

Service No.	Operator	Destination	Frequency
30	Andybus	Town Service	Half hourly 09.00-17.00
31	Andybus	Swindon via Little Somerford	Hourly 06.45-17.55
41	Andybus	Yate	Two hourly 07.45-16.25
76	Coachstyle	Bath	Wednesday one service
91	A. D. Rains	Chippenham via Dauntsey Vale	Hourly 08.34-17.25
91B	A. D. Rains	Sutton Benger	Two hourly 10.25-17.25
92	Andybus	Chippenham via Hullavington	Hourly 07.25-18.00
93	Andybus	Cirencester via Crudwell & Oaksey	Two hourly 07.50-17.45
278	Dolphin	Tetbury	Monday, Wednesday & Friday two or three per day

With increased Council budget cuts, services were reduced from 1 April 2014, Service Nos. 91/91B came to an end. Coachstyle became the operator of Services 30, 31, 41, 92, 93 and a single service on Wednesday on new route 37 from Hullavington via Malmesbury, Sherston & Castle Combe to Bath. Hatts returned to scheduled services by running a daily bus from Dauntsey to Malmesbury on route 97 but this came to an end after the Company unexpectedly closed in July 2014.

Housing

Council Houses

In 1913 The Borough Council commissioned a report which showed the following: the average number of house occupants was 3.75, the lowest of any Wiltshire borough; there was not one large owner of houses and many were owned by the occupier; there were very few houses built back to back, some being near the Market Cross; two thirds of the houses with a rental of less than £15 had been inspected; there were not more than five cases of serious overcrowding; if cases of overcrowding were to be reduced more houses had to be built as there was no spare accommodation; and there were only two vacant cottages with rental under £5 but these were not in a fit state to let. Councillor Thompson said the cause of poor housing was *the labouring man not having sufficient wages to keep their families and pay rent.* No action was taken.

Following the First World War the Housing Act 1919 required Councils to provide 'Homes fit for heroes'. Sites in Gastons Lane (now Bremilham Road) and Park Road were considered but in 1920 the Borough Council bought land on Reeds Farm for £621 17s 6d., spending another £100 on architect's fees. This site was chosen because it was inside the borough boundary. 20 houses were to be built but problems soon arose with flooding and disposal of sewerage. The scheme was abandoned and the site sold for £390. In 1930 the Vicar, Rev. J. Deane and the Roman Catholic Priest, Father Grorod, led the formation of a Housing Association. This prompted the Borough Council the following year to buy land in Gastons Road for £140 and Pool Gastons for £500. On these sites 13 houses were built before the end of 1932, five at the top of Gastons Road and eight in Pool Gastons Road, for a cost of £5,514 plus fees. These houses were originally lit by gas and had no electricity supply. A path leading to 44 allotments had to be diverted. Another 14 houses were built the following year, some in the new Athelstan Road. 12 more were added in 1935 and 14 3-bed houses in Athelstan Road completed the pre-war programme. These last cost only £4,942 as prices had fallen. Rent was 8s. per week.

The Workhouse, which had closed in 1933, was bought by the Borough Council three years later for £400. The main block was converted into 19 tenements for £2,737. The name of the development was changed to Bremilham Terrace and over two years the hospital block, tramps' ward & porter's lodge became another eight tenements.

This 1964 view of the old Workhouse shows the size of the main building.

Nos. 2, 4 & 6 Burnivale were ruled to be insanitary in 1933 and were to be demolished after the first Pool Gastons Council houses were completed. However in 1937 they were presented as a gift to the Council by A. Rice. It seems they were not subsequently occupied and were demolished to widen the road.

After the Second World War began, extra housing for Ekco employees was required. This was provided by the Borough Council even though the factory was in the Rural District. This led to some resentment when peace came as Ekco staff remained priority tenants for this part of the housing stock. Four new houses were built in Pool Gastons Road and 20 in two stages in Athelstan Road. A new road linking Burnham and Park Roads was named St. Aldhelm Road. Further sites were acquired – 2½ acres at Cowbridge were bought from Ekco for £200 where 12 prefabricated bungalows were built in 1941 and 7.345 acres at Corn Gastons bought for £650.

As the war came to an end the Borough Council tried to deal with increased demand for housing, sometimes being frustrated by material shortages and restrictions placed on the numbers approved by the Ministry of Health. As central Government provided funds for building and grants to subsidise rents, all plans and tenders had to be submitted to the Ministry. In 1946 E. A. Hider Ltd.'s tender of £26,780 was approved for 20 more houses on the Pool Gastons site which now covered Pool Gastons Road, Athelstan Road, Alexander Road and Avon Road where 13 homes were added the next year. 130 people applied for this extra housing. The Council decided not to take over ex-army huts near the bacon factory containing two squatter families as they were unfit to be adapted. Building in Pool Gastons continued. E. A. Hider tendered £19,104 for 12 houses which would be rented for 15s. a week. When completed in 1950, Councillors were dismayed to find the final price was £20,867 increasing the subsidy needed from the Rates. Also in 1950 a site adjacent to St. Aldhelm Road was bought for £530 from Adye & Hinwood's Bacon Factory. 24 'Cornish' units were built there at a total price of £30,258 and named Hobbes Close. The Pool Gastons scheme was completed by 1952, but delays were experience at St. Aldhelm Road.

At Cowbridge 40 permanent aluminium bungalows (pre-fabs) were allocated by the Ministry in 1947. Ekco gifted the land to the Borough but they were unable to buy an extra 1½ acres so only 20 could be built. These were all occupied by 1948.

Pre-fabs in Cowbridge Crescent, 1964.

There was very little private housing at this time. Of the 1947 allocation, 13 were allotted to the Borough Council and only three for private builders. It proved difficult to find sufficient applicants even for this small number. The Rural District Council built a pair of houses at Burton Hill which were completed by 1951. Another pair at Cowbridge were held up by lack of windows. The RDC also took over Charlton Park Camp, home to many Polish families, and spent £6,381 to convert four 5-bed, 10 3-bed and 13 2-bed dwellings. The use of the Camp for housing came to an end in 1958 when the families were moved to Parklands.

In 1953 the Borough produced plans for 57 houses in Corn Gastons. The Ministry of Health required the cost of the first 24 to be reduced by £58 each. They were built starting from the Bristol Road end and were completed for £34,961 in 1955 by which time 20 more houses there and five bungalows in Hobbes Close were also finished. Within two years the Rural District Council had begun building 34 houses and 21 bungalows on a site to the west of Corn Gastons which was named Parklands.

At the start of the 1960s the Rural District drew up plans for more housing along the Foxley and Bristol Roads. 50-60 were planned for Parklands but these were delayed until the sewerage scheme was implemented. They also agreed to extend a road to help the Borough develop Corn Gastons. The Borough had built 155 houses since the war, the latest being three two-bed homes on a small site named Newnton Grove. They cost £1,832 each and had a weekly rent of £2 0s. 7d. but there were still 50 names on 1961's housing list. As the sewage scheme was finished in 1964 a project jointly funded by the Borough and Rural Councils was started for accommodation for the elderly. This comprised ten bungalows either side of a warden's flat with a communal room connected by covered way. The next year the Rural Council began developing ten acres in White Lion Park. It was said this was *halfway to Sherston* and the need for a town bus was highlighted. In the late 1960s 84 more houses, bungalows and sheltered homes were added.

Although Councils were building many houses by the early 1960s, only 33 had been completed by private developers in 33 years with six more under construction. Some developers were frustrated, a Public Enquiry in 1963 refused permission for a small isolated site in Park Road. Then there was a controversial scheme for 39 acres between Daniel's Well and Arches Farm. This led to much debate and the formation of Malmesbury Civic Trust to oppose it before a Planning Inspector ruled against it. However the same decade saw around 100 private houses erected in White Lion Park.

West Street before renovation.

The Government was encouraging slum clearance and it was reported that many people here were living in shabby houses – *there are a number of cases where two or more families have to share the same toilet.* The redevelopment of West Street was intended to be part of the clearance. Several houses there were owned by the Warden & Freemen which the Council wanted to buy. In 1967 the Council obtained outline planning permission to develop the area to the west of West Street and widen the road. To be demolished were the terraced houses at the south end of the street together with houses in Bristol Street including the cottage subsequently identified as the Saxon St. Helens Chapel. Malmesbury Civic Trust appealed for renovation rather than demolition. Further planning applications were made and granted but little work was done. In June 1974 the Civic Trust and the Council for the Protection of Rural England achieved listing of 4-12 and 32-38 (even numbers) West Street to protect them. Notwithstanding this the new North Wiltshire District Council applied for demolition of 2-30 West Street. Fortunately they experienced difficulty in financing the project and a Stroud builder came up with an alternative scheme. After further problems were encountered the southern end of the terrace was renovated and 18 to 22 were sympathetically rebuilt. The final plan incorporated a number of changes including no connection of Hudson Road to Bristol Road.

In 1972 the old Workhouse in Bristol Road was demolished and 27 council houses built in Bremilham Rise. Two years later 22% of the town's housing did not have a fixed bath or an inside WC. Three localities were identified for improvement, centred on West Street, Lower High Street and Abbey Row. Government grants of up to £1,900 per house were available in these areas. The 'prefabs' in Cowbridge Crescent were redeveloped. However towards the end of the decade there were still 171 on the housing list. The local government reorganisation of 1974 moved the responsibility for housing from the Borough and Rural District Councils to the newly created North Wiltshire District Council.

Persimmon Homes, a Yorkshire Company founded in 1972, obtained permission to build 251 houses on Reeds Farm in 1983 and immediately started work. After Linolite moved from the Postern Mill site, plans were drawn up for housing there. In 1988 a scheme for 41 homes for those over 55 and a warden's flat was agreed. Unfortunately the developer, Brampton Homes, went into receivership two years later with the site partly built. Amended plans removing the age restriction for occupants and greatly increasing the number of car parking spaces were vigorously opposed which led to at least one prospective developer dropping out. However in 1992 a Planning Inspector finally approved the construction of 34 houses and two flats with 81 car parking spaces for the development called the Maltings.

Reeds Farm in the foreground with Tetbury Hill behind before development began.

Town Councillor Ken Silveston became concerned about the lack of social housing and in 1990 formed the Malmesbury & District Housing Association. They wanted to build 36 affordable homes behind Parklands Close but ran into many difficulties with backers pulling out and planners being concerned over unsympathetic extension into open countryside. The original intention was to call it Paynter's Mead after the man who willed the land to be used for the benefit of the people of the town in 1938. However when work finally started in 1997 just after Cllr. Silveston's death, it became Silveston Way in his memory.

Reeds Farm has now grown to over 380 houses. 168 further houses were built by Persimmon on the old Filands Secondary School site to the north of Reeds Farm with 38 in Poole Road on part of the old Primary School site. Redrow have redeveloped the Cowbridge House site and built 143 homes with more planned. In several places around the town older houses have been demolished and infill sites have been found for more development. Wiltshire Council's planning strategy for the period up to 2026 requires another 270 dwellings to be built and the community is formulating a Neighbourhood Plan to deliver these.

Local councils used to build most new houses but with increased personal wealth central government decided that the majority of future projects should be private. After 1979 council houses were offered to tenants at heavily discounted prices and many Malmesbury residents have taken advantage of this. North Wiltshire District Council transferred their remaining housing stock to North Wiltshire Housing Association Ltd. on 11th December 1995. This company was renamed Westlea Housing Association in June 1999 and has been part of the GreenSquare Group since 2008.

Abbey House

This house was either built by William Stumpe (c1497-1552) or his son Sir James around 1550. It was built on the undercroft of the 13th Century Abbot's house. Windows that were part of the original building are visible from the north side at ground level. A French priest in the Stumpe household was probably responsible for laying out the grounds and gardens. The porch bears the arms of Sir James and his wife Isabel Baynton. In the 17th Century a low eastern wing was added with a long two-storey range running south from the western corner. This is the only large house in town to have survived from the 16th Century.

Thomas Ivy (d1672) occupied the house during the middle of the 17th Century. He acquired his wealth working for the East Indies Company but on his return found that his wife had died. In 1649 he married Theodosia Stepkin, a widow said to have spurned a suitor favoured by her father after he had been sick in her lap following a bout of drinking. Both parties to the marriage felt wronged by the other and Thomas published a pamphlet *Alimony Arraigned*. It was said that *he was knighted after the King's return but merited a whipping rather*. The family coat of arms is still over the chimneypiece.

During the 18th & 19th Centuries the house was divided into separate apartments. Dr. Joseph Jennings, the Borough's Receiving Officer, lived in the house from 1857 until 1900. After his death the whole house was bought by Mr. (later Captain of the Lanarkshire Yeomanry and Household Cavalry during WWI) Elliot Mackirdy Scott Mackirdy. The Drill Hall near the base of the Water Tower was pulled down. He enclosed the area of the cloister with iron railings and turned it into a kitchen garden as well as carrying out extensive modifications to the house. Harold Brakspear (1870-1934), an architect from Corsham who worked on most of the area's important historic buildings (as well as others further afield such as Windsor Castle) superintended the works. This included the demolition of both extensions with the eastern one being replaced by a two-storey wing with attics similar to the original building. The cellar floor level was excavated by six feet to return it to the same level as in the 16th Century. The house was occupied by the Deaconess Community of St Andrew from 1968 to 1990 to whom ownership passed after the death of Lady Eva Scott MacKirdy (1883-1971), but is now owned by Ian and Barbara Pollard. They opened the

gardens to the public in 1998 and these have proved to be a strong attraction for visitors, drawn perhaps not only by the flora but also the Naked Gardeners! At the time of writing, the future of the gardens is uncertain.

Almshouses

These attractive buildings are on the corner of St Johns Street. Facing the High Street is

Abbey House from the south.

a 12th Century archway originally part of the Hospital of St. John the Baptist which was incorporated when the structure was rebuilt in 1694. There was reputed to be a chapel here in Saxon times. After the Knights Hospitalers were suppressed by King Henry VIII in 1540, the Corporation bought the site for £26 13s. 4d. The almshouses existed in

The Almshouses with a gas steet lamp on the corner.

1622 with the Corporation taking responsibility for maintenance soon after. The building was derelict from the early 1950s until restored in 1968. Although not exactly used for its original purpose the rents for the dwellings, owned by the Old Corporation, are less than the market value. The plaque over the arch reads:

Memerand that whereas King Athelstan
did give unto the free school within this
Burrough of Malmesbury Ten Pounds and to
the poor people my Almshouse at St John's.
Ten Pounds to be paid yearly by ye Aldermen
and Burgesses of ye same Burrough for Ever.
That now Michael Weekes Esquire, late of
this said burr, and now citizen of London,
hath augmented & added to ye afore sd gift.
viz, to ye sd Free School, Ten Pounds, and to ye
sd Almshouse, Ten Pounds only, to be paid
yearly at St John's, afore sd, within this sd
burr, and by his Trustees for ever, and hath
also given to ye Minister of this Towne
for ye time being 20s only, by ye year for life
to preach a sermon yearly on ye 19th day
of July, and to his sd Trustees 20s by the
year beginning on ye 25th day of March,
Anno Dom 1694.

Avon House, 25 Abbey Row

The present Avon House, Grade II* listed, was rebuilt in 1798 with a Georgian facade on a much older smaller cottage. John Alexander (1824-1910) lived here and his obituary from the Wilts & Gloucestershire Standard tells his story: *Mr. John Alexander, of Malmesbury and Cleveland, Ohio, Malmesbury's oldest retired resident, passed away on Tuesday morning at the ripe old age of 86 years. He was a native of this town, born in 1824, and in early life worked in Malmesbury and Bristol. We learn that he worked his allotment with other comers, at King's Heath, and was finally so disheartened by one disastrous season that he suddenly decided to seek his fortune in the United States, then the El Dorado of the British working men. Possessed of the keenest business instincts – which remained with him right up to his death – his phenomenal success*

Avon House and John Alexander.

in Cleveland, where he settled in 1848, reads like a romance. He was employed in an oil refinery for many years, but rose rapidly up the ladder of success until he at last set up in the business himself, prospered for many years, and ultimately sold out to the Standard Oil Company, of which Mr. John D. Rockefeller was the head. With a fortune amassed he returned to Malmesbury, having previously purchased his present fine residence on the Abbey-row in the year 1875. It is rather ironic that having been involved in the development of a new fuel he built up a business selling coal, coke, wood, salt and artificial manure with premises in Gloucester Road as well as at Somerford and Tetbury. He is buried along with his first wife Sebella (1823-1881) and second wife Hephzibah (1843-1920) in the Abbey churchyard to the south west of the west end. His nephew Walter (1844-1907) took over the business, living at Westport House, 116 Gloucester Road opposite his coal yard at No. 97. Joseph Moore (1858-1947) moved to Avon House with his daughters when he sold the Old Bell. One of them (Mary Moore 1882-1978) created 25A, the attached former carriage house, which on her death was left as a home for the elderly together with a legacy of £10,000. By 1983 it was occupied by the charity's administrator. The May Moore charity has moved and provides a parson to minister to the elderly. The main house from at least 1973 was used as a dentists by Barker, Tufft, Brown and partners and in 1980 it became a retreat run by Mollie & Harry Raiss for eight years.

The Beeches, Burton Hill
This house was built in the late 18th Century. Esau Duck and his family lived here from the early 1880s until his widow's death in 1910. It was then rented to Mrs Ramsay, niece of the Dowager Countess of Suffolk who lived here until World War II, for the grand sum of £45 per annum. Later Alfred Beutell occupied the house when he was running Linolite during and after the war. It was turned into a guest house in 1968, becoming a private nursing home from 1980 until 1999 and is now a private house again.

Bremilham Rise
This was the site of the Workhouse. The Poor Law Amendment Act 1834 promoted fundamental changes in local administration although its purpose was simply to provide a new system of poor law relief. Previously this had been the responsibility of individual parishes and the standard of care varied. The three Malmesbury parishes had their workhouse in what is now called Tower House. Under the new law parishes were gathered into Unions and the Malmesbury Union, formed in 1835, comprised – Abbey (Malmesbury), Alderton, Brinkworth, Brokenborough, Charlton, Crudwell, Dauntsey, Easton Grey, Foxley, Garsdon, Great Somerford, Hankerton, Hullavington, Lea & Cleverton, Little Somerford, Luckington, Malmesbury St. Paul, Minety, Norton, Oaksey, Sherston, Sopworth and Westport St. Mary. The new Board of Guardians met for the first time on 5th December 1835, but it was not until September of the following year that they decided to replace the four workhouses at Minety, Malmesbury, Crudwell and Sherston. It was built on

Bristol Road just outside the Borough's boundary in Brokenborough and was completed in 1838, costing £2,800.

The conditions were deliberately unattractive with married couples being separated. Up to 230 inmates could be accommodated. Work had to be done to earn one's keep and typical tasks were breaking stones for use on the roads (there was a quarry opposite) or chopping up old railway sleepers into firewood that was then sold. A separate hospital was built in 1850/1 at a cost of £630. A large bell rang at 6.45 am, 8 am (for breakfast), 12 noon (dinner), 5 pm (tea), and 7.45 pm (supper). The workhouse had its own covered hearse used to return the dead bodies of inmates to the parish from which they came for a pauper's burial. After the Great War Sydney Kite from Park Lane Farm provided the horse for these journeys.

When the County Council took over responsibility for poor relief on 1st April 1930 Malmesbury's Workhouse was an early casualty closing in 1933. It was bought by the Borough Council for £400 who between 1936 and 1938 converted it to lower rent council houses. Demolished in 1972, 27 council houses were built on the site. The main building overlooked Bristol Road. The only remains being the stone wall to the west of Holford Rise. A few feet up the pathway you can see the outline of the Porter's Gate.

Burnham House, Burnham Road.

This house was built in the late 1880s by James Barnard and bought by Fred Poole (1866-1907) in 1899, one of five famous brothers who ran Myrioramas. Their grandfather Richard Poole, a fuller of cloth, moved to Malmesbury before 1841 and seems to have been employed at Avon Mill as he lived in the Lower High Street. He had three sons John (1817-1889), Charles (1821-1877) and George Walter (1828-1877). Moses Gompertz started touring the country with 'Panoramas' of colourful events like Artic expeditions, battles and fires which he called Myrioramas. Charles and George joined his company as musicians until 1863 when, in partnership with Anthony Young, they took over the business. They developed the shows which involved scenery painted on canvas rolls being wound from a reel on one side of the stage to the other as the story progressed. This was accompanied by music and fireworks with the whole illuminated by special lighting effects powered by gas! John had five sons – Joseph (1847-1906), George (1849-1929), Henry (1850-1925), Charles (1858-1918) and Fred. Joseph joined his uncles in 1865 and later built Verona House on Tetbury Hill. Fred began work with Joseph in 1878 but in 1896 formed a partnership with Henry. After Fred died his widow moved away from the town.

'Nipper' Constance moved to Burnham House in 1949. He developed his veterinary practice here until he left Malmesbury in 1964. By 1968 the house was unoccupied. Town Councillor Jim Owen felt that it would make a good facility for

Burnham House in 1985. (Malmesbury Chronicles)

local old folk and persuaded the County Council to buy it in 1971. Unfortunately they did not have the capital to convert it so the property was plagued by vandals and boarded up. In 1977 it was finally opened as a day centre for the elderly. Jim Owen raised money to furnish it and arranged for pupils from the Corn Gastons School to decorate it. It was such a success that in 1981 the County Council and Health Authority shared the cost of £442,000 to add residential facilities for 50 people. Some 40 to 45 staff were employed in the home. The project also received support from charities. In 1977 Mr. C. H. Barnes, a former railway worker, left money in trust for the project and later the estate of a resident, Mrs. Hale, was added to it. This fund paid £31,500 to expand the day care areas of the sitting room and dining room during 1995. The Malmesbury Community Trust now administers these funds. The County Council sold the house to the Order of St. John and in June 2008 residents were transferred to the new Athelstan House Care Home at Burton Hill and it was boarded up. It is now planned to demolish the building and provide more sheltered housing on the site.

Burton Hill House

The original house was probably built in the early 17th Century. In 1787 Timothy Dewell, a doctor who practised in Malmesbury, bought it for £2,650. Following his death the property was auctioned on 3rd November 1792 when Francis Hill, a lawyer and clothier from Bradford-upon-Avon paid £3,610. He had bought the mill by the Town Bridge two years before and was rebuilding that. Five years after his death in 1828 brothers Simon (1800-1851) and Isaac (1805-1849) Salter of Kington Langley purchased the house together with Burton Hill Mill (later to become the Silk Mill) for £7,500. The Salters then sold Burton Hill House with 35 acres to John Cockerell (1785-1869) from London in 1842 for £7,050. Cockerell pulled the house down and employed his brother Charles Robert Cockerell (1788-1863) to design a new house. Charles was a most gifted and knowledgeable architect. At the same time as he was supervising the construction of his brother's home he was completing one of his finest commissions, the Ashmolean Museum in Oxford. Unfortunately the house burnt down on 14th March 1846 with the damage estimated at £10,000. Rebuilding started immediately using the same Tudor-Gothic design but three years later Charles William Miles (who was known as Peter!) bought the house.

Burton Hill House around 1900.

Miles was a member of an old family of bankers and merchants from Bristol, had been a Lieutenant Colonel commanding the 17th Lancers and hunted with the Quorn before coming to Malmesbury. He became High Sheriff of Wiltshire and High Steward in 1856. He wanted the house to be known as Ingleburn Manor and made many changes to the structure notably an extension to the west including a ballroom. The famous architect George Gilbert Scott Junior (1839-1897) oversaw the works and some of his moulded plaster ceilings survive. After Peter Miles died in 1892 the house passed to his son Charles Napier Miles (1854-1918), who was also an army officer, commissioned into the Life Guards in 1875. Napier served in Egypt during 1882 and in the South African War, being mentioned in dispatches. He commanded 1st Life Guards from 1895 to 1902 and became a CB and MVO. He also became involved in local affairs being a magistrate and the High Steward of the Old Corporation from 1893 until his death. His wife Emelye converted to Catholicism, and this is commemorated by a crucifix in St. Aldhelms Church dated 1903. They had no children and Napier's brother Audley Charles Miles (1855-1919) inherited but died. Later in 1919 parts of the estate amounting to 200 acres were sold off at auction in the Kings Arms, presumably because of double death duties. The heir was Thomas Gordon Audley Miles (1885-1960) who advertised the house and the remaining 174 acres in Country Life during 1921.

However it was not until 1924 that H. L. Storey bought the estate. He moved from Burton Hill Manor opposite. Again more improvements were made including the construction of a large lake in the grounds, apparently work instigated to provide employment during the depression. After his death in 1933 his widow moved and sought to sell the house. Eventually it was sold to the Shaftesbury Society in 1945 and their school's history is recounted later. Soon after the school closed in 2007 Malmesbury Civic Trust ensured the building was listed. The main house has been sympathetically converted into luxury housing.

Burton Hill Manor House
Originally a farmhouse, by 1823 it was called the Manor House. It was rebuilt later in the 19th Century in Tudor style, probably by Colonel Peter Miles who incorporated it into the Burton Hill Estate. Colonel Charles Miles allowed the Red Cross to use the Manor House as a hospital for the duration of the Great War. In 1919 it was bought by Herbert Lushington Storey (1853-1933), the eldest son of Sir Thomas Storey, who with his brother, William (1823-1879), had started a painting, japanning and tablecover manufacturing business in Lancaster. In 1887 Sir Thomas purchased the Bailrigg estate, Lancashire comprising 784 acres, four farms and other properties. In 1898, the year of his father's death, Herbert began to build a 12 bedroomed mansion on the estate. The house and garden were designed by Thomas Hayton Mawson a noted Lancastrian architect. Herbert was a keen horseman and huntsman and wanted to join the Beaufort Hunt. Therefore he bought the Manor House and spent part of the year here. After a couple of years he decided to dispose of Bailrigg which was sold at auction on 1st November 1921. The Manor House had seven bedrooms, two bathrooms, a bath dressing room, five servant's bedrooms with one bathroom, five reception rooms and 'Domestic Offices' comprising a lofty kitchen, scullery, butler's pantry, brushing room and servants' hall. However Herbert found the Manor House was not big enough for his expanding stable and in 1924 moved across the road into Burton Hill House (see also under the Hospital).

Cowbridge House
On the north western side of the bridge is a modern office. By 1773 there was a large house and mill (Cow Mill) on this site. In 1839 Samuel Bendry Brooke (1792-1869) bought the property and in 1849/50 he rebuilt the house in an Italianate/French style. When he died his nephew, Rev. Charles Kemble (1819-1874), Rector of Bath, inherited. Kemble carried out some improvements (his initials can be seen on railings that used to be part of the bridge over the mill stream at the entrance) but is best known for dealing with the restoration of Bath Abbey 1864-74 using George

Cowbridge House showing the picturesque front garden over which Ekco built a large brick building.

Gilbert Scott Junior as architect. On Kemble's death his widow Charlotte settled Cowbridge on their son Stephen. He offered it for sale from 1893 and in 1899 Baldomero de Bertodano (1845-1921), a retired solicitor of Spanish descent who had practised in Swindon, purchased it. The mill, previously used by a brewer, was now generated electricity for the house. Two years after Mr. de Bertodano's death the property was sold to Philip (later Sir Philip) Hunloke, King George V's yachtsman. Hunloke moved to Malmesbury to hunt with the Beaufort. A day before war was declared in September 1939 the property was bought by E. K. Cole Ltd. to be used as a shadow factory. This story is told later but the house was later badly neglected and was demolished in 2007 to make way for a modern housing estate.

32 Cross Hayes

This is a late 18th Century town house of two storeys with dormers and cellars. Mary Dewell, a native of Purton, widow of Charles who died in Jamaica, bought the property for herself, her two daughters and a son, Timothy. Timothy became a doctor who in 1787 moved to Burton Hill House and apparently rebuilt No. 32. On his death five years later he was in debt and was buried in the Abbey churchyard at night to avoid the attentions of creditors. His estate was left to his widow, Elizabeth and his sister Mary. They had to sell Burton Hill House and return to 32 Cross Hayes. Timothy had at least six children and his eldest son, Charles who was vicar of the Abbey in 1817/8, inherited his mother's estate. Mary left her interest in this house to her nephew, Thomas, a younger son of Timothy. By the time Charles died in 1826 he had accumulated much property including Wynyards Mill, the Black Horse Inn, various cottages, several miscellaneous pieces of land, Cross Hayes House (described under Places of Worship) and another house in Cross Hayes. All of this was left in trust to his second wife, Sarah and daughter, Jane for their lives and on the last death would pass to a child of Jane's or if she died without issue the first son of his brother Thomas. Jane died before her father.

In 1874 the house was bought by Esau Duck (1828-1908). He was the son of a miller, born in Blackland near Calne. At the age of 16 he walked to Malmesbury looking for work. He found a job at Crabb Mill (near Southfield Farm beyond the sewage works). He was a resourceful young man and eventually took over the business. Through his milling he accumulated wealth enabling him to move into this prestigious address in the centre of town. As well as the house he bought the brewery at its rear. In the early 1880s Esau moved to the Beeches, Burton Hill and his son in law Thomas Reed lived at No. 32 until 1911 when he moved to Swindon. After Esau's death his

No. 32 Cross Hayes in 1964, with the bus shelter next door and Tilley & Culverwell's office at No.34.

eldest son Harry (1876-1950) continued as brewer and after the Reeds left, lived here. However the bulk of the estate valued at £72,000 (a fortune then) was inherited by the younger son Arthur Monte Jacob Duck (1888-1975).

By 1920 32 Cross Hayes was rented by Henry Beak (1865-1936) who ran Rich & Beak wine and beer merchants at 45 High Street. Later Henry bought the house and it remained in his family for around 50 years. A basement at the rear was used as a Drill Hall for the Wiltshire Yeomanry and a detachment of the 4th Wiltshire Regiment (TA) in the 1930s. After the war Athelstan Coaches had a garage in the old brewery. More recently John Kadwell ran an antiques business from there until the premises was converted into prestigious offices and a flat in the new millennium. The house itself remains a family home.

Culver House, Culver Gardens, Ingram Street
Presumably containing a former dovecot, this 16th Century house was divided into four tenement houses at the beginning of the 19th Century when the outbuildings were converted into cottages. Culver means dove or pigeon, which was used as a source of meat. The house is reputed to have been the residence of Parliamentary Military Governor Col. Nicholas Devereux, from 1644-6. Later it was the home of the notorious Dr. Edmund Wilkins (1726-1804), Alderman, Receiver General, magistrate and an apothecary. At first he was a supporter of Henry, 12th Earl of Suffolk who served as High Steward 1762-8. He then became Deputy High Steward to Charles James Fox and carried out many of Fox's duties. In 1775 he was elected High Steward and remained so until his death. He was the first Malmesbury resident to hold this post in over 100 years and when he took over the town had been solidly Whig since the beginning of the 18th Century. He controlled the election of the town's two MPs in the following manner. Ten of the thirteen electors (the Alderman and twelve Capital Burgesses) gave him a bond of £500 for which he then paid them an annuity of £30 (provided that they supported his candidates and annually re-elected him as High Steward). Towards the end of his life he got behind in making these payments and left £500 in his will to be distributed between the Capital Burgesses to clear the debt. He sold the Parliamentary seats to the highest bidder. In 1796 there was a contested election for the first time in half a century. The Whigs put forward Mr. Vassar as candidate. Although he had much support in the town he received only one vote. He petitioned Parliament to overrule the election but failed.

Wilkins held dinners for the Capital Burgesses which were always sumptuous affairs. At one of them he introduced the latest import, cigars. Unfortunately his guests did not know what to do with them – they saw Mr. Wilkins bite the end off his but he was then distracted and they thought they had to eat them! This amusing tale comes from a speech made by A. Fraser to the Malmesbury Literary and Debating Society long ago; *THE EFFECTS OF A GOOD DINNER, followed by trying to chew, and smoking cigars and drinking wine, this select company got right happy and jolly, and when they departed many had difficulty to get up and walk or get to the door, and when they got outside the fresh air had a most singular and strange effect on the feasters, for they began to go reeling round and round like spinning tops, knocking one another over. Also the cigar had the same result on their stomachs as it has on naughty boys when they have smoked their first pipe - it made them retch.*

Mr. Wilkins had a statue of St. Aldhelm, which formerly stood in the Abbey, erected on a pedestal in his garden. One of the Burgesses, endeavouring to go home, happened to wander off the path into the garden, and went up to where the statue stood and addressed it as follows:-"Bisent thee coming whoam?" Getting no reply he said "Don't stick up there like a dumel, you girt gawney you, come on" and suiting the action to the word he put his arm around it and gave a lurch, when both rolled over on to the ground together, where he went to sleep with his arm around the prostrate statue. Early next morning, Isaac Cook, Mr. Wilkins' groom, going through the garden with his lantern to the stables (which have since been converted into cottages), thought he heard someone snoring, and going across the garden to see who or what it was, found this worthy Burgess fast asleep by the side of the statue. Recognising him by the light of his lantern, he addressed him thus: "Jumes, what bist thee doing here, you drunken slipot?" (at the same time giving him sundry kicks to wake him). "Get up. Why, thee hast bin an' pulled St. Old 'un off his perch. Did'st thee thenk as how thee had'st the Missus alongside on 'e? Thee had'st better shamock off and make thyself scarce afore the Squire gets about, for 'e sets main store on thuck image as 'e used to be in the old Abbey," (and giving the sleeping Burgess more kicks,) "for if he finds thee here, Jumes, thee wotent find nothing under thee plate when thee dost come to supper next turn." "Thee bide a' quiet, Isaac," said Jumes, rubbing his eyes, "and doesn't thee let on to the Squire as how thee's found I here, for he 'ull send round for I to put the 'Saint' on his stand again - well, thur now, one job makes another - I'ull stand thee a quart of Saml. Hanks' 'stingo'" (his best beer) "when I sees thee round at The Bear." "Mind thee doesn't forget it then, Jumes," said Isaac, and with the light of his lantern turned on to the garden, old Isaac exclaimed, "My blessed, what a rucket! and what a feegarie all on 'em must have had last night - the husbirds (or whosbirds) - a scrambling and hocksing about - and the messes all over the pleace, for when I turns the dogs out they'ull find their own bre'kfusts, and it'ull take I main of the mornin' to put it all in track agen. Bless my heart and soul if it won't," said Isaac, making his way to the stables.

It was said that hardly any of the Burgesses knew how they got to their homes from this banquet, and many were not seen for several days after. Also it was said for a fact that none of them brought away with them anything that was put on their plates, only that which they found under their plates! This is a reference to the Trinity Tuesday dinners when the annuities would be paid.

Euclid Villas, 62 & 64 Abbey Row

These rather incongruous houses were built in 1881 by John Alexander (of Avon House opposite) to block his neighbour's view. He had been upset by a new building being erected in the back garden of the Mundens. Apparently the neighbour was so incensed that he sued but lost and the case established the principle that you cannot prevent the obscuration of a view by a new building.

Halcombe (now erroneously called **Malmesbury Manor**), Foxley Road

A smaller house existed on this site before Charles Richard Luce (1829-1926) bought the premises in the 1860s. He rebuilt the house and lived here until his death. The house was requisitioned in 1942 for Ecko workers and not released until 1951. It remained a private home until 1982 when it became an Old Peoples' Home. There were complaints that the town had become *a dumping ground for old people*. Five years later there was a plan to build a house in the grounds of the home which was refused and unsuccessfully went to appeal. In 1989 Major & Mrs. Jackson reputedly gave the residents five days notice to quit a short time before Christmas. A plan for a 62 bed extension to the Home was refused. The vacant property was occupied by squatters and vandalised before it was sold in 1995 with the intention to refurbish it as a Nursing Home. In the event it was put on the market later that year and sold as a private house.

Kings House, Kings Wall

The listing particulars note; *an exceptionally fine and interesting early 18th Century town house, the sash windows being very early examples.* Built in two stages the main house differs in architectural style from its west wing. There are two possible explanations for the name. First it is reputed to have been the site of King Athelstan's palace but it is outside the town's defences. More likely it was the site where Matthew Kyng, MP and clothier lived in the 16th Century. He was an unscrupulous character who always seemed to be on the wrong side of the law, frequently appearing in the civil and criminal courts although he represented the town in Parliament between 1554 and 1558. Early in the 19th Century Benjamin Coffin Thomas (1776-1840) owned the house and he invited William Cobbett (1763-1835) to stay. Cobbett wrote the following account in *Rural Rides* on 11 September 1826 and being so engaging it is reproduced in full:

When I got in here yesterday, I went, at first, to an inn; but I very soon changed my quarters for the house of a friend, who and whose family, though I had never seen them before, and had never heard of them until I was at Highworth, gave me a hearty reception, and precisely in the style that I like. This town, though it has nothing particularly engaging in itself, stands upon one of the prettiest spots that can be imagined. Besides the river Avon, which I went down in the south-east part of the country, here is another river Avon, which runs down to Bath, and two branches, or sources, of which meet here. There is a pretty ridge of ground, the base of which is a mile or a mile and a half wide. On each side of this ridge a branch of the river runs down, through a flat of very fine meadows. The town and the beautiful remains of the famous old abbey stand on the rounded spot which terminates this ridge; and, just below, nearly close to the town, the two branches of the river meet; and then they begin to be called the Avon. The land round about is excellent, and of a great variety of forms. The trees are lofty and fine: so that what with the water, the meadows, the fine cattle and sheep, and, as I hear, the absence of hard-

Kings House has changed little since 1964.

pinching poverty, this is a very pleasant place. There remains more of the abbey than, I believe, of any of our monastic buildings, except that of Westminster, and those that have become cathedrals. The church service is performed in the part of the abbey that is left standing. The parish church has fallen down and is gone; but the tower remains, which is made use of for the bells; but the abbey is used as the church, though the church-tower is at a considerable distance from it. It was once a most magnificent building; and there is now a doorway which is the most beautiful thing I ever saw, and which was, nevertheless, built in Saxon times, in "the dark ages," and was built by men who were not begotten by Pitt nor by Jubilee George. – What fools, as well as ungrateful creatures we have been and are! There is a broken arch, standing off from the sound part of the building, at which one cannot look up without feeling shame at the thought of ever having abused the men who made it. No one need tell any man of sense; he feels our inferiority to our fathers upon merely beholding the remains of their efforts to ornament their country and elevate the minds of the people. We talk of our skill and learning, indeed! How do we know how skilful, how learned they were? If, in all that they have left us, we see they have surpassed us, why are we to conclude that they did not surpass us in all other things worthy of admiration?

This famous abbey was founded, in about the year 600, by Maidulf, a Scotch monk, who upon the suppression of a nunnery at that time selected the spot for this great establishment. For the great magnificence, however, to which it was soon after brought, it was indebted to Aldhelm, a monk educated within its first walls, by the founder himself; and to St. Aldhelm, who by his great virtues became very famous, the church was dedicated in the time of King Edgar. This monastery continued flourishing during those dark ages, until it was found to be endowed to the amount of sixteen thousand and seventy seven pounds, eleven shillings and eight pence. of the money of the present day! Amongst other, many other, great men produced by this Abbey of Malmsbury, was that famous scholar and historian, William de Malmsbury.

There is a market-cross in this town, the sight of which is worth a journey of hundreds of miles. Time, with his scythe, and 'enlightened Protestant piety,' with its pick-axes and crow-bars; these united have done much to efface the beauties of this monument of ancient skill and taste, and proof of ancient wealth; but in spite of all their destructive efforts this cross still remains a most beautiful thing, though possibly, and even probably, nearly, or quite, a thousand years old. There is a market-cross lately erected at Devizes, and intended to imitate the ancient ones. Compare that with this, and you have, pretty fair, a view of the difference between us and our fore-fathers of the 'dark ages.'

I set off from Malmsbury this morning at 6 o'clock, in as sweet and bright a morning as ever came out of the heavens, and leaving behind me as pleasant a house and as kind hosts as I ever met with in the whole course of my life, either in England or America, and that is saying a great deal indeed. This circumstance was the more pleasant, as I had never before seen, or heard of, these kind, unaffected, sensible, sans-façons, and most agreeable friends.

Cobbett was a Radical who had scathing words for any small example of corruption and mismanagement he found on his tours. The hospitality he received must have been excellent for him not to mention anything about this rotten borough or that his host was one of the chief aides of the borough-monger. Thomas was Town Clerk, Clerk to the Magistrates, to the Lieutenancy and to the Commissioner of Taxes and carried on that business here so that may be the reason for the Old Corporation's arms on the roofline nearest the river. The crest closest to the road is probably that of the Anderson and Yeaman families but it is not known what their connection was with the house. The house was later divided into several separate dwellings but is now two.

Knoll House, Swindon Road
Commander William Luce RN (1793-1874), brother of Thomas who managed the bank, moved here around 1840 to enjoy the local hunting. He rebuilt it in the 1860s to replace the 17th Century

house. Thomas' eldest son William Hollis Luce (1822-1912), who had made his fortune trading tea in China, moved in after his aunt left in 1875. He had four daughters, Gertrude (1871-1962), Jane (1872-1937), Ursula (1874-1965), Amy (1879-1967) and two sons, Thomas (1877-1925), William (1880-1900). Before World War II the sisters distributed

A postcard of the Knoll at the beginning of the 20th Century.

vouchers worth 5s. to the poor of the town at Christmas redeemable at Adye's Grocers at 52 High Street. Ursula would park her car outside the shop, toot her horn and expect David Adye to serve her at the kerbside! Gertrude was a JP and School Governor. Amy smoked Turkish cigarettes and organised local National Savings. She expected to be able to jump the queue at the Post Office but at least one assistant sought to thwart her! The four sisters led separate lives each with their own sitting room and only joining together for meals. They had a car each and even during the war would drive separately to the Abbey. They never married and thus there was no family member to inherit the house at Amy's death. It later became an hotel.

Manor House, 6 Oxford Street

This building is thought to originate from about 1580. It is Grade II* listed and still has its original Elizabethan staircase. It is not clear why it is called the Manor House – before Dissolution the Lordship of the Manor belonged to the Abbey. The history of the Manor is difficult to follow (Luce has more details), most names of the Lords and dates of their Lordships are known but it was often sold, sometimes inherited and none of the incumbents seemed to live here. Maybe it was used for administration or for the Estate Manager. However in 1743 the Manor was bought by Sir John Rushout and thereafter it remained in his family.

The Manor owned much property around Malmesbury. This was either rented out or let on Copyhold. This curious form of ownership dated back to feudal times and was so called because a copy was made in the Court Roll. An annual rent was paid to the Manor with the land let on the lives of up to 3 individuals who did not have to be in any way connected with the property or Copyholder. The copyholder would pick people with long life expectancy but also those whose deaths he would hear about - often members of the Royal family were named. On death a new life had to be added and a heriot or fine paid to the Manor which could not prevent the nomination. If the holder failed to put in the new life a third party could do so and might eventually become the copyholder if he held all 3 lives. This type of ownership was abolished in 1922, but by that time the Manor had sold the freehold to all its properties.

Two brothers, William and William Henry Lockstone established a grocery business at the Market Cross in 1808. At the outset they were also chemists and tallow chandlers – makers of candles from animal fats. Two years later they moved into the Oxford Street premises where the business grew into a substantial wholesale and retail grocer. Part of the premises was still known as the Candle House long after oil and gas had become the main forms of lighting. The premises were

The Manor House in its sorry state. The puzzling marks on the chimney can be seen at the top of the photograph.

extended towards the road; you can see the shape of the original roof in the stonework on both gable ends. If you inspect the chimney stacks the stonework suggests that a roof was built against each gable, but roofs did not abut, the profile is the same on each end and is puzzling. At the rear, visible from the car park to Abbey Brewery, is an original window.

Before the last war Lockstone's provided cigarettes as wholesalers to the workers constructing Hullavington aerodrome. Wartime rationing was based on pre-war usage and so Malmesbury never ran short of fags! After the grocers shut in 1968 it became two shops used by various small retailers for around 30 years but the building has been vacant and neglected for ten years. Hopefully a recent change of ownership heralds better times.

Mundens, 27 Abbey Row

This stone house has an inscription on a rainwater hopper on the eastern end with some initials and the date 1811. At the rear there was the purported Castle Well, now filled in. Revd. James Moffat (d1804) in his *History of Malmesbury* stated that the well was *large, of great depth and the workmanship neatly executed*. From the late 19th Century for nearly a hundred years this was one of three surgeries in the town, the others being Tower House and 10 Gloucester Street. One of the main parts of the Welfare State introduced by the Labour administration after World War II was the provision of free medical services. However it was not welcomed by all, the British Medical Association bitterly opposed it with doctors voting 9:1 against it in March 1948. A patient from Foxley wrote to Dr. Winch on the subject saying *A few years in the Civil Service and all doctors will become bureaucrats and patients just numbers* and *I believe the fears are justified for it has been the avowed intention of the Socialists to have complete control over the medical services*. The National Health Service Act 1946 created the 'nationalised' health service which was implemented with effect from 5th July 1948.

The Priory

Unfortunately nothing now remains of this house. It was sited to the east of the southern approach to the Priory roundabout at the junction of the A429 and B4040. In the 13th Century the hospital of St. Mary Magdalene stood here. The chapel survived and was later used as a private house. In the early 18th Century this was demolished and a new house, Canister Hall, was built on

The Priory in 1964. The Swindon Road junction is hidden by the house with the Black Horse opposite. The houses in the background are still there on the old road past Parliament Row.

the site. In 1809 Richard Robins bought it. Obviously finding it unfashionable and not suitable for his status, he built a new three-storey brick house, changing the name to the Priory. His widow, Hester, sold the house to Simon Salter in 1842 who lived there until 1865 when Thomas Henry Chubb (1815-1888) bought it. He was a solicitor whose father Thomas set up a practice which became Chubb & Sons with an office at 36 Cross Hayes.

At the beginning of the 20th Century Lewis Edward Morrice (1853-1933) bought the Priory. He had served with the Royal Warwickshire Regiment in the Boer War where he was awarded the Distinguished Service Order. After his death his widow lived here until she died. Priory Farm to the north of the Swindon Road before WWII was also owned by this household. The farmer at that time, Bill Woodward, is remembered for sitting in the dairy ladling out creamy milk to children who came to collect it. During the last war workers at Ekco used the house and it was converted into flats. In 1967 a fire caused substantial damage which was not repaired. The remains were demolished in 1971 to make way for the bypass.

Stainsbridge House, 101 Gloucester Road

In the middle of the 19th Century solicitor Thomas Chubb (1792-1869) lived here. Capt. Richard Coote (1836-1875) bought the property for £600 in 1870 and rebuilt it the following year. Unfortunately he did not live long enough to enjoy his new residence fully, his memorial faces you on entering the Abbey. The widowed Mrs. Julia Clark (1848-1902) in 1893 turned the house into a day and boarding school for girls called Stainsbridge College. This closed in 1930. After closure the house became the residence of solicitor Frederick Ernest Smith (1844-1939) until he moved in 1937. The House became a National Children's Home until 1953 when the Superintendent and 40 children moved to St. Leonards on Sea. The following year it was turned into an Hotel. In 1978 its use changed to that of a residential home for the elderly with accommodation for 29. A large extension was added in 2006 which increased the capacity to 45. It specialises in dementia and Alzheimer cases.

Tower House, 13 Oxford Street

Although this has been a single dwelling since the 19th Century, it comprises a Medieval Hall with a Tudor rear wing and to the north a terrace of 4 houses greatly altered with the addition of a 19th Century service wing. The site has a varied history. The earliest known use was as an Abbey hospitium (guesthouse). The merchants' banqueting Hall, now the garage, was built around 1490. This has a 3-bay roof (formerly 4) with collar trusses and chamfered arch braces forming continuous arches, wind braces to the lower 2 registers and a through diagonal ridge beam.

William Stumpe, the wealthy clothier who bought the Abbey at Dissolution, lived in the Hall whilst building Abbey House. He added the southern rear wing possibly using stone from the Abbey, a trefoil window being an example. Stumpe was in royal favour: *King Henry VIII, hunting in Braydon Forest, came with all his court train, unexpectedly, to dine with this clothier. But great housekeepers are as seldom surprised as captains with enemies. Stumpe commands his little army of workmen, which he feeds daily in his house, to fast one meal until night, and with the same provision have the king and his court train most wholesome and plentiful entertainment.* Stumpe kept his head!

Charles I later briefly stayed here during the Civil War. It is suggested that the parliamentarians set out to capture him but he was rescued in the nick of time by Prince Rupert coming from Cirencester. The 1647 'bird's-eye' map of the town shows an enclosed courtyard at the back of the Hall. A workhouse was established here from the 18th Century until 1838. It seems that this started in the Tudor wing (later the stables) but expanded to include the Hall, probably due to unemployment following the end of the Napoleonic War, problems in agriculture and the failure of Francis Hill's new factory at the Town Bridge. By 1838 a new workhouse for 24 parishes around the town had been built on the Bristol Road.

Tower House in 1964 with the covered shelter still in place.

Prior to 1803 the northern part of the terrace was a post house known as the Salutation Inn. Until recently there was a right of way from the garden of Tower House to Holloway, maybe allowing access for travellers with their horses to the rear courtyard of the inn. There is a basement and well under the present living room in the northern wing. Folklore suggests that a secret tunnel ran from there to Nuns Walk by the town wall but no trace of this has been found.

The tower was added in 1834 by Dr. Player (1756-1864) a keen astronomer. This was built over the 4th bay of the old Hall. A large gateway was made through the hall to allow coaches to enter. It seems that the Handy family (lawyers who lived in Gloucester Street) owned the property from at least the early 19th Century although it was occupied by Dr. Alfred Jeston (1800-1869) after Player's death. Around this time it is likely that the doctor's surgery was established with its street entrance underneath the tower. When Jeston died it was bought at auction in 1870 by William Thompson. By then all the extensions to the northern part were complete. Dr. Richard Kinneir (1842-1922) started as Dr. Jeston's assistant but took over and finally bought the premises for £1,650 in 1897. Barbara Kinneir scratched her name on the glass of one of the bedroom windows.

The property was purchased by Arthur Heaton in 1919 whose widow sold it in 1929. Dr. Battersby (1895-1937) ran the practice from then but after he was called out on a cold night he caught pneumonia and died. He was followed in 1938 by Dr. Willie Winch who is remembered for making his rounds in a 2 door open Bentley accompanied by his Siamese cat on the front seat! He was not particularly enamoured of the National Health Service and had many private patients. Despite this, having discovered a gravely ill farm worker he brought him back to health and engaged him as a gardener. Dr. Winch moved out but used the house as a Nursing Home with staff living at Eastgate House two doors away. A number of rich eccentric residents were attracted by this facility including an ex Indian Army Brigadier who would demand champagne and sandwiches during the night. Mentally ill patients could, as an alternative to being committed to an asylum, lodge with a General Practitioner and one such lady with her keeper resided here.

Before World War II the tower became an Observer Corps post designated M1, M2 being at Chippenham and M3 at Marshfield. Dr. Winch strongly objected to the disruption caused as access to the tower was through the house close to his bedroom. The new access from the garage was installed as a result. An electricity supply was installed (no doubt arranged by Ron Young of Wessex Electricity who was an Observer) and a canvas screen erected around the viewing platform. The first winter of the war was bitterly cold and a more permanent screen was built to protect the Observers. This was made of blocks with half of the platform open and the other half forming a covered shelter for 2 men.

At the end of the war the Royal Observer Corps stood down but was reactivated in 1947. The tower was still used and personnel climbing the stairs early on weekend mornings would often disturb the occupants of the house. This came to an end following another reorganisation in 1968 when the ROC's responsibility for plotting aircraft ceased.

Dr. Winch did not want a partner and would employ doctors as associates to help with the residents. However he spent more and more time in Guernsey and first employed Dr. Michael Pym as a locum in the winter of 1955. Three years later whilst suffering from mumps he decided to retire and sold the house and practice to Dr. Pym for £5,000. As mortgages were not readily available Dr. Winch gave him an interest free loan.

There were still a number of private patients including the Earl of Suffolk who expected to be seen even when he arrived without notice. The practice was expanding and Dr. John Rycroft became a partner. Unfortunately there was insufficient room in the house to provide the new facilities that modern medicine required. Several redevelopment schemes were considered until in 1979 the practice moved to Laystalls (so called because in earlier times dung collected from the streets was kept there), near the south west corner of Cross Hayes. Tower House was sold to finance the move and for a time the old surgery was used for an antiques business by Mrs. Fidler. In the late 1980s A. Nielson, who ran Athelstan Coaches, owned it and ran a guest house. André Ptaszynski, the theatre impresario, lived here for a year until 1992 when it was sold again.

Until the 1990s Tower House was the last property in the town paying a Quit Rent to Jesus College, Oxford. This was a charge made to release the house owner from feudal duties but it is not clear how this connection arose.

Verona House, now Poole Road

This is another elegant Victorian villa gone without trace. It was built by Joseph Poole, the myriorama proprietor, in 1883. He chose this site close to the railway so he could oversee the loading of his shows. Next door to the house was a large building where Joseph's artists painted the scenery on rolls of canvas. This was later used as a school gymnasium and then as the Cartmell Youth Centre. Joseph became Mayor in 1890 and at the end of his term of office presented road name plates to the Borough inscribed **JOS^H. POOLE** ^ESQ **MAYOR 1890-91** and a number of these still can be seen around the town. In 1921 Verona House was bought by the County Council for use as the Secondary School Headmaster's home. By 1984 it was vacant but then converted into offices by Persimmon Homes who were building the nearby Reeds Farm estate. They ensured that many of the internal features were preserved but in 2005 they demolished the building despite efforts to have it listed. It is ironic that their inelegant new office at the top of Tetbury Hill has been named Verona House.

Verona House was the most elegant Victoria villa in the area and deserved protection.

Westhill House, Bristol Road

This area was originally an isolated small pocket of the parish of Bremilham but became part of Westport St. Mary in 1884. It seems that this arrangement arose because the Holford family

Westhill House as a Nursing Home in 1985. (Malmesbury Chronicles)

where the white line is in the middle of the road! Mrs. Langley purchased Westhill in 1962 and converted it to a Nursing Home. Dr. and Mrs. Coleman took over in 1965. This was closed due to difficulties in the late 1980s. Dr. David Jackson and originally 3 partners reopened the New Westhill Nursing Home in 1989. Just 10 years later due to the need to upgrade facilities it was no longer economically viable and this well-used local amenity closed. The following year the building was converted into 3 town houses.

Education

Malmesbury has a proud tradition of education following the establishment of the monastery as a seat of learning. There have been many schools here over the years and only the most important of these are described.

Old Corporation Boy's School, St. Johns Street

In St. John's Street the archway next to the Almshouses is known as School Arch because it led to the Old Corporation's School, held in the Old Courthouse (on the left through the arch). The earliest document relating to this is dated 22 June 1629 signed by the Alderman and 12 Capital Burgesses *for the payment of twentie pounds for the mayntenence of a schoolmaster and five poor pepell, to be mayntaynd at St. John's according unto the decree formerly made ...* £10 was paid to the master. Pupils were not required to pay for their education. Michael Wickes in a deed of 1695 added another £10 from land at Great Somerford *the better to procure an able diligent schoolmaster*. In 1714 the master was dismissed because he lived outside the town and appointed a deputy who presumably was badly paid because he demanded fees from the pupils! By the early 19th Century the teacher was earning £50 a year, £40 paid by the Wickes' charity and the balance by the Capital Burgesses. Between 60 and 70 boys attended in winter but only 50 during the summer and they were first admitted at the age of six with *no time limited for their learning*. The school, also known as St. Paul's Free, closed in 1888 when the 20 scholars were transferred to the National School. The master's salary payments were made to the National Society until free elementary education was introduced following the Elementary Education Act 1891.

The Girls' Free School, the Abbey

Robert Arch through a deed of 19 July 1634 provided land in Lea, the rents and income from which were to be used for the general good of the borough. In 1834 income of £34 was used to run a girls' school. This was established in the parvise of the Abbey which could only accommodate 45 girls. The schoolmistress Mrs. Anne Hanks (1799-1878) received £25 a year for instruction in reading, writing and sewing and Lucy Hitchins received £13 to teach lace-making. The deficit was met by the Wickes' charity. Later the school was moved to the vestry so capacity increased to 60 pupils but when Mrs. Bessie Angell (1850-1932) was mistress the average attendance was 20. The school closed around 1886.

Elizabeth Hodges' Boys School, 40 Gloucester Street

By her will Elizabeth Hodges left £30 per year each for the augmentation of charity schools in the towns of Tetbury and Malmesbury. From 1730 schools for the education of 15 poor boys were established in both towns. In 1836 Jeremiah Webb (1799-1873), a carpenter and parish clerk, bought 40 Gloucester Street. He was then awarded the contract to run the school and built an extension at the rear of his terraced cottage. This comprised 2 storeys, a workshop on the ground floor with the classroom above. A number of modifications were made to the house, for example a staircase leading straight from the front door to the school rooms, locks on doors denying access to the boys and high level spy holes for adults to see what was going on in the next room. Some of these changes are still in situ. This school was amalgamated with the Westport National School in 1869. The charity remained dormant for many years but in 1990 Malmesbury Town Council restarted the disbursement of its funds as bursaries.

National Boys' School, Gastons Road

The 'National Society for Promoting the Education of the Poor in the Principles of the Established Church' (founded in 1811) established a boys' school in the Guildhall, Oxford Street by about 1820. This was popular and larger premises were needed. The Church was grateful to be given land in Crab Tree Close in the detached part of Bremilham parish off Bristol Road by Robert Stayner

Holford (1808-1892) of Westonbirt. The name Crab Tree Close has been reused for new housing adjacent and Robert Holford is remembered through the development called Holford Rise at the end of Bremilham Road. Originally it was intended that both girls and boys would be taught here. However on 2nd February 1857 two new schools were opened, one

The pupils of the Gastons Road Boys' School in the playground c1910.

for boys on this site and the other for girls in Cross Hayes. When the schools opened it was proclaimed:

The object has been to provide what has long been wanted, a place of education in this town, upon such a footing that no one need be excluded on account of a religious difference; and that all classes, without distinction, may here find sound instruction, suitable to fit their children for their own sphere of employment, trade or business.

Therefore, not only Reading, Writing, Arithmetic, and Needlework for girls will be taught, but Farmers and Tradesmen, who can afford to keep their children at school to an age when their minds become capable of application to higher studies, such as Geography, Mathematics and History, may provide for them a competent course of Education in this school at a moderate expense.

Mr. Henry Onesimus Moyse and Miss Facey will be the Master and Mistress of the respective schools.

The rate of payment will be as follows:

For children whose parents are poor, 2 shillings per quarter, if paid in advance, or, if paid weekly, 2 pence halfpenny per week.

For children of Farmers, Tradesmen and others in a position superior to that of a day labourer, ten shillings per quarter, paid in advance.

Within a few years there were about 100 pupils at this school. Gardening was

The gardening class. (Athelstan Museum)

an important part of the syllabus with land nearby used for this purpose. The Infants had their school on the first floor until 1922 when they moved to Cross Hayes. The flooring was declared unsafe before World War II (is that why the Infants moved?) and it was only used for light storage. However with the influx of evacuees in 1940 more space was desperately needed and classes were once again held upstairs but the strengthening work was carried out a year later! It was not until the new Secondary Modern School opened in 1954 (taking pupils from age 11) that Gastons Road became a mixed Junior School. In 1966 after the Grammar School had vacated the site on lower Tetbury Hill, this school (combined with the Infants' School) moved into the old Grammar School building. The old Boys' School became the Arts Centre for the Secondary Modern School but fell into disuse in 2001. The building has now been converted into flats known as Westport Manor.

National Girls' School, Cross Hayes

This school was built thanks to the munificence of Samuel Brooke (of Cowbridge House) and his nephew Revd. Charles Kemble and could accommodate 300 pupils. Children between 5 and 14 were offered education but the parents had to pay for it as explained above. No. 22 Cross Hayes was the home of the schoolmistress and S. B. Brooke's arms are over the door. The girls were taught reading, writing, arithmetic and needlework. Older children could be employed as Monitors to supervise the younger ones and would receive a salary of £6 a year.

Government grants were available after the passage of the Education Act 1870. Unfortunately Revd. Kemble was unable to accept the Act's Conscience Clause (which allowed parents to withdraw their children from religious studies) and the school was unable to receive any such funding. The school had some support from the Poor Law Guardians. After Kemble's death in 1875 the school was able to benefit from the government money.

The Infants at Cross Hayes Girls' School c1900.

Prior to the opening of the Secondary Modern in 1954, Cross Hayes lacked classroom space. Two classes were held in St. Mary's Hall and one in the Silver Street Congregational Church. It then became the Infant's School until in 1966 it combined with the Junior School on Tetbury Hill using new buildings in the grounds.

St. Joseph's Primary School, Holloway

Father Larive started an evening school for working class men in 1867. This proved so successful that his parishioners urged him to open a free day school for children of parents who could not afford the fees of the National Schools. This, called St. Joseph's, was established in two rooms in Cross Hayes House the following year. When the new church opened they moved into the old building, able to accommodate 100 children. In 1932/3 new premises, costing around £6,000, were built in Holloway on the site of a kitchen garden owned by the Kings Arms. In 1955 a Roman Catholic Secondary Modern School opened in Swindon which allowed St. Joseph's to become part of

The pupils of St. Joseph's School 1907.

the primary system. It continues to be very successful, one extension was added in 1965 and another in 2012. Only having a small hard courtyard to play in, the field on the escarpment below the school was made into a green space for the children's use in 2012.

Ragged School, Burnivale

Following the establishment of St. Joseph's free Roman Catholic School in 1868, the nonconformists reacted violently and set up a committee to have it closed down. They failed to do so and instead sought to open their own school. Subscriptions were raised and the support of Walter Powell MP enlisted. He provided a wooden building put up on land donated by Charles Luce. The Ragged School, which had operated on Sundays and evenings since 1866, opened as a free day school in Burnivale (where there is now a block of garages) in February 1870 with 53 pupils, 13 of whom had come from the Catholic school. Despite a rule that no child eligible to attend the National School could be admitted, some were. The Ragged School flourished for a time with a new building being opened in June 1873. It was soon in financial difficulties but obtained its first Government grant in 1877. However as more funding came from the State so the cost of meeting their standards rose. Funds were so scarce that parents were charged 1½d. per week. Apparently if not all of this could be afforded then the pupil attended for part of the week. By 1886 it was too expensive to comply with current requirements and the school closed with the pupils transferring to the National Schools.

Stainsbridge Ladies College,
Gloucester Road

The widowed Mrs. Julia Clark (1854-1902) took over a small girls' school run by the Misses Dale in Gloucester Street in

Stainsbridge House in 1964. A large extension has now been added for its Care Home residents.

1883. She moved it to 32 Cross Hayes two years later where she took in boarders. By 1893 she had moved to Stainsbridge House, Gloucester Road and it was renamed Stainsbridge College. The school had a good reputation and attracted pupils from all parts of the country. Infant day boys were admitted in the 1920s. Miss Geraldine Elder who was one of the original Assistant Governesses took over as Principal after Mrs. Clark's death. She returned to Londonderry in 1930 to look after her sick father and the College closed soon afterwards.

Malmesbury Academy, Corn Gastons

At the end of the 19th Century Elementary Schools catered for children up to the age of 13. The first secondary school for children aged between 8 and 14 was the Technical School which opened in the back of the Council Chamber, Silver Street in September 1896. The premises were described as *three classrooms approached by a long narrow passageway; a small chemical laboratory, a shed for practical work and a caretaker's room made of corrugated iron and matchboard registering 81°F when inspected*. In the beginning there were only five scholars with two teachers, Mr. Cameron and Mr. Eatell, covering a wide syllabus with the expected Arithmetic, English, History, Latin etc. but also including subjects such as Agriculture, Bookkeeping, Euclid and Land Surveying. Other 'Sub-Centres' for learning and examinations were set up in many surrounding villages. The Executive Committee chaired by the Earl of Suffolk arranged for pioneer lectures to be held in the villages *in order that an interest in the subjects of Instruction may be awakened*. The school was soon popular and new premises for up to 75 scholars were opened for classes on 7th January 1903 at the foot of Tetbury Hill at a cost of £5,192, financed by grants of £1,800 each from the Rural District & County Councils, £500 from the Borough Council with the balance from subscriptions and donations. Parents had to pay for their children to attend but contributions also came from Councils with the Borough Council agreeing to levy a rate of 1d. in £1 and the Rural District Council $^3/_8$d. This building was described as having *two classrooms on*

The Tetbury Hill premises after it had become the Primary School. The building was fenced off and a porch added to protect pupils from falling masonry!

the ground floor, a cookery kitchen, woodwork shop, Headmaster's and Mistress' room, boys' and girls' cloakroom and offices. On the first floor another classroom, an Art room, two laboratories and a lecture theatre.

Not long after this Wiltshire County Council took over responsibility for education and the school was renamed the Malmesbury and District County Secondary School. Even though this was the official title it was generally known as the 'grammar school' although it did not become one until 1954! Parents were required to commit to keep their children here until age 16, although the school leaving age under the Education Act 1918 was 14. In 1921 Verona House was bought to provide accommodation for the Headmaster and space to allow the school to expand to 120 pupils. The County threatened to close the school in 1935 but despite this expansion took place in the late 1930s and 1944. Riddick's Year Books during the late 1930s contained the following information:

The Malmesbury and District County Secondary School - Headmaster, Mr. K. Willmore, B.SC.., B.COM. (B.A.). Staff, Miss M. M. Browne, M.A., Miss E. M. Bevan, B.A., Miss R. M. Wise, B.A, Miss M. E. Oatley, Mr. J. J. Chipchase, B.SC.., Mr. J. W. Davies, B.A., Mr. S. L. Hockey, M.A.., Mr. G. W. Tracy. Art Master, Mr. A. F. Hayward.

The School, established in 1903 as a Secondary School for boys and girls, is maintained by the Wiltshire County Council. It is administered by a body of 21 Governors. Chairman of the Governors, Alderman J. A. Jones; secretary to the Governors, Mr. C. Bradshaw, 10, High Street, Malmesbury.

Boys and girls whose parents wish them to enter the school should see that they sit for the County Examination held in the early part of the year. On the results of this examination, supplemented by an oral test or interview, will be awarded a number of County Junior Scholarships carrying complete exemption from school fees. Other children who reach a sufficient standard in the examination will be admitted at fees of three, six, nine or twelve guineas a year according to the income and financial responsibilities of their parents. Parents are required to sign an agreement promising to keep the pupil at school until July of the year in which he (or she) attains the age of sixteen

A number of maintenance allowances are awarded from time to time by:—
> *(a) The Trustees of the Elizabeth Hodge's Charity.*
> *(b) The Trustees of the Michael Week's Charity*
> *(c) The Capital Burgesses of Malmesbury.*
> *(d) The Trustees of the Warner Bequest.*

The arrival of evacuees at the beginning of World War II created a shortage of teachers and one of the original teachers Mr. Eatell returned at the age of 86! In 1944 secondary education became free.

A Practical Instruction Centre was opened at Corn Gastons in 1950 to teach cookery and woodwork. This was used by pupils from the two Church of England Elementary Schools. In 1954 the Bremilham Secondary Modern School was opened in a new building at Corn Gastons. This started with 30 teachers and 450 pupils. At the same time the County Secondary became the Grammar School and pupils had to pass the Eleven Plus examination to gain entry. This School outgrew its premises and in 1964 moved to a new site at the junction of Tetbury Hill and Filands (now a housing estate).

Whilst the benefits of the new site were just being enjoyed, the Labour government implemented the Robbins Report which recommended comprehensive schooling. In 1971 both secondary schools were combined into the Malmesbury School. The Lower School (junior scholars) being at Filands and the Upper School at Corn Gastons. In the late 1990s the high cost of the school

The new school at Filands under construction in 1964.

being on two sites led to the decision to move onto one site at Corn Gastons. This was financed through the Private Finance Initiative, in other words without the help of state funds. Contractors put up the buildings necessary and became leasehold owners of the buildings with the County Council paying rent. This project, combined with others at Chippenham and Wootton Bassett, obtained Government approval at the end of 1998 and was completed in 2001.

Burton Hill House School

After the death of her husband in 1933 Mrs. Sylvia Storey moved out and tried to sell the house. Finding no buyer it was leased to Misses 'Zoo' and Hilary Hunt around 1936, who set up a private school. Nursery education was provided for local children, both day and boarding. This establishment closed in 1945. By this time the estate incorporated over 150 acres which was sold in lots. Shortly afterwards Mrs. Storey was finally able to sell the house, which included Arches Farm, to the Shaftesbury Society for £11,000. Burton Hill House School for up to 50 Seriously Crippled Girls opened on 1st May 1947. Summer fetes were used as annual fundraisers which

Burton Hill School, the corridor to the pool on the right.

drew many local people. 1961 proved to be an important year – Bob Arnold, Tom Forrest of the Archers, opened the fete which raised a record £540 and boys joined the roll for the first time. In 1964 a hydrotherapy pool costing £10,500 was built. An extension containing two classrooms and storage space was opened in 1977, called the Brocklebank Wing after the principal donor. By 1984 the fete could bring in £3,500 in just a few hours. £120,000 was needed to pay for a Field Studies Centre intended to attract groups from other schools. Six bedrooms, kitchen, drying room and toilets could accommodate 24 who could study local history, geography and the environment. Changes in funding and the ambition to integrate handicapped children into mainstream schools led to difficulty in attracting pupils and the school closed in 2007.

Other Schools

Sunday Schools

In his 1876 History of Malmesbury James T. Bird (1843-1898), a printer who lived in Abbey Row, wrote; *Among the various methods which have been practised to ameliorate the condition of the lower ranks of people, there is none perhaps more praiseworthy or effectual than the well-known institution of Sunday Schools. These seminaries have been the means of rescuing many individuals from a state of ignorance and barbarism, and making them valuable members of society.*

Malmesbury can boast of ten such Schools, one of which is connected with each of the following places of Worship. Independent Chapel, Back Hill; Moravian Chapel, Oxford Street; Friendly Sabbath School, Market Cross; Baptist Chapel, Abbey Row; Congregational Chapel, Westport; Primitive Methodist Chapel, Westport; Ragged School, Burnivale; Roman Catholic Church, Cross Hayes; Westport Church; and two belonging to the Abbey Church.

49 The Triangle,

In 1596 there is mention of a grammar school in the Sheepfair opposite the Three Cups and it was probably at no. 49. The master, Robert Latimer, instructed Thomas Hobbes and later taught John Aubrey. This became the Oddfellows Inn.

Athelstan School, Ingram Street

Mrs. Ellen Hawxwell was persuaded in 1940 to restart teaching which she had given up on her marriage. She had come to Malmesbury from Kent to teach at St. Joseph's. She began with six pupils in her home, the Willows, Park Road. Again demand from parents led to her having to move the school to a room in Stainsbridge Mill. In 1952 it moved into a classroom in Ingram Street. The school catered for all pupils aged between 4½ and 11. Mrs. Hawxwell retired in 1976 and two years later F. J. Carrigan and his daughter Miss M. H. Carrigan bought the school. However in 1981 the new Headteacher Mrs. Dorothy Braun had to close the school. The premises had been moved to Mundens Close, Mill Lane and although 47 pupils had been expected a third of them did not arrive. The fees were around £100 per term. Four full time and two part time teachers lost their jobs.

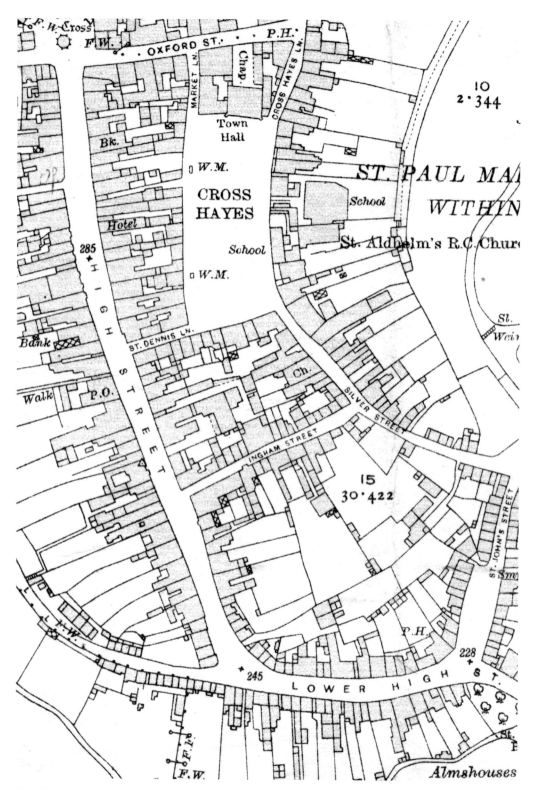

The 1921 Ordnance Survey showing the High Street and Cross Hayes. Note the weighing machines used for the market in Cross Hayes and the Three Horseshoes on the corner of Cross Hayes Lane and Oxford Street.

High Street Shops

West side

Cherry Tree, 1 High Street
This is believed to have been part of the produce and poultry market built over at the beginning of the 19th Century. The shopfront was added towards the end of that century. Combined with No. 3.

By 1875 James Barnard, watchmaker, jeweller and silversmith occupied the shop here but left the town in 1892.

c1895-1936 Edward Jones (1870-1945), goldsmith and jeweller. The Jones family lived at No. 3. Edward's younger son Leonard also became a jeweller and optician whose main premises were in Cirencester although he held a weekly optician's clinic in his father's shop.

1936-1959 Norman Lewis, goldsmith and jeweller. Norman was recruited by Edward Jones as a watch repairer in 1923 from Maidstone. He bought the business in 1936 and continued until 1959 when he took over a general store in Corn Gastons.

From the 1970s this was a ladies' clothes store which between 1980 and 2005 was called Number One Clothes. Thereafter it was combined with the Cherry Tree of 2 Gloucester Street.

Halls Bakers, 3 High Street
This small shop was combined with No. 1 until the 1960s when E. & J. Phillips, baker and confectioner from Tetbury took the premises. They closed in 2004 and the following year Halls Bakers moved in. John Hall and his son Edward opened a bakery in Minchinhampton in 1902, the company still being run by the family from larger premises in Woodchester. They have five shops and supply customers over a wide area.

Vacant, 5 High Street
A late 17th Century building with unusual chimneys, it was refronted c1869 but the shopfront is modern.

1915 Charles White, cycle agent. Kelly's Directory includes this listing but no others have been found.

c1923-c1947 Albert Strange (1874-1933) ran a wireless and electrical supplies shop here which was continued by his widow Amelia (1874-1960).

After a period as Wayfarer Antiques, the Tarantula coffee shop, popular with young people, operated from here in the late 1950s and 1960s. It

In 1964 the Tarantula at No. 5, the basement being a popular place for teenagers to meet, Wakefield's electrical store at No. 7 and Hodder's at Nos. 9 & 11.

became Pot au Feu, a kitchen & china shop, from c1971 for at least a couple of years before that moved to No. 6.

1976-2006 The Cheltenham & Gloucester Building Society established a branch here in December 1976. Since closure an art gallery and Pattini's shoes operated from here for short periods.

Oxfam, 7 High Street

A late 17th Century building which was refronted in the middle of the 19th Century with a shopfront added shortly afterwards.

c1905-1961 Joseph Burton & Sons Ltd, a grocery business from Nottingham established a grocery store here which traded for a time under the name India & China Tea Stores but for most of the period was simply called Burton's Stores. This was the first national chain store in the town. They had a garage in Olivers Lane for their delivery van. In 1961 they wished to expand and built the supermarket at No. 8.

1962-c1966 Edwin Wakefield (b1925) converted No. 7 into an electrical store with a *well stocked record department*. Again after a few years he moved into larger premises across the road

1966-1968 Sketchley, dry cleaners.

1970-1986 Wyles Shoes. This was owned by the same company as the Frisby shop at No. 31 but this branch closed first.

1986-present Oxfam. In July of that year this became the first permanent charity shop in the town. The freehold was purchased in 1989.

9A Barbers, 9a High Street

Prior to 1985 Nos. 9 and 11 were combined. The building dates back to the early 17th Century with a timber frame and jettied first floor which was refronted in 1849.

c1885-c1927 Thomas Bower (1847-1923) & Son, drapers & outfitters; Thomas retired before the Great War and the business was carried on by his surviving son Percy (1878-1960), daughters Bessie (1884-1959) and Alice (1886-1956).

From the left H. J. Hodder at No. 11, Burton's Stores, No. 9, A. F Strange, No. 5 and Norman Lewis Jeweller on the corner during the 1930s.

c1929-1984 Harold J. Hodder (1878-1968), draper & outfitter. Harold's son Donald (1906-1983) joined the business after the war. Before Donald's death his son Roger took over the business until it closed. The property was then bought by J. Saville Gordon Properties of Birmingham. The building was converted into smaller units with flats above and behind named Hodder's Court.

No. 9a

1986-1991 Willsdon's confectioners moved here from No. 22 but competition from supermarkets caused Mrs. Ruth Hayward, the owner to close.

1991-1993 Haybens Footware, after refitting Mrs. Hayward reopened but the new business only lasted two years.

1998-2009 Malmesbury Bookshop, established by Sandra Allen who within a few months left to look after her father and continued by Nick Buchanan.

2013-present 9a Barbers, launched in December 2013, owned by Kristian Trimble.

Spoilt for Choice, 9 High Street

1986-1995 Rompers children's clothes.

1995-2000 West Country Cleaners (from 1 Oxford Street and moved to 40 High Street).

2000-present Spoilt for Choice, novelty soaps & costume jewellery.

Fruits, Roots & Shoots, 11 High Street

Combined with No. 9 prior to 1985.

c1987-1994 Country Crop, greengrocer, later called Joys.

1995-1996 Portway Ceramics, gifts.

1996-2006 Aladdin's Cave, toys.

2006-2011 Bishopstone Trading, adult and children's clothes.

2011-2013 Malmesbury Rocks (from No. 15), toys.

2013-present Fruits, Roots & Shoots, greengrocers.

Capers, 13 High Street

No. 13 was combined with No. 15 until 1985 when it was redeveloped at the same time as Nos. 9 & 11. This is a 17th Century building which was refronted in the 1820s.

c1900-1973 Riddicks, stationer, printer & bookbinder. Nathan Riddick (1858-1926) took over the printing works of William Hatcher in St. Dennis Lane behind 34 High Street in 1889. Until 1880 this was owned by J. T. Bird, author of a comprehensive History of Malmesbury. In 1914 Nathan's nephew, Joseph Riddick (1873-1959), took over and in 1946 it was passed on to his son, Harold (1907-1985).

1973-1985 Wood & Co., printers & stationers.

No. 13

1986-c1987 Minerva in Malmesbury. Art gallery.

c1987-2009 The Fromagerie (from No.43), delicatessen.

2009-present Capers, delicatessen & coffee.

B & Co., 15 High Street

Combined with No. 13 prior to 1985.

1986-1987 Cornucopia (from 7a Gloucester Street), gifts.

1988-1990 Claire's, wool.

1992-2007 Cotswold Cobblers, cobbler & key cutter.

2008-2011 Malmesbury Rocks, toys. Run by John Lawton and expanded by moving to No. 11.

2011 Sweet Memories, sweets.

2013 Abbey Taxis, for a few months this was used as an office.

2014-present B & Co., dress shop.

H.J. Knee Ltd., 17 High Street

At the beginning of the 20th Century there were two shops on the site, Walker's grocers and John Lyne's (1809-1901) butchers on the corner but before 1907 one larger shop had been built.

c1905-1958 Jones and Son, cycle agents & ironmongers. James A. Jones (1868-1966) began work as a barber in his father's business (at No. 6) but at the age of 30 changed career and established a cycle and musical instrument

Lyne's butchers had a slaughterhouse behind the shop in Olivers Lane, but when the photo was taken they and Walker's grocery had moved.

Boots the Chemist on the corner of Olivers Lane, H. J. Knee and Riddick's in 1964.

shop at No. 10 Oxford Street. He then opened a cycle store at 36 Gloucester Street which suffered a catastrophic fire in 1913. After the Hospital moved from the Market Cross in 1925 he converted those premises into a furniture store. He was Mayor in 1911, 1923-24, 1930 and 1939. At the age of 96 he became the oldest Alderman and longest serving member of any Council in Great Britain. No. 17 High Street was sold around 1930 first to P.M. Rhodes, later to Mr. Richards and finally to Mr. and Mrs. Charles Hazell in 1947. It continued to trade under the name of Jones and Son. Charles Hazell was one of the sons of the Railway Hotel's licensee. He and his wife built up a very successful greengrocer's business in Corsham. Shortly after the end of World War II they sold up, moved to Corston and ran the department store until retiring.

1958-present H.J. Knee from Trowbridge then took over the business. Henry John Knee had opened a corner shop in Trowbridge in 1879. Originally selling ironmongery and furnishings, the business expanded to become at one time or another a removal firm, building contractor, restaurant, hairdressers, undertakers and department store with premises in Bradford-on-Avon and Melksham. Noel Knee (1914-2005), grandson of the founder, negotiated the purchase in Malmesbury, being more favourably disposed after Mrs. Hazell served him the best tea he had ever eaten! After Knees took over they knocked down cottages at the rear and extended the shop.

Cancer Research UK, 19 High Street

A 17th Century building refronted in 1815 but with a modern shop window.

c1886-c1919 Henry Norman Ratcliffe (1857-1922), chemist, brother of Edwin who founded the Westport Foundry.

c1920-1936 Howard William Bryan (1877-1964), chemist.

1936-1989 Boots the Chemist, this business was founded as a herbalist's by John Boot in Nottingham in 1849. After becoming a limited company it expanded, opening its 1000th store in 1933. This branch moved to the larger premises at No. 39 in 1989.

1992-present, Cancer Research, the town's third charity shop following Oxfam and the Abbeyfield Society at the Market Cross.

Frederick Compton proudly stands in front of 21/23 High Street. Gents' shirts and hats feature in the window on the left, the door advertises Dent's Gloves and the windows on the right contain Ladies' and Children's clothing.

Woodward's, 21 High Street

These premises were rebuilt in 1854 but with a modern shopfront.

c1855-1896, Thomas Denney (1802-1862) and later Mrs. Elizabeth Denney (1823-1896), grocer.

1896-1920 incorporated into Compton's at No. 23.

1920-1950 Mrs. Jessie Marmont, costumier and ladies' outfitter.

1950-c1983 Beryl's Fashions, Mrs. Beryl Sheppard.

1985-present Alan Woodward, watchmaker & jeweller, moved from 10 Oxford Street where he started his business in 1976.

HSBC Bank, 23 High Street

The present building was built in 1920/1 by Messrs. Chivers and Son of Devizes.

c1875-1920 Frederick Compton (1839-1920), linen draper and outfitter.

1921-1999 London Joint City & Midland Bank later shortened to Midland Bank. The Birmingham & Midland Bank was founded by Charles Geach in 1836. In the 1890s the company expanded into London and by 1918 was the largest bank in the world. Further branches opened during the 1920s including Malmesbury's.

E. S. T. Cole's original premises can just be seen on the left edge of this photo with the London Joint City and Midland Bank in the centre.

1999-present HSBC, this company took over the Midland in 1992 and renamed the whole network a few years later.

Haine & Smith, 25 High Street

Nos. 25 and 27 were built in the 17th Century with two shops on the ground floor.

c1880-c1902 John Painter (1832-1914), chemist.

c1902-1920 Thomas Willsdon (1844-1916), tobacconist & confectioner moved here from 2 Gloucester Street where he had established his shop around 1880. Carried on by his widow Emily who moved to No. 22.

1920-1930 Edwin Stuart Travis Cole (1895-1984) established a motor business here after being demobbed from the R.A.F., having won the Military Cross as a pilot in 1917 His sister Eveline was married to Edward Jones, the jeweller at No. 1, and Stuart had been his apprentice prior to the First World War. The garage benefited by taking over plant, equipment and premises owned by James Jones (who owned the town's first motor car in 1903), his sister's brother in law. James' eldest son Monty, the manager, had been killed during the war. Jones' business included the old Primitive Methodist Chapel in Bristol Street. As the business grew Stuart moved to No. 26.

1930-1950 Dennis Sydney Morse (1906-1962), chemist. Dennis was born in Malmesbury and after completing his studies at the London College of Pharmacy returned here to set up his business.

1950-1985 The history of this period is incomplete although W. T. Goodfield, jeweller & gifts, was here between 1955 and 1980 and F. Wartnaby trading as Willsdon's, tobacconist, 1983-6.

1986-present Haine & Smith, opticians. Mrs. Sue Haine, from Crudwell and Barry Smith, from Devizes began their partnership in 1975 with practices in Westbury and Marlborough. It has now grown to 19 premises.

The Old Bakehouse, 27 High Street

This building has a 19th Century shopfront.

c1855-1885 William Kent Hanks (1832-1917), saddler & harness maker, moved to No. 12.

Yarnold's and Goodfield's shops in 1964 with an Austin A35.

c1886-c1905 Thomas Carr (1859-1940), fishmonger, ice & game dealer

c1905-1917 Tom Rich (1877-1940), the butcher from No. 34 seems to have taken over this fishmonger's business and employed a manager to run it. He closed the shop in August 1917 with the intention of reopening.

c1919-1945 Frederick William Yarnold (1883-1945), watchmaker & Jeweller moved his business here from 7 Gloucester Street where he had been since c1905.

1945-1976 Frederick's son Frank (b1912) turned the shop into a men's outfitters which also sold gifts.

1977-present Colin Witts (b1948) established the Old Bakehouse here, the first to bake on the premises for around 20 years. Now owned by John Brunner.

K Shoes, 31 High Street

c1840-1859 Henry Garlick Hanks (1789-1879), Watchmaker & postmaster .

1859-1875 John Hook Hanks (1829-1876) son of Henry, bookseller, stationer, newspaper agent, watchmaker, jeweller & postmaster.

1875-1881 Emma Hanks (1839-1886) widow of John, postmistress & stationer.

1881-1890 Albert Pugh (1858-1890). Albert was employed as Clerk and was living on the premises so was a natural successor.

1890-1902 Miss Ruth Bartlett (1859-1902), postmistress who managed the move to No. 41 but died shortly afterwards.

c1902-1923, Francis Herbert Summers (1877-1942), photographer & stationer moved here from another High Street address. Bizarrely he began selling boots and shoes before he moved to Worthing.

1923-1987 Joseph Frisby Ltd., boots & shoes. In 1923 Ernest Bowring opened the branch and managed it until he retired in 1965. Aubrey Ashby was then the manager until 1984.

1987-present K Shoes, the retail arm of C. & J. Clark, a shoe manufacturer founded and still based in Street, Somerset.

Vacant, 33 High Street

c1857-1908, Charles Thrush (1827-1908), bootmaker whose wife Elizabeth (1823-1890) began selling china & glass which became the main business.

1908-1923 Charles' & Elizabeth's daughter Catherine (1862-1923) continued the business until her death.

c1929-1931 C. Leonard Hitchings, house furnisher until he moved to 36 Gloucester Street.

1931-1947 Edgar Elphege Basevi (1887-1967), photographer moved here from 32 Gloucester Street where he had lived since arriving from Cambridge around 1908. He retired in 1947 and moved to Bournemouth.

1950-1969 D. S. Morse, chemist moved here from No.25 until he retired.

1969-1986 M. D. Whiteoak, chemist took over and enlarged the shop.

1986-c1993 R. Gordon Drummond Ltd., chemist, seem to have taken over Whiteoak's.

c1993-2008 Cooks Chemists, renamed Lloyds in 1999 and closed in September 2008.

The original Wilts & Dorset Bank building around 1890. Note that No. 41 had not yet been rebuilt as the Post Office.

Lloyds Bank, 35 High Street

These premises were rebuilt in 1924.

c1840-present The first bank in Malmesbury was opened at the beginning of the 19th Century somewhere in St. Dennis Lane. The proprietors were Messrs Hanks, the Deputy High Steward, J. S. Ody, Daniel Smith, both brewers, Richard Robins (1762-1836), a solicitor and Young, the owner of the cloth mill at Cowbridge. They issued banknotes payable at their premises in Malmesbury or at Pastons, Cockerell, Trail & Company, Pall Mall, London. They recruited Thomas Luce (1790-1875) as Manager in 1813 who moved to the town from Bristol. Thomas later became a partner when the name changed to Robins, Luce and Young. Not long after that he became the sole owner. However in 1836 he sold the business to the Wilts and Dorset Banking Company which was founded in Salisbury the previous year and was seeking to expand quickly. Thomas was retained as branch manager living at the bank and his son, Charles took over from him in 1863. In 1914 the Wilts and Dorset was taken over by Lloyds Bank. After the First World War Lloyds took over Capital and Counties and thus had two branches in the High Street. After rebuilding at No. 35 the branch at No. 10 closed.

Geddes Carpets, 37 High Street

A 17th Century building with changes made at the front and rear a century later.

c1891-1915 Henry Mussell (1851-1921), clothier, boot & shoe seller. In 1915 Henry moved to 43 Triangle. After his death the business was continued by his widow Sarah (1851-1934) at 29

Abbey Row and then by their daughter, Ruth until she was evicted in 1960.

1915-1994 Hinwood & Son, this business began in No. 39 but they expanded to include this shop in 1915. The drapery business was sold in 1955 and Hinwoods became just outfitters. James Thornbury bought the business in 1965 and continued it until December 1994 when the premises were sold.

1995-present Geddes Carpets moved here from No. 47.

Boots, 39 High Street

During 2003 the upper stories of No. 39 were renovated revealing the building dates back to c1500. Originally there were two timber framed houses each with a single central window on the upper two floors of the gables which were jettied into the street. These façades were probably highly decorated. In the 18th Century the frames were cut back to align with the ground floor to create a single typically Georgian frontage.

c1885-1955 Hinwoods, outfitter. Thomas Lot Hinwood (1838-1926) came to Malmesbury from Ramsbury in 1859 to open a linen draper's in the High Street. Later Thomas concentrated on the bacon curing business (see the Bacon factory) and moved his family home to Ferndale Terrace, 85 Gloucester Road. By the 1890s the name of the business was Hinwood and Son with a gentlemen's outfitters at 39 High Street run by one of Thomas' sons Frederick Louis (1865-1901), whose family lived above the shop. Frederick died from tuberculosis. His widow, Martha (1862-1952), carried the business on until their son Harry (1887-1971) joined. As it expanded they took over 37 High Street. By 1923 their adverts proclaimed they were outfitters and tailors who specialised in sports wear. In 1949 Jim Thornbury joined the business. The shop was a favourite with children as it had a pneumatic tube to shoot the takings to the cash office.

1955-1969 Bailey Brothers Ltd., a Cirencester company which specialised in selling furniture bought No. 39 until the company went into liquidation.

1969-1974 vacant.

1974-1978 North Wiltshire Exporters, an antiques business run by Michael Hinwood but this moved to the Rattlebone, Sherston.

Frederick Hinwood outside the shop at No. 39. The globe gaslight can be seen in the photo on the opposite page.

1978-1988 The Trade Centre, an indoor market which started out with up to 14 stalls selling antiques. Over time the range of goods on offer expanded to include clothes, toys, pottery, sweets, electrical appliances, toys and a cafe. There was much disquiet when the owner closed the premises.

1989-present Boots the Chemist who moved from No. 19.

ASM, 43 High Street

Originally 43/43a was a pair of houses built in the late 18th Century but is now one house and two shops. They are constructed of limestone rubble with a brick right-hand party wall stack and stone slate roof.

c1852-1890 Jacob Vizard (1804-1890), draper & outfitter. Jacob (actually christened John) moved to Malmesbury from his birthplace in Reading.

1890-c1895 Nicholls & Co., general grocers. Although not listed in any directory a photograph taken at the time of the 1892 election shows this name.

c1900-1940 J. E. Ponting & Sons, furnishers, see No. 44 for their story. A three storey warehouse was built behind to store the stock.

1940-1960 E. K. Cole Ltd., Western Development Unit worked from here during the war when a small greenhouse-like structure was constructed in the warehouse roof to test air interception radar sets. After the war it was used as a showroom and store with an employee living in the house.

1962-1967 Bailey Brothers of No 39, used this for storage.

1967-1997 A variety of enterprises used these premises including (in chronological order): J. E. Nunn, fine upholstery; Athelstan Coaches; Patrick Fry Insurance Brokers; A. L. Projects, precision engineers; Fromagerie, until it moved to No. 13; Poppys, gift shop owned by Mrs. Marion King of the Fromagerie; Dale & Gorey, estate agents; P. J. Carpenter, accountants; Chippenham Motor Components; Motorcraft.

1997-1998 CLS Autoparts, from this date the northern part was used as a separate shop, No. 43a.

A large crowd supporting John Dickson-Poynder at the 1892 election passes Randell & Son at No. 45 and Nicholls & Co. at No. 43

2000-2002 The Art Workshop, Howard Wright who moved here from No. 53.
2002-present ASM Outfitters, run by A. S. (Stan) Malpass whose business had been at No. 6 Oxford Street since 1984.

Vacant, 43a High Street
1997-2000 The Fringe, ladies hairdresser moved to 1 Abbeyfield House, Market Cross
2002-2008 Venture Portraits, photographer.

Vacant, 45 High Street
These premises have a late 19th Century shopfront.
c1860-c1904 Samuel Randell (1826-1888) started off as a grocer but by 1867 was also a plumber & glazier. In 1875 painter & paperhanger was added. By 1885 the Randells were no longer grocers. After Samuel's death his widow Mary (1828-1915) carried on – she gave her profession as plumber and decorator at the age of 73 in the 1901 census!
c1904-c1918 J. E. Ponting & Sons (see No. 44). The Randells' plumbing and decorating business seems to have been taken over by Pontings and their manager, initially Henry Price, lived here.
1918-1920 Food Office. The combined Urban and Rural District Food Office moved here in April 1918 until the end of rationing.
1922-1979 Rich & Beak, wine merchants. This was founded by Henry Beak (1866-1936) who had been head brewer of Luce's Brewery and William Rich (1874-1930), a horse dealer who had been the landlord of the Railway Hotel. Bill Rich retired from the partnership in 1927 and after Henry's death the business was carried on by his widow Alice (1873-1955) who was joined by her son-in-law Sidney Farmer in 1938. On Alice's death a limited company was formed owned by her three daughters. Sidney retired in 1979 when the business closed.
1979-c1982 Malmesbury Vintners, Peter Law moved his business from No. 125 where it had been established in 1974.
1983-2011 Threshers, off licence, the name changed later to Wine Rack.

Vacant, 47 High Street
A 17th Century building originally combined with No. 49 but divided 200 years ago.
c1907-c1933 William Charles Miles (1865-1939), tailor who moved to Bath.
c1933-1937 Herbert William Wheeler (1888-1965), greengrocer
1938-c1947 Florence Waite (1879-1961) seems to have moved her tobacconist's from No. 49. Her father Charles (1855-1946) lived with her after he sold his cycle business. Who occupied these premises between the 1950s and 1990s is unclear but it seems to have been a private house for some time.
1992-2012 Various enterprises including: Pizza Takeaway; Geddes Carpets, before moving to No. 37; Green Gallery; Beales who moved from 36 Gloucester Street but closed in 1999; Simply Style; The Blue Door; Clobber Clothing.
2012-2014 Maisey & West Ltd., accountants. Lisa West having traded on her own for seven years set up this company in 2012. However by 2014 the company was renamed Thyme West Ltd. and relocated to Crudwell.

Malmesbury Tandoori, 49 High Street
c1896-c1903 Henry Barton (b1861), jeweller & watchmaker. Henry, born in Suffolk, started his business in Ingram Street but traded under the name Edwin Barton.
c1912-c1923 Arthur Mattick (1874-1956) and his wife Ada (1878-1964) lived here and she ran a milliner's. After the fire at No. 12 in 1922 Arthur moved his saddler's here until made bankrupt.
c1929-c1938 Florence Waite started a tobacconist's here which seems to have moved to No. 47.
c1938-1947 Miss Christine Waite, confectioner. Christine was the eldest daughter of Florence's

Cowern's shop at No. 49 in 1964.

uncle Victor (1881-1967) who also lived here with his wife Frances.

1947-c1955 Joseph and Elizabeth Hirst, but it is not clear if they were in business.

c1955-1982 K & M Cowern, tobacconist & confectioner.

1983-c1989 Hong Kong Centre, takeaway.

c1989-present Malmesbury Tandoori, Indian takeaway with permission given to become a restaurant in 1990.

C. H. White & Son, 51 High Street

A mid 18th Century building with a shop window added in 1839.

c1860-1894 Thomas Austin (1836-1894), butcher

1894-c1913 Henry Charles Clements (1872-1934), butcher & game dealer who moved to Tetbury.

c1913-c1920 Sydney Herbert Keene, refreshment rooms who moved to 63 Gloucester Road.

c1920-1928 Charles Waite, cycle dealer & fishmonger moved here from Gloucester Street and retired to live with his daughter.

1928-present C. H. White & Son, cycle dealer. Charles Henry White (1890-1986) worked as a cycle repairer for Jones & Son before he bought the business from Charles Waite. He was later joined by his son, Frederick Charles (1923-2010). In turn Frederick's sons Timothy Charles (b1957) and David Haywood (b1959) have taken over so this High Street shop has been owned for the longest period by a single family. Sadly it would not seem it will pass to a fourth generation.

The Old Bear, 53 High Street

The pub closed in January 1963.

This photo of game and meat joints hanging on the front of Austin's butcher's shop could not be left out. (T. & D. White)

1963-1987 Clifford Drewett and Co., auctioneers and estate agents converted the premises into offices with shopfronts on the street. Mr. Drewett (1913-1965) became the sole proprietor of Messrs. Howes, Luce, Williams and Panes (Malmesbury) and changed the name. This company moved here from No.63. In 1984 it was taken over by Pocock & Lear from Marlborough and moved to No. 52 three years later.

1988-1991 Bloomers Dried Flower shop, later Abbey Flowers

1991-2012 Wiltshire & Gloucestershire Standard. The first edition of this newspaper was printed and published in Malmesbury on 28th January 1837. However it moved to Cirencester in July 1840 but their local reporter had an office here until June 2012. Previously located at 32 High Street until 1958 when it moved to 36 Cross Hayes and later 38 Cross Hayes from where it moved to No. 53.

2012-present Strakers, estate agents.

Private house, 55 High Street

This and its neighbour at No. 57 were constructed in the early 19th Century.

c1880-c1923 Mrs. Salome Harris (1846-1934), milliner & dressmaker. Mrs. Harris must have been a talented woman as the 1881 census records she employed five women.

It seems this property became a private house and was George Weeks' home, the Town Clerk during WW2.

J. M. Forss, 57 High Street

c1892-1931 Frederick Weeks (1864-1931), plumber, painter & decorator.

1931-1959 Frank Weeks, plumber (1904-2000) carried on father's business until 1959 when he went to work for Westinghouse in Chippenham.

1956-1966 Chippenham Laundry Ltd.

1967-1999 D. Ivel Rees, optician.

2000-2001 R. J. Maums, optician.

2001-present J. M. Forss Ltd., optician.

Private House, 61 High Street

An early 19th Century building.

c1897-1906 Emma Anstee (1858-1906), dairy shop

1907-1916 Jacob Mortimer (1871-1916), dairy. Jacob and his cousin William bought the business begun by the Misses Anstee but William left Malmesbury after marrying.

1916-1921 Mrs. Eva Mortimer (b1884), dairy. Jacob had four children but his first wife died. He employed Eva Scott as housekeeper and married her in 1915, but he died the next year.

1921-1942 Frederick Strange (1888-1956), Malmesbury Dairy. Frederick married Eva and took over the dairy. During the Second World War he became a painter & decorator and retired just before he died.

1948-1990 Alfred James (Jim) Strange (b1923), seedsman. On returning from war service his son, Jim, reopened the family shop selling seeds which he bought in bulk and put into smaller packets. On retirement the front room returned to domestic usage.

Private House, 63 High Street

A 17th Century building altered c1800. This seems to have been a private house occupied by Mrs. Westlake in the 1920s and Miss B. Godwin from the 1930s until the 1950s. It then became an office.

c1960-1963 Howes, Luce, Williams & Panes, auctioneers & estate agents who ran the market. Taken over by Clifford Drewett the office moved to No. 53.

1966-c1990 Shrimpton, Montgomery & Co., accountants.

c1998-2011 Malagola, antiques. The business was run by Francis Marshall and after his death it reverted to being a private house.

Private house, 65 High Street

An 18th Century house with the name Cordy still etched into the glass over the front door.

c1840-1882 Joseph Cordy (1816-1882), cabinet maker and upholsterer. Joseph's father (also Joseph was the landlord of the Black Horse at Burton Hill.

1882-1936 Henry James Cordy (1850-1936) Joseph's eldest son, cabinet maker and upholsterer. After Henry's death his widow Mary (1855-1942) lived in the house and it seems not to have been used as a shop again.

Private house, 67/69 High Street

c1914-1927 The Bonnet Box, Mrs. Hilda Newman, milliner. Hilda was Frederick Louis' wife (see No. 2). Her business occupied both Nos. 67 and 69 until c1925 when Frederick opened a grocer's at No. 69. The couple then moved away.

1927-c1931 The Bonnet Box, Mrs. Gladys Beckerson, milliner. Arthur Beckerson continued the grocer's at No. 69. Mr. & Mrs. Beckerson seem to have come here from Shepton Mallet but only stayed a short time.

c1935-c1949 Wheal & Ireson, upholsterers. Miss Ireson worked at No. 76 before pairing up with Mary Wheal c1933 at 79 Gloucester Road. They then moved here. By 1950 Charlotte & Mary Wheal seem to be living at No. 67.

Private House, 71 High Street

c1895-c1941 Lillian (1874-1906) & Agnes Helen Gore (1878-1957), dressmakers and milliners. Their father was Levi Gore (1849-1932) who spent 44 years working as a printer for Riddick's until a few months before his death. Lillian and Helen had a dressmaking business in their home. Helen with her youngest sister Jessie seem to have lived in the house after retiring.

East side

The Bird Cage, 2 High Street

This building was constructed c1793 but has a modern shopfront.

1824-1840 James Messiter, mercer and draper took the lease of a messuage and shop, described as the corner house near the Market Cross at the Upper end of High Street and Upper Oxford Street, erected on ground where the Red Lion Inn formerly stood. His widow Sarah took over in 1829.

1840-1859 A new lease was granted to William Gale, timber dealer, from London and Thomas Martin, dissenting Minister but it is unclear what the property was used for.

1859-1866 George Edwin Wall (1818-1898), general dealer.

1866-1869 Thomas Lyne, draper.

1869-1884 Edward Harris of Lacock Brewery took the lease and rented out the property. It seems to have become the Red Lion Inn again and was so named in the 1881 census.

1884-1919 Frederick Newman (1857-1934), grocer. He rebuilt the roof of the Oxford Street part of the premises so that it was the same height as the High Street frontage. Frederick had three sons: Frederick Louis (1890-1965) started in this business but then became manager for Burtons at No. 7 before opening his own grocers at No. 69; Reginald George (1891-1916) became an ironmonger before volunteering to serve in the First World War, dying of pneumonia in Egypt; Victor Garnett (1894-1916) worked for his father before moving to Stroud and was killed in action on the Western Front. Frederick retired at the end of the war.

1919-1969 Chippenham Co-operative Society.

1973-1989 Flower Service which moved to No. 4.

1989-2010 Halifax Estate Agents. The premises were redeveloped so that a banking counter was provided in the Oxford Street portion.

2011-2012 French Grey, kitchen goods with the same owner as Greene Grey at No. 6.

2013-present The Bird Cage, pizza restaurant.

Summer Cafe, 4 High Street

c1848-c1883 Henry Hankins (1817-1903), grocer. Hankins was born in Witney and in the 1851 census gave his occupation as manager of grocery business.

c1883-1930 Alfred and later Walter Jones, see No. 6.

1930-c1964 London Central Meat Co., butchers. This firm was started by G. E. Lowe selling meat from a stall in Tamworth market and despite the company name most of its branches were in the Midlands. Their first Malmesbury shop was at No. 18. The firm specialised in selling chilled or frozen imported meat.

c1964-1986 Baxter's Butchers, the company was renamed after its Chairman.

1986-1988 Dewhurst's Butchers, Baxter's were taken over by the Vestey Group and renamed. Rationalisation saw the closure of the Malmesbury branch.

1989-1995 Flower Service (from No. 2) then renamed Malmesbury Flowers.

1995-1998 The Basset Baker (called Lunchlines for a time), baker & tea shop from No. 6.

1998-present Summer Cafe

Greene Grey, 6 High Street

c1860-1865 James Stephen Jones (1814-1865), perfumer & hairdresser established a shop here which on his death was taken over by his son Alfred Stephen Jones (1841-1913).

1865-1911 Alfred's trade was originally listed as hairdresser & toy dealer, then hairdresser & general dealer before concentrating on hairdressing, stationery, bookselling and mineral water manufacturing. Alfred became collector of taxes in the 1880s and agents for Sutton & Co., carriers based in London. He was father of James (see No.17), Edward (No. 1-3) and Walter (1883-1945) who joined him in this business and eventually took it over.

1911-1935 Walter Jones, Stationer & newsagent and collector of taxes

1936-1964 Adye's Radio Supplies. Brothers Reginald Victor Adye (1901-1962) and Norman Ernest Adye (1905-1983) took over their father's garage business and entered into a partnership. Reg ran the garage whilst Norman opened a Radio Shop at 6 High Street. From here the Radio business relocated to Adye's Garage in Bristol Road but moved to 57 Gloucester Road in 1975 until that shop closed in 1996.

1965-c1975 E. J. Wakefield Ltd., electrical appliances. Mr. Wakefield bought the freehold of this property and then refused to renew Norman Adye's lease. Alterations were carried out to increase the floor space. The company seems to have been in financial difficulty and after an attempt to put it into liquidation in 1973 it was finally dissolved in 1978.

c1975-1987 Pot au Feu, china shop. Edwin Wakefield's wife Joan was a joint owner of this property. She closed her shop at No. 5 and moved here. When she retired due to ill health the property was sold to a developer and split into two units. The second unit was used by the Basset Baker until 1995 when it moved to No. 4 and the unit became part of;

1987-2011 That New Shop, gifts.

2011-present Greene Grey, gifts.

Co-operative Store, 8 High Street

The present supermarket built in 1960/1 replaced an early 19th Century house with a slaughterhouse behind facing on to Cross Hayes.

1801-1831 James Garlick, butcher, took out a lease on a decayed messuage and cooper's shop

At the start of the 20th Century Florence Jones occupied No. 14, William Hanks No. 12, Capital & Counties Bank No. 10, Henry Garlick about to retire in No. 8, Alfred Jones Nos. 4 & 6 with the barber's pole and Newman & Sons on the corner.

at the upper end of High Street. A new lease was granted in 1805 for the *messuage newly built with butcher's shop*. It is not known when James died but Rachael Garlick (1765-1844), a spinster is shown as a butcher in 1822.

1831-1865 James' son also James (1810-1891) took over the business.

1865-1874 James Junior's son, Henry (1842-1924) continued the business.

1874-1883 The name changed to Garlick Brothers after Henry's brother James (b1846) joined. James emigrated to New Zealand in 1883.

1883-1909 Henry Garlick carried on until he retired in 1909. He was a Town Councillor, being Mayor in 1893 and 1899.

1909-1931 The premises now became Henry's private house. He married Emily Walker (1850-1928) at the age of 67 and she lived here until her death.

1931-1960 Mrs. Natalia Clark (1854-1940), a baker's widow, her daughter Louise (1879-1965) and Elsie Wood made these premises their home. When sold it was still lit by gas, the butcher's shop and slaughterhouse little changed since closure.

1960-1988 Fine Fare, supermarket. Burtons Stores were taken over by Fine Fare Ltd., a company only established in 1956 with a single supermarket in Brighton. The small shop at No. 7 did not fit in with the new owner's mode of operation and it was decided to demolish this fine 19th Century house and build a large (for the time) supermarket. John Betjeman remarked that this building was quite the most disgraceful thing on a High Street in the south of England. In 1986 the chain was sold to the Dee Corporation which also owned International Stores (see No. 28) and Gateways who had just built a larger supermarket near Stainsbridge. They wanted to close this store but public opinion forced them to sell it as a going concern.

1988-1994 Circle K. This company jointly owned by an American company and News International bought the store. Circle K won the contract to run the Post Office Counters concession in 1990 when the Post Office at No. 43 became just the Sorting and Delivery Office.

1994-2003 Alldays. Although this company took over Circle K in 1989 this store was not renamed for some years.

2003-present Co-operative Wholesale Society which took over Alldays.

Castle Sundborn Insurance, 10 High Street

This is a fine example of a brick building from the time of George I, 1714-27, made from 2" bricks with stone window dressings and roof parapet.

c1850-1870 Thomas Brooke (1818-1860), grocer and baker seems to have moved here from the Market Cross. His widow Mary (1819-1883) continued the business for ten years after his death before moving to No. 28. Mary held a licence to sell wine.

1870-1878 North Wilts Banking Company. By 1839 this company, founded in 1835 at Melksham, had taken over a bank run by William Walker (1822-1900), who farmed during the day but spent two hours each evening conducting the business. He was retained as manager. As the bank expanded it required new premises which underwent *a complete renovation and now presents an elegant appearance*.

1878-1924 Capital and Counties Bank. North Wilts Bank was taken over and the new owners kept on William Walker until he retired in 1892. In 1918 the Company amalgamated with Lloyds and after their premises at No. 35 were rebuilt this branch closed.

1927-1974 Malmesbury Rural District Council.

1985-1988 David Butler, estate agents, from Gloucester Street, who let offices in the building to others.

1988-1990 Ham Jackson Brown, accountants

1990-2010 Moore Stephens, accountants. This large company begun in London in 1907 maintained a branch here for a decade.

2013-present Castle Sundborn financial advisers and insurance brokers. Malmesbury Brokers

Ltd. was incorporated in 1964 and Tim Bather joined the company in 1975, taking it over a year later. In 1980 Patrick Fry and Co. was taken over and new offices at 4 Gloucester Street opened. To accommodate growth another office was opened at Laystalls, Cross Hayes in 1990, the Gloucester Street premises being vacated in 2002. The company name changed in 1989. Tim's son Anthony joined in 1987 and is now Managing Director.

E & S, 12 High Street

c1835-c1872 William Ponting (1805-1885), furnishing ironmonger, moved here from Bristol. Towards the end the business was called William Ponting and Son but after William retired his son John developed his business at No. 43.

c1872-1885 William continued to live here until he died.

1885-1915 William Kent Hanks, saddler & harness maker moved here from No. 27.

1915-1922 Arthur Mattick, saddler bought the premises from William Hanks with a loan of £50. A fire burnt out the shop on 28th January 1922. He continued his business from his home at No. 49 but was underinsured and made bankrupt.

c1925-1927 Malmesbury Electricity Supply Co., later taken over by Western Electricity Supply Co. which moved the showroom to No. 18.

1927-1948 Percy Grainge Jackson (1882-1950) moved his family's outfitter's business from No. 16. The shop was kept open by his widow, Isabelle (1902-1952).

1948-present E & S, ironmongers. Edwards & Son, coachbuilders of Holloway moved into retailing. Shops were bought in other North Wiltshire towns but in 1984 the others were sold. No. 14 was bought so its garden could be turned into a yard and that shop was then sold.

A4 Stationers, 14 High Street

This is a 16th Century building with a late 19th Century shopfront which at one time was a pub called the Black Swan and also had been part of the Griffin Inn.

Edwards & Son, Evett's and Stan Hudson's shops in 1964.

c1800-1864 John Player (1776-1864), originally listed as saddler & harness maker, later adding grocer but by 1861 had changed to tobacconist.

1864-1870 The son John (1810-1870) continued as a tobacconist.

1870-1874 In 1869 John married Sarah Paginton (1815-1874), who had served as the household's domestic servant for many years. She lived here listing her occupation as retired tobacconist.

1874-1908 Thomas Sharpe (1841-1901), boots & shoes, continued by his widow Ellen (1844-1928).

1908-c1914 Florence Jones, restaurant & fruiterer

c1914-1923 Star Restaurant, run at first by Mrs. Elizabeth Brown, then by Ernest Canning.

1923-1949 Arthur John Evett (1873-1949) continued the Star Restaurant but built up the fruiterer and greengrocery.

1949-1976 Evetts, greengrocer & confectioner. The business continued under several owners.

1977-1985 R. S. Fruiterers Ray Symons changed the shop's name.

The premises were renovated in 1988 and part of the 14th Century timber frame was exposed.

1990-1992 Parker MacPherson Kitchen Design.

1990-1996 Briggs & Chapman, antiques & gifts.

1996-1999 Eat & Sleep, kitchen & bedroom equipment.

1999-2008 DAC Stationers.

2008-present A4 Stationers.

Flowers Galore, 16 High Street

The site of the Griffin Inn with a 16th Century building to which many modifications have been made since.

c1830-1842 Harry Head Alexander (1811-1842), bookseller, stationer & printer.

1842-1867 His widow Mary (1812-1867) continued the trade assisted by their son Richard Alexander (1837-1861).

1867-c1878 The Golden Boot, William Chappell Thompson (1824-1900) began as a bootmaker in Gloucester Street and moved here as a bootmaker, draper & gentlemen's outfitter.

c1878-1894 William senior retired from the business and his sons William Grainge (1844-1894) and Joseph Thompson (1846-1889) continued the business until their deaths.

1895-1929 Mrs. Bessie Jackson (1850-1924), outfitter. The business continued to be known as Thompson's, The Golden Boot. Her son Percy continued the business but moved to No. 12.

1929-1964 Stanley Walter Hudson (1897-1979), the shop originally concentrated on cycles but eventually sold motor cycles, cars, accessories and petrol. He used the slogan 'The Push 'em in and Ride 'em out Shop'. He was co-opted on to the Borough Council in 1942 and was Mayor from 1946 to 1948, serving for over 31 years. He was made a Freeman in 1974 at the same time as Dr. Hodge. Stan retired in 1964 and moved to No. 43.

1964-1976 Reginald Ivor Adye (1930-1971) bought the garage and continued trading using Hudson's name. After Ivor's death the business was carried on by his widow, Madeleine (b1932). Unfortunately new regulations prohibited the sale of petrol here which led to its closure. It was thought that new petrol tanks with pumps in Cross Hayes at the rear would be acceptable and Mrs. Adye was shocked to learn this was not so.

1977-1986 Malmesbury Building Supplies. A DIY store owned by Les Reynolds.

1990 Irene's Pet Pantry, which moved to 34 Gloucester Street.

1992-present Flowers Galore. On the closure of the Building Supplies shop Karen Rudman decided to open a flower shop in Griffin Alley. Within a few years the business had prospered and was able to move into the High Street.

George Vets, 18 High Street

At one time this was the Griffin Inn's stables and Stan Hudson used the rear as part of his garage.

c1839-c1868 William Croome (1814-1885), originally listed as hairdresser & wig maker, the occupation given in the 1851 census was house & sign painter which changed to writer & engraver in 1861 and finally stone mason & seedsman in Kelly's Directory of 1867. In a lease the property was described as a cottage, bakehouse and stables, with ½ the court and passage and free use of the well, in High Street, extending backwards to Cross Hayes.

c1868-c1878 Henry Borton (1840-1915), seedsman & stationer.

c1878-1908 James May (1840-1908), antiques dealer, who was the town crier and billposter for about 50 years.

1908-1930 London Central Meat Co., first established a shop here before moving to No. 4.

1930-1947 Wessex Electricity

1947-1996 Southern Electricity, following privatisation in the 1990s the retail arm was renamed Powerhouse and sold to the Hanson Group in 1995. Within six months they closed the Malmesbury shop.

1997-present incorporated into the George Veterinary practice (see the George Hotel).

Mistral Clothing, 22 High Street (north unit)

c1919-c1968 Yorkshire Insurance Office. James D. Curtis (1869-1929) was the inspector for Yorkshire Insurance Co. Ltd. covering Wiltshire and East Gloucestershire from around 1900. His son, Percival James Curtis (1893-1943) also joined the company being based in Cirencester but moved to Malmesbury on his father's death. However his tenure was shortlived and a series of managers ran the office until closure. Harry Porter worked here for 44 years before retiring in 1966.

1993-present Walton Design Ltd., ladies clothes. This company was started in Malmesbury by John H. Lewis and his daughter Tracey Garreffa in 1988. Its Head Office is now in Calne and runs 28 stores in the south of England. The trading name changed to Mistral

The Wild Food Company, 22 High Street (south unit)

c1875-1911 William Pitt (1831-1911), general dealer, later china & glass.

1911-c1915 Maurice Pitt China & General dealer

1920-c1983 Willsdon, tobacconist & confectioner, Mrs. Emily Willsdon (1871-1951) moved here from No. 25 and was still running the shop with her daughter Doreen in 1950. Afterwards new owners continued to use the name before moving to No. 25 and then 9a.

1986-2005 Dowding & Son, television, radio & electrical supplies & repairs. George Dowding's (d2003) business was continued by his son Philip until relocating to Dauntsey Lock.

2007-present Wild Food Company, organic grocer.

The Workbox, 24 High Street

c1898-c1910 William Curtis (1864-1936), clothier & outfitter. William came from Hereford and only seems to have stayed here for a few years.

c1910-c1919 James D. Curtis (1869-1929) resident inspector for Yorkshire Insurance Co. Ltd. had his office here for a few years before moving to 22a. James does not seem to have been related to William.

1927-c1935 Teagle & Sons, auctioneers. This firm was begun by William Teagle (1840-1913) who lived in Seagry brought several members of his family into the business but his son William Rich Teagle (1869-1933) became its next head. The firm of Tilley & Culverwell took over the business and continued to use this address on market days up to the war.

c1935-1972 The Workbox, fancy repository. Miss Muriel Beak (1913-1972), daughter of Henry who founded Rich & Beak at No. 45, ran this gift shop

1973-2007 The Workbox. Mr. & Mrs. M. Pullin bought the shop and were succeeded by their daughter Mrs. Sue Bush.

2007-present The Workbox, Mrs. Sandra Baker.

The Workbox and E. S. T. Cole in 1964 when the petrol pumps were still in use. The refurbished self-service International Stores can just be seen on the right.

Hyams Autos Ltd., 26 High Street

c1880-1888, Coles & Drakeford, grocer, wine & spirit merchant. Charles Drakeford (1855-1928), born in Coleshill, Warwickshire, was living here at the 1881 census. The business employed three men and one boy as well as two domestic servants but seems to have only lasted a few years.

1888-1930 Henry Farrant (1864-1933) ran the grocer's shop here originally in partnership with J. C. Coles of Chippenham whose interest he later

Farrant's with William Curtis, clothier, on the left and Thomas Brooke, grocer and confectioner, to the right.

bought out. Around 1900 the shop advertised the products of W. & A. Gilbey, a large London wine importer and gin distiller. Farrant was known as 'Split Fig' as he would do that to make the correct weight. His turnover in 1928 was £7,373 but £6,857 the following year when his wage bill came to £443 12s. 11d. He retired at the age of 66 in 1930 and sold the business to Adye & Son (No. 52). They did not want the premises and sold them to E. S. T. Cole who had been at No. 25 opposite since 1920.

1930-1980 Stuart Cole introduced several innovations including the installation of the first hydraulic ramps in the South West and using a special concrete mix for the workshop floor to stop it absorbing oil. His son Richard Stuart Travis (Dick) Cole (1918-1988) continued running this dealership until 1973 when it amalgamated with Tony Lloyd Jones' Athelstan Garage. Car sales continued here for a couple of years but the greater space available on the corner of Gloucester Road and Park Road caused the business to concentrate there and to sell this site.

1980-present Hyams Autos. The business was bought by Mrs. Joan Hyams and her son Paul. They had no previous experience of the motor trade, Paul having been an apprentice electrician who became a burglar alarm engineer! Initially they traded second hand cars but slowly recruited a number of mechanics and became Renault dealers in 1982. In 1998 they changed to being Ford dealers.

Lloyds Chemist, 28 High Street

1870-1883 Mrs. Mary Brooke, grocer moved here from No. 10.

1883-1923 Thomas Brooke (1849-1923), Mary's son carried on until his death.

1924-1985 International Tea Stores Ltd., tea merchants and grocers. Mr. H. E. Kearley (1856-1934), whilst working at Tetleys, began selling tea to shops on his own account. In 1878, having been joined by two partners, their first shop was opened in Brentford, Middlesex. Within 10 years they had opened 200 International Tea Co. branches. In 1960 after refurbishment this became Malmesbury's first self-service store, which was opened by Norman Painting the actor who played Phil Archer in the radio serial. In 1984 Gateway Stores took over International and after acquiring Fine Fare the following year, had two High Street shops as well as the new supermarket in Gloucester Road. It was decided to close No. 28.

1986-present Lloyds Chemists. This chain of pharmacies only began in 1973 with Allen Lloyd opening one in Poleworth, Warwickshire. The style of the store was different with most goods being available on a self-service basis with only prescription medicines behind the counter. By 1985 the company was owned by Gateway which had also acquired R. G. Drummond (see No. 33).

Barclays Bank, 30-32 High Street

It seems that Charles Reeves (1801-1888) ran a saddler's at No. 30 but after his death this was incorporated into No. 32.

c1860-1899 Josiah Emery (1824-1899), baker & cornfactor. Josiah was born in Wotton under Edge and it is unclear when he moved to Malmesbury although he married a woman from Somerford. The year before he died he was injured by a gas explosion. A gas pipe had broken in Cross Hayes and gas had flowed through the old drock drains into the bakehouse at the rear of the premises. Smelling the gas, the ovens were turned off but another ignition source caused an explosion which overturned the dough troughs, shattered the oven door and injured three men on the premises.

1899-1913 Isaac Emery (1861-1913), Josiah's nephew managed the business before his uncle's death.

1913-c1925 Mrs. Annie Emery (b1879), carried on until she sold the premises.

c1925-1942 George Tanner (1878-1954) worked for and then took over Chappell's bakery at 46 Gloucester Street, then bought out Mrs. Emery. George retired in 1942 and left the town only to return a year later.

1942-1958 Tanner's Bakery. It seems the business carried on under new owners, one of whom was Mrs. B. L. Philp in 1952 when the manager was J. H. Irving. Upstairs Messrs. Barker-Tufft and Brown had a dental surgery in the late 1950s.

1959-present Barclays Bank. The dutch roofed building was demolished and replaced by a banal modern design.

Malmesbury Rendezvous, 34 High Street

c1860-1870 John Robins (1809-1870), butcher.

1870-1881 Mrs Jane Robins (1838-1881), John's widow continued until her death. It seems as though their son Bryant (1856-1917) moved away from the town.

c1885-c1900 Bartlett Brothers, tailors & outfitters. Moved to No. 48.

c1900-c1922 Tom Rich, butcher, also had a fishmonger's at No. 27. The field to the north of the Bowling Green is still known as Tom Rich's. Access to the field was next to Frank Sharpe's blacksmith's shop in Holloway where there was a slaughterhouse. On retiring he lived at Cowage Farm.

c1922-c1924 George Harold Cordy (b1893), butcher. Harold, son of Henry at No. 65, seems to have owned the shop for a short period.

c1924-c1925 W. H. Evans, butcher. Mr. Evans was refused a licence for a slaughterhouse behind the shop.

c1925-c1932 James Watkins, butcher. Watkins moved to Portsmouth.

c1932-c1934 C. T. Robinson, fishmonger.

c1934-1980 Norman Richards (1911-1964) carried on the business during the widening of St. Dennis Lane in 1936 which halved the shop's High Street frontage. He retired several years before his death but his name continued to be used by new owners.

c1980-1984 Loveridge, jewellers

1984-1992 Duchess, jewellers. Mrs. Phyllis Hall opened a tea room upstairs in 1988.

The funeral procession of Willy Thornbury in 1915 passing Tom Rich's. Note the narrow width of St. Dennis Lane. Arthur Cooke's is on the opposite corner.

1992-1999 Oriental Chef, Chinese takeaway.

1999-present Malmesbury Rendezvous, Chinese takeaway.

Sport & Leisure, 36/38 High Street

There is a stone on the north gable dated 1763.

No. 36 as a separate shop.

c1897-1920 Arthur Cooke (1873-1944), hairdresser, tobacconist & umbrella maker. There was a sign advertising Hot Baths.

1920-1962 William James (Bill) Wheadon (1891-1978), started as an assistant to Walter Jones in 1911 and after service in WW1 set up in business here. In addition to hairdressing he distributed newspapers. Before the Second World War this was also the Wilts Gazette office. From about 1950 the barber's was in St. Dennis Lane behind the enlarged Rawling & Phillip's shop which combined Nos. 36 and 38.

No. 38

c1910-1931 James Walker (1864-1932), jeweller moved here from No. 58.

c1932-1938 George Clark, saddler. Mr. Clark's career came to a premature end when he was poisoned by gas.

c1941-1947 Mrs. Beak, corn merchant & forage contractor, moved here from No. 40.

1948-c1970 Rawlings & Phillips Ltd., agricultural merchants. This Calne based company bought the business and also had premises at Stainsbridge Mill. In 1970 they merged with James & Co. of Marlborough.

c1973-present Sport & Leisure, clothing & sports equipment.

Cross Hayes Antiques, 40 High Street

A late 18th Century building with two shopfronts, No. 40 being very small but made into a separate shop c1930.

c1870-1905 William Hanks (1830-1905), bookseller, stationers, newsagent & photographer.

1905-1925 William's daughters Louisa (1863-1942), Lizzie (1866-1944) & Kate (1869-1926) continued the business but sold it to W. H. Smith & Son Ltd.

1927-c1933 Drew & Co., corn dealers.

c1933-1937 Ronald Beak (1891-1937), corn merchant. Ronald ran the business at his home, West Hill, Bristol Street but opened an office here.

1937-c1941 Mrs. F. M. Beak, corn merchant, Ronald's widow who moved the office to No. 38.

c1955-c1967 Athelstan Coaches, bus & coach operator.

1968-c1971 Army & Navy Surplus Store.

1973-1980 Dale & Gorey, estate agents.

Hank's newsagents with No. 42 still looking like a house and J. E. Ponting's newly built premises at No. 44.

1983-1992 Cotton On, haberdashers & fabrics.

1994-1998, RSPCA, charity shop.

2000-2005 West Country Cleaners, moved from No.9.

2013-present Cross Hayes Antiques.

W. H. Smith plc, 42 High Street

Owned by the Hanks family these premises did not have a shop window until W. H. Smith took
   over.

1925-present W. H. Smith & Son Ltd. This enterprise dates back to 1792 when Henry Walton
   Smith opened a small newsvendor's in London. The name changed after William Henry Smith
   and his similarly named son went into partnership in 1846. Soon afterwards they developed
   a network of kiosks on railway stations which led to them becoming the country's largest
   newspaper distributor.

Hair & Nails, HEALS Malmesbury, 44 High Street

John Edward Ponting (1834-1906) began his career working for his father William (1800-1874)
in the ironmonger's at No. 12. By 1865 *& Son* had been added to the title of that business.
John was originally a brickmaker and timber merchant but he expanded to incorporate builders,
carpenters, painters, blacksmith, tinsmith and shops at Nos. 43, 44 and 46 which sold furniture,
carpets, china, glass and ironmongery. In the 1890s he lived at No. 43 behind which was later built
a large furniture warehouse. He later bought No. 44 on the other side of the street and rebuilt
that in 1901. He also intended to redevelop No. 46 which was known as the Cannon Works due to
two cannons in the entrance. For some reason he did not rebuild but established a large working
area at the back extending into Ingram Street for trades of nearly every description as well as
running two unreliable electricity generators. The building & timber merchant's business based
in Park Road was transferred to the eldest son Henry Ernest Ponting (1869-1914) on his marriage
in 1905. Shortly afterwards John retired (although his death was only a few months later), making
over the High Street businesses to the other sons Frank Edward (1875-1951), Arthur John (1881-
1951) and Walter Ward (1871-1939). Walter left the business when he married in 1918.

Unfortunately the whole enterprise was put into voluntary liquidation in 1940. All of the premises
were taken over by the Western Development Unit (WDU) of E.K. Cole Ltd. Because of the secrecy
surrounding radar development many rumours persisted about their work. More than 50 years
later people thought that ammunition had been produced in the centre of town!

1946-1972 Public Library. In 1926 Wiltshire County Council first supplied the town with books for
   free loan to the public. The premises and volunteer librarian were provided by the Borough
   Council. At first the library was housed in the Town Hall and opened between 6 and 7.30 p.m.
   on Tuesday and Friday evenings. During the war it moved to the corner of Oxford Street and
   Cross Hayes Lane. After the move to the High Street it was still run by volunteers for limited
   hours. The first professional librarian was appointed in 1949 and with the voluntary help
   extended opening became possible. In 1972 the facility moved to the vacant Cross Hayes
   School.

After the Library moved, Robin Clark, architectural & building consultant took over the building.
   The frontage was used for two shops, the incomplete history is;

1976-1985 Swindon Permanent Building Society.

1980-1983 Lane Fox & partners, surveyors & estate agents.

1984-1988 Olivers Travel, travel agent (northern shop). Started by Peter and Sally Brown the
   previous year in Olivers Lane the business moved to Market Cross where it now trades under
   the name Miles Morgan.

1985-1995 Stitchcraft, sewing materials (southern shop). Maureen Starr who previously worked
   for Hodder's started this shop.

1990-1995 Aspens, china & glassware (northern shop).

1995-2012 Stitchcraft took over both halves and expanded the goods stocked to include clothing & lingerie. The business was bought by Mrs. Franchesca Caton who moved it to 32 Gloucester Street.

2012-2013 Andrew Carnegie Lighting occupied the northern unit but closed due to lack of footfall.

2012-2013 County Jewellers was in the southern unit and during its tenure was robbed at knifepoint.

2014-present Hair & Nails, opened by Sarah Clover in July 2014 in the north shop

2014-present Heals Malmesbury, not for profit organisation founded by Alison Cross-Jones moved into the south shop in February 2014.

Offices, 46 High Street

The building is dated 1671 with 18th Century and c1890 rear extensions. The interior was rebuilt behind the facade in the mid 1980s. After Ekco vacated these premises in the late 1940s Edward Albert Hider (1905-1977), Ekco's maintenance manager, set up as a builder here. Peter, Edward's only son, took over in 1970 and the firm became P. J. Hider Ltd. Unfortunately the company went into liquidation in 1986 with the loss of 27 jobs. The premises were vacant for a year before the doctors opened this as a combined surgery.

1987-2008 Gable House Surgery

2009-present Converted into offices and let to various businesses.

Maison Let, 48 High Street

c1900-1932 Bartlett Brothers, tailors & outfitters. J. Gee Bartlett (1845-1920) ran this business which was sold on his death to Frederick W. Hitchcock.

1932-1959 Maison D'Arcy, ladies and gents hairdressing. Hugh D'Arcy Vicker (b1910) He sold the business to Mrs. Hannall from Mayfair.

1960-c1963 House of Lorraine, court hairdresser. Mrs. Lorraine Bole moved to 1 Market Cross by 1964.

c1966-c1969 Peter Heaven (Carpets). This business also had a shop in Tetbury and supplied

Towards the end of the 19th Century H. C. Taylor, draper, occupied No. 50.

carpets by mail order.

1973-c1982 Minerva Galleries, antiques & books.

c1982-c1983 Mike Heath Antiques

c1983-2003 Andrew Britten Antiques. Tim Tyler (b1937) ran an antiques shop in London for many years before coming to Malmesbury in 1982.

2004-present Maison Let, residential letting agent. Jane Maslin formed this company in 1996 and moved here from 48 St. Dennis Lane.

Blount & Maslin, 50 High Street

c1870-1885 Thomas Lot Hinwood, draper moved to No. 39.

1885-1892 H. C. Taylor, draper.

c1892-c1919 Ernest William Bonner (1861-1907), draper. His widow, Florence (1858-1930) continued the business.

c1920-1926 William Horace Beeston (1888-1965), draper

1927-1941 Thomas Thomas, draper. It seems Mr. Thomas continued to live above the shop.

1941-1992 Wiltshire Gazette office.

1994-2001 Christopher Blount & Co., estate agent. Having worked for 20 years as a chartered surveyor Mr. Blount opened his own business.

2001-present Blount & Maslin Ltd., estate agent. Keith Maslin joined the company in 1997, becoming a partner four years later.

The Gazette office in 1985 with their reporter Malcolm Sandars. (Malmesbury Chronicles)

Lockstones Estate Agents, 52 High Street

During the 18th Century the site of the White Horse Inn.

1827-1868 Thomas Rogers (1786-1868), grocer.

1868-1887 Alfred Adye (1841-1912), grocer. Alfred started as an apprentice to Mr. Rogers and on his death took over the business, bringing his brother Albert (1854-1932) to join him. They were the sons of William (1792-1867) who was born in Dover but married a Malmesbury woman and set up in the High Street as a Brazier. William's other two sons Sidney (1838-1910) and William (1843-1929) were also Braziers, Coppersmiths and Tin-platers at 100 and 75 High Street respectively. A pig killing business was started behind the shop in Ingram Street to sell the meat in the shop. This expanded and In 1877 Alfred joined his neighbour, Thomas Lot Hinwood in forming Adye & Hinwood Ltd. to build the bacon factory in Park Road. To raise capital Alfred sold out to Albert for £929 2s. 7d. which was payable in instalments with the final payment made on 29th April 1882. Alfred remained the owner of the premises and was paid rent of 16s. per week.

1887-1901 Albert Adye, grocer. Alfred concentrated on his new business and Albert's name was listed in trade directories for the first time. Between April 1900 and July 1901 the shop was substantially rebuilt with four storeys instead of two by Henry Wilkins of 98 High Street. The total bill came to £1,204 16s. 6d. One of the boasts of the business was *No foreign Bacon or Cheese ever enters these premises*.

1901-1983 Adye & Son. The name was changed to Adye and Son to reflect Albert's son Sidney (1883-1972) starting work. In 1930 they took over the business of Henry Farrant (but not his premises which they sold) from 26 High Street. More staff had to be taken on to deal with the extra customers. After the last war it was the turn of Sidney's son David

Adye's shop at its reopening n 1901.

(1915-1993) to join. Between the wars the Luce sisters of The Knoll distributed vouchers worth 5s. to the poor at Christmas, which were redeemable at Adye's. Miss Ursula Luce would park outside and toot her horn for service! David Adye retired in 1983.

1983-1985 Young's Grocers. Mr. and Mrs. Edward Young took over the business as their first shop but after a year decided they could not compete with supermarkets.

1987-1988 Dennis Pocock & Drewett, estate agents, moved across the road from No. 53.

1988-2008 Hamptons, estate agents. This London firm took over the company and renamed the shop.

2010-present Lockstones, estate agents.

Paul Newton, 54 High Street

Dating from the 18th Century this building has a modern shop window.

1979-1993 Feathers, ladies clothing. Mrs. Jeanne Handford (1930-1993) having worked as a model, fashion compere and for Vogue magazine came to Malmesbury to end her career in the retail trade.

1995-present Paul Newton, goldsmith & silversmith. Maker of bespoke jewellery.

Private house, 58 High Street

A late 18th Century building. The pierced vent holes over the window installed whilst this was a butcher's have been retained.

1889-c1910 James Walker, jeweller. Moved to No. 38.

c1910-1932 Ernest Hill (1868-1935), boot & shoe maker.

1932-1950 William Caudell (1895-1950), butcher. Born in Oxford he became an apprentice with the London Central Meat Co., being sent to Malmesbury as manager in 1929. He then set up his own business.

1950-1992 Ivan Caudell (b1927), butcher. William's son took over helped by his widow Edna who lived at No. 60. Another shop was opened in Great Somerford for a time.

1992-1995 Adrian Saunders, organic butcher. Mr. & Mrs. Saunders bought the business hoping to keep the same traditional service (such as offering bacon sliced from whole sides). Unfortunately it was shortlived and the building became a private house once more.

Commerce

Until the 20th Century most local businesses were agriculture based. The rivers provided power to process grain or wool and create employment. A selection of businesses past and present are described in this section.

Avon Mill

This is one of the sites around the town where there a mill had existed for centuries. Schotesbure Mill stood here in the 13th Century. By the middle of the 16th Century the millers came from the Cannop family and the mill took their name. Nicholas Archard, whose family owned the Burton Hill estate built a new fulling mill here around 1600. Fulling was the process whereby cloth was thickened and shrunk by pounding it in a solution of fullers earth. The outbreak of the Thirty Years War in 1620 cut off exports causing a crisis in the woollen industry leading to the spectacular failure of Archard's business in 1622. However these premises were still known as Archard's Mill when the Bird's-Eye map was prepared in 1648. The first building south of the bridge is the Mill House which dates from 1720.

The woollen industry was cyclical and a century after Archard's collapse it had closed down in Malmesbury. At that time machinery was being introduced in the face of the workers' fierce opposition. Francis Hill, a Bradford on Avon clothier and lawyer bought this Avon mill in 1790 to reintroduce the trade to the town. He moved his business from Bradford following riots there after his proposal to use machines, a matter described to a Parliamentary Select Committee in 1803. He built the two factory buildings in 1793 only 20 years after the first factory had been built by Richard Arkwright in Derbyshire. Factories organised labour in one specialised workplace giving the employer total control over the means and cost of production. Hill pioneered the use in Wiltshire of water power to drive fly shuttles and some 50 or 60 spring looms for weaving. Although vast quantities of cloth could be produced, the quality was poor and much was returned to the factory. It was fortunate that he was able to supply cloth to the government for uniforms during the Napoleonic Wars. Although Hill's business was innovative it was unsuccessful and closed before his death in 1828.

C.S. Taylor & Co. of Chippenham then rented the factory for a short period. They introduced spinning mules but went bankrupt in 1830. In 1831 when the town was surveyed by Benjamin Ansley for Parliament in relation to the Great Reform Bill he noted; *a cloth factory was established about 20 years ago; but is now abandoned, and has been converted into a corn-mill. It* (the town) *contains very few Houses which appear to be occupied by persons of independent circumstances, and has altogether the air of a place on the decline, it must now be considered as entirely an agricultural Town.*

After a wrangle over Francis Hill's will, the mill and estate was bought by Simon Uncles Salter (1800-1851) and his brother Isaac (1805-1852) in 1833. Five years later a steam engine was employed. This was unusual as a lot of coal was needed to power the engine. There was no canal, the normal way of carrying heavy or bulky goods and the road network to the town was none too good. Around 1840 a Highland regiment camped on the Worthies and proved such an attraction to the young women who worked in the factory that it had to shut until the soldiers moved on!

Thomas Bridget & Co. of Derby bought the mill in 1852. They were silk manufacturers and Richard Jefferies described the operation in 1867; *the silk arrives here in a raw state and is unpacked in the upper storeys of the building. Much of it is Chinese, and the packages often contain small slips of paper stamped with Chinese characters. The operation of cleaning employs a large number of children who tend the machinery used for that purpose. Most of these are very young and sing at their work. Overseers superintend them, and talking is not allowed, for the simple reason*

Avon Mill. Steam wagons would often stop here to draw water from the river.

that attention is required to be exercised to manipulate the silk properly. Beneath is the winding department; lower still the looms where the ribbons are made. The machinery is of an order impossible to describe. There is a sameness in it. Apparently the greatest attention is paid to the comfort of those employed. The rooms are very large, well lighted, and though necessarily warm, not overheated. Nevertheless, from being so early put to work the children have an old look; but nothing of that careworn expression sometimes seen in factories. The machinery is driven by water power. Silk ribbons were much in demand during the Victorian era and at its peak the factory employed around 400. A tariff on silk products was removed in 1860 and it was difficult to compete with imports, particularly from France. A new owner, Joseph Davenport & Co. also from Derby, bought the factory in 1867.

Davenport's business failed in 1888. It was reported there had been works at Sherston and Tetbury which had employed between 300 and 500 hands including those at Malmesbury. An advertisement was placed in the *Methodist Times and Methodist Recorder* for a Methodist capitalist to purchase the mill. John W. Herivel of London, whose brother William was the Steward of the Malmesbury Methodist Circuit, bought the premises which William managed. Three years later extra capital was needed to buy 50 looms and a prospectus was issued for a new limited company. This promised to help liquidate the debt of the Rouen Mission and subscribers would *help consolidate Methodism in Wiltshire ... besides helping Methodism in France.* Within a short time Mr. Herivel was declared bankrupt. It was then bought by Charles Jupe of Mere (a Congregationalist!) and by 1900 there were 150 workers. Japanese competition forced another closure that year and the factory remained vacant for 13 years. In 1913 production was restored by Shuttleworths Ltd. who installed a large boiler weighing over 30 tons which was successfully brought down the High Street and over the bridge by two steam tractors. This huge investment was unsuccessful, the factory closed for six months in 1915 and the company went into voluntary liquidation a year later. A new owner was found, Avon Silk Mills Co. Ltd. In 1917 the factory was reported to be in a *flourishing condition.* During the 1920s and 30s demand was curtailed and at times the mill opened for just three days a week or on alternate weeks. Residents of the town could tell the time by the Silk Mill's bell which first sounded at five o'clock in the morning, then for breakfast at eight o'clock, lunch at one o'clock and finally at six in the evening. Silk production continued until 1941 when the Ministry of Supply closed it down. Most of the 50 workers were transferred to Ekco.

In 1946 Messrs. K. and H. Kattan wanted to restart production but failed to do so. Dryden & Son bought the premises in 1950 to use it for dressing rabbit skins. Unfortunately myxomatosis which was introduced to control the rabbit population instead decimated it and brought that business to an end in 1954. The owners then opened an antiques showroom which carried on until 1980. Other businesses operated from the site, between 1974 and 1979 Manco produced battery chargers but made 30 workers redundant when they closed. In 1984 both buildings were converted to flats.

Postern Mill, the Maltings
This is one of the few sites in the old town where an archaeological investigation has been carried out. During the Roman period there was a brick kiln here and Roman coins have been found. The Saxons also had a kiln and tiles similar to those discovered under the Abbey floor were found. It became a tannery & slaughterhouse for 400 years during medieval times with many animal bones in evidence. Later there was a corn mill, followed in the 16th Century by a woollen mill owned by Matthew Kyng MP. He lived where Kings House is and it is thought that the name Kings Wall is associated with him, perhaps a corruption of King's Walk. With the decline of the woollen industry it reverted to the milling of grain. In 1836 the site was bought by Thomas Luce and developed into a brewery and malt house.

Thomas Luce, the Bank Manager, had started brewing in 1821 when he entered into a partnership with John Brooke. They bought the brewery to the north of Cross Hayes for £2,200, with only £200 put up by Brooke who managed the business. By the time Luce sold the bank in 1836 the partnership had ended and he reinvested the proceeds in new premises. His son Charles took over the brewery and became the Bank Manager, succeeding his father in 1851 about the time Thomas was elected to Parliament. Because his main concern was the bank, Charles took a partner Mr. Harris, who oversaw the brewery. This relationship broke down 12 years later when a private auction was held between the partners in the Kings Arms. With the support of his brother-in-law, Charles made the highest bid. He then hired a manager, Edgar Farrow (1840-1922) who remained with the business for nearly 50 years. In 1865 a serious fire necessitated much rebuilding. A new malthouse was erected in 1887.

Charles groomed his eldest son Edward (1863-1887) to take over the business however he died from typhoid. Then his youngest son Cecil (1873-1901) who was an enthusiastic Volunteer officer joined the Wiltshire Regiment for the Boer War. Unfortunately in South Africa he too succumbed to typhoid. So with no one to succeed him Charles sold the business to the Stroud Brewery Company in 1912. Stroud's main interest was in the 42 licensed premises owned by Luce including 13 in Malmesbury. Licensees often had little money and bought beer on credit from brewers. To safeguard their position the supplies would be secured on the main asset – the pub building. If the publican was unable to pay the brewery would foreclose on the pub. The Stroud immediately closed the brewery but continued to use the malthouse and bottling department.

In 1923 the mill was turned into an electricity generating station and Wessex Electricity became owners. The Ministry of Food requisitioned the malthouse in 1940 which had been unused for 15 years and it became a National Reserve Food Store. Linolite Ltd. moved into the old mill early the following year. Alfred Beutell had patented a tubular electric lamp in 1901. After making some himself he contracted Edison and Swan to manufacture them. In 1933 he formed his own company, Linolite Ltd., to take over production. They made filament strip lights often used for displays and later

Linolite's modern building on the left with the Malthouse on the right, 1971.

Linolite staff leaving work just before this factory closed. (Malmesbury Chronicles)

for illuminating bathroom mirrors. During the Second World War they became the main supplier of hose clips for bomber aircraft de-icing systems. Unfortunately their factory was in Victoria - they were finally told by the Ministry of Aircraft Production to evacuate from London and they chose Malmesbury. A lease was granted by Wessex Electricity. During the war Linolite made 7.5 million hose clips in a workshop on the third floor of the mill. The second floor was their canteen with offices on the first. In 1944 there was a disastrous fire that badly damaged the upper part of the building and the adjacent Electricity Manager's house. The building was covered with an asbestos roof but the top two floors were never reused. After the war Linolite reverted to making electric lights and new buildings were erected. The brewery was unoccupied and deteriorated over the years.

The family sold the company to Rotaflex Ltd. in 1978 although Peter Beutell, grandson of the founder, remained a director. Eight years later Rotaflex merged with an American telecommunications group G.T.E. Corporation. In 1985 the company moved to new premises at the top of Tetbury Hill at which time the workforce was around 250 with hopes of increasing this number. Finally the factory, then part of Sylvanian Lighting International which had taken over just six months before, closed in 1993 putting the last 90 employees out of work. Later the factory was taken over by Dyson. The Maltings housing project, originally proposed for older people, was finally completed in 1993 after the first contractor went out of business.

Breweries

Abbey Brewery, Market Cross

Presumably the brewery here originally served the monastery. The present building dates from 1672 with a 19th Century façade and was restored by Malmesbury Preservation Trust in 1989. The North elevation has two storeys, the overhanging first floor supported by five stone columns with slightly tapering shafts. The brewery, sold by J. S. Ody in 1845 to William Randall, was then sold to John Harris before being taken over by Luce in 1871. As a sideline the maltster would dry clothes overnight for 1d. Edgar Farrow, Luce Brewery's manager, lived next door in Brewery House. When the business was sold to the Stroud Brewery they disposed of the House and used the brewery's office as a Sales Office where the Manager, Mr. E. Marmont was liberal with his samples. Apparently ginger beer and lemonade were also stocked here. The Stroud Brewery closed its office in 1941 and sold it in 1946. By 1928 the Stroud owned 420 pubs and was taken over by Cheltenham & Hereford Brewery in 1958 to form West Country Brewery which was swallowed up by Whitbread in 1967. In 1989 breweries were forced to sell a large number of tied houses. The Kings Arms and Three Cups became part of Enterprise Inns.

Cross Hayes Brewery

Harry Duck, the head brewer for his father c1880.

Confusingly there were two Cross Hayes Breweries, one at the north and the other south of the square. The northern brewery was owned by Daniel Smith at the start of the 19th Century. Thomas Luce and John Brooke leased this in 1821 before Thomas bought the freehold in 1835. Having developed the Postern Mill brewery he sold part of these premises to the Market House Company in 1848 which built the Town Hall. The Malthouse in Market Lane was taken over by Esau Duck in 1886. In 1926 the Stroud Brewery sold part to the YMCA and part to the Borough Council.

The southern brewery was run by Joseph Reynolds until about 1852 when Frederick Parsloe took over until Esau Duck bought 32 Cross Hayes and the brewery in 1873. During the construction of the new railway line Esau had seen the opportunity to sell beer to the navvies for 1d. a pint. Esau retired from the business in 1892 when he leased it to his son-in-law Thomas Reed and it was renamed Duck & Reed. However Thomas broke the lease before it expired *because of the heavy burdens imposed upon the trade by the budget* and moved to Swindon in 1911 so the firm became Duck & Company. The brewery owned an office and bottle store on the other side of Silver Street and stables in Cross Hayes Lane. After Esau's death in 1908 his sons Harry and Monte kept the business going throughout the First World War but in 1922 sold to the Stroud Brewery. The Stroud just wanted the tied houses leaving the brewery with Monte who turned it into a cinema for a short time.

Abattoir, Park Close

The new Borough Council in 1887 issued slaughter licences to Messrs. Henry Garlick, John G. Lyne, Thomas Austin, Arthur Portch, all High Street butchers; W. & E. Lockstone, Oxford Street; Adye & Hinwood, Park Road; Edward Savine, Horsefair; and John Rich & Son, Burton Hill. After the First World War public health regulations prevented licences being approved for any slaughterhouse within 100 yards of any dwelling house. In 1924 W. H. Evans, wishing to buy 34 High Street, was refused a licence for the slaughterhouse behind his premises then for one in St. Dennis Lane. The following year only three licences were renewed, unfortunately the report provides no more detail. James Watkins who had moved to 34 High Street was unable obtain a licence for other premises in Ingram Street or Kings Wall. In 1932 a By-law was proposed to forbid school children to visit slaughterhouses and 17 men were granted licences to slaughter.

The Newman brothers outside the new buildings at the Abattoir in 1985. (Malmesbury Chronicles)

George Frederick Day (1877-1948) opened a butcher's shop at 2 Market Cross just before 1911 and in 1920 built an abattoir in Park Road. He and his son Arthur (1910-1953) ran this facility which was the only local supplier of butcher's meat. When Arthur died, Victor (1903-1963) and George Newman (1905-1976) took over. George farmed at Winkworth Farm, Lea. In 1960 an extension was added but within a couple of years there were complaints that the river was running red with blood and there was a disgusting smell. George's sons Anthony and Timothy continued the business and in 1979 got permission to renew all the buildings on site despite 77 objections. During the 1990s a number of robberies occurred including the theft of a lorry containing meat. At the same time new European legislation increased costs. In January 1998 two pigs escaped, swam the river and evaded capture for a week. Named the *Tamworth Two,* the plight of Butch and Sundance made headlines across the world. They were bought by the Daily Mail and lived out their lives in an animal sanctuary. Planning Permission was granted for 33 houses and although assurances were given that the abattoir would not immediately close, within a few weeks it did. Crest Homes then submitted plans for 24 four and five bedroomed houses but were refused. However a fresh plan for 2 flats, 11 three bed, 19 four bed and 2 five bed houses was approved.

Bacon Factory, Willow View Close

This was site for the factory opened in 1877 by Adye and Hinwood Ltd. The principals were Alfred Adye, grocer of 52 High Street, who raised his portion of the capital by selling that business to his brother Albert and Thomas Lot Hinwood, outfitter and draper, 50 High Street. On the ground floor was the slaughter house, hanging room, sausage room, lard room and smoke chamber with the smoke room and storeroom on the first floor and the curing cellar and salt store in the

Looking south across Park Road (hidden behind the wall) at the bacon factory from the site now occupied by bungalows.

basement. The railway station just a few hundred yards away was well placed for the transport of produce. To increase production this was one of the first plants to have refrigeration just after the Great War and for the next 20 years much was exported. In 1938 it was described as *an old Factory ... rather rambling ... being situate in Malmesbury, it is too far off the beaten track to go in for Sausage Making etc., on a large scale.* As a result it was recommended for a lower rateable value. During World War II much of the premises was requisitioned. When the war ended up to 500 pigs were processed every week but within a few years the number shrank to around 200. The factory finally closed in 1964 when only eight people were employed and the company wound up the next year. Eventually houses were built to form Willow View Close and the rubble from the demolition was dumped in the 'factory field' across Park Road so that bungalows could be built along the riverbank.

Cinema

One puzzling aspect about early cinemas here is that there is no explanation as to how the electricity for the projector was generated, as unless a large bank of batteries was employed the power would decrease as the film progressed. The first experience town dwellers had of this new wonder was in 1912 when Messrs. Lever Brothers' travelling cinema visited the Town Hall to show a *finely illustrated* lecture on soap making facilities at Port Sunlight. The admittance charge of 1s. or 6d. was given to aid YMCA funds. In 1913 J. H. Fielder (the leaseholder of the Town Hall) made an application for a cinematograph licence, which was granted subject to an iron exit staircase being erected at the rear and fire extinguishers provided. So Powell's cinema began but within a year it became the Electric Picture House run by A. E. Smith. In February 1914 11 year-old William Saunders sliding down the banisters whilst a cinema show was in progress (although he *had several times been ordered to desist*) fell 16 feet causing cuts and bruises, rendering him unconscious. Fortunately he suffered no lasting harm. That October the programme for Monday, Tuesday & Wednesday was; *The Sheriff and the Rustler* and *England's First Line of Defence,* and on Thursday, Friday & Saturday; *Under the Daisies (Two-reel drama)* and *England Declares War.* At this early stage of the war *the Electric Picture House is better patronised than ever and the Territorials have found it a haven of enjoyment ... There was an amusing incident on Monday evening. One of the pictures showed the hero of the play admiring the scene from the top of a precipice. Behind him stealthily crept the villain, whose intention was obvious. Just as he was about to spring at the hero a young soldier in the front seats gave a loud whistle and then called* out, *"He's coming behind you, mate."* It is unclear when this cinema closed but in 1915 only a single report has been found, in November announcing the Picture House was reopening for one show.

In May 1918 a cinema van visited the town to show views of the war following a lecture in Cross Hayes. *At the close some clever pictorial appeals for the financial help of the working man whose war savings loaned to the State would help to "down" Kaiserism once and for all made people realise the value of the last mite in turning the scales of justice in favour of John Bull and Co.*

After Monte Duck sold the Cross Hayes Brewery business the building behind 32 Cross Hayes at the top of Silver Street became vacant. He turned this into a cinema and the new premises opened in November 1919. It *will seat 240 people in the most up-to-date lounge chairs, well upholstered, with tip-up seats. It is electrically lighted, warmed by an efficient steam plant, is perfectly draught-proof, and is all on the ground floor. Teas and light refreshments will be provided in an ante-room adjoining ... and ... with its silver-screen – the only one in the West of England – will be found the most modern and up-to-date in the district.* It opened with *Tale of Two Cities* followed by a two part comedy. Miss Isabel Wilkins was the first pianist to accompany performances but she was succeeded by Mr. Phelps. Youngsters could attend a Saturday matinee for 3d. At this time films were often shown as serials with the last show on Saturday night maybe depicting the hero (or more likely heroine) left helpless in dire straits, so patrons were obliged to attend next week to see how the drama played out! Monte then had to rewind the reels and drive them to Kemble station for dispatch to the next cinema in the circuit. Unfortunately this was another example of considerable investment which did not pay dividends because Monte Duck left Malmesbury within a few years and his enterprise closed.

In 1927 a travelling cinema arrived in town run by John Mott (1899-1981), who set up a portable wooden building in the old Unicorn Inn yard off the High Street near the South Gate. Electricity was provided by a Lincoln Imp steam engine operated by two of the town's part time firemen, George Vanstone and Dick Bishop. Mains electricity was eventually connected, films with sound introduced and the cinema was named the Malmesbury Electric Picturedrome. The business

John Mott's first premises in Lower High Street.

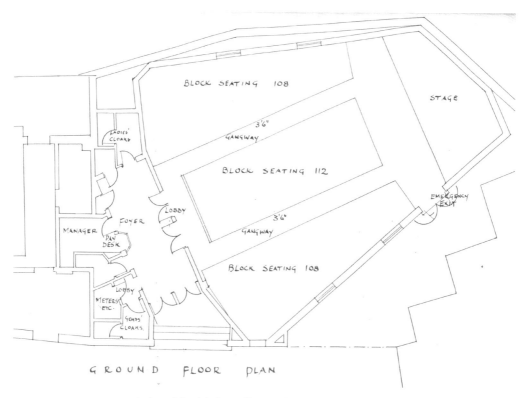

A plan of the Athelstan Cinema, Market Cross (J. Mott).

prospered and a permanent site was sought. It was first proposed in 1927 to erect a structure with walls of corrugated iron and an engine room behind the old hospital close to the Abbey but this had been vigorously opposed. Jack Mott then sought to gain public support by having shows with proceeds being donated to the hospital and inviting the trustees of the public assistance institution to attend. Matters came to a head when lightning struck the old cinema in 1934 and hailstones as large as pigeon's eggs caused serious damage. A Council election was in progress at the time in which Jack Mott was a candidate and the main talking point was his proposed new cineam. Two silver and two copper birches were planted in the churchyard to screen the cinema from view. With the support of Councillor Jimmy Jones, the Athelstan Cinema was opened in March 1935. The vicar, Rev. Arthur Beaghen (1887-1977), supported the cinema even though many of his parishioners did not. This position was repeated in 1941 when the Ekco cinema club wanted shows on Sunday over which there was much argument until it was agreed with the Vicar not to open before 7.30pm. Pressure from some members of the public led to Sunday performances ending in December 1943. Before and during the war many fund-raising events were held in the cinema. In 1954 a new wide screen was installed, *the prelude to the provision of stereophonic sound,* Malmesbury was the first with such facilities in the area.

However the popularity of cinemas was declining and in 1961 Jack Mott closed two other cinemas he owned, the Tudor, Chipping Sodbury and The New Palace, Tetbury, the latter being just 10 years old. In Malmesbury Sunday evening bingo sessions began the following year. Jack's son, also John, took over but in January 1973 he closed the cinema as he and his wife had not had a holiday for 11 years. Roger Harwood took over and reopened in September 1976 with films on three evenings a week alternating with bingo sessions. Films did not seem to make any money although bingo did and films were no longer shown by 1980. At this time 500-600 people per week attended bingo and a liquor licence was granted. However it closed in 1990 and when a proposal for offices on the site was being considered, the building was demolished in 1994.

Cinema returned to the town in December 2010 when the lottery funded Rural Cinema Pilot Scheme provided equipment for digital films to be shown in the Town Hall. At first a projector was shared with Melksham and Calne but after this suffered a major breakdown the project was threatened. Fortunately Dolby Europe from Royal Wootton Bassett came to the rescue, providing equipment and support which has enabled the Town Council to continue beyond the end of the Pilot Scheme.

Coal Merchants

Some excitement was caused in the early 19th Century when it was suggested there were substantial deposits of coal on Kings Heath. A meeting of Trustees of the Common was held in October 1837 and it was resolved to make enquiries on the subject. It was said at least one person had been mining coal there. However hopes had been raised by *an ignorant collier* who maintained there definitely was coal there but some 60 years previously shafts had been sunk without finding anything. So coal continued to be transported from outside the district which meant it was not widely used until the arrival of the railway network.

The first coal merchant here seems to have been Thomas Pinnell (1816-1899) of High Street who lists this as his trade from 1841 but in 1867 he was also a tea dealer and Vestry clerk. He left Malmesbury before the 1871 census. Robert Bishop (1809-1892) of St. Johns Street gave his occupation over the years variously as agricultural labourer, haulier, coal merchant, farmer and finally labourer. For a brief period in the 1870s Francis Bailey (1817-1888), an Ingram Street builder who in 1881 employed 10 men, sold coal. With the arrival of the railway branch line larger businesses appeared, the most prominent of which was founded by John Alexander of Avon House. He started the Malmesbury Coal Company around 1880 jointly owned with his nephew Walter Alexander (1843-1907). They sold coal, coke, lime, salt, wood and artificial manure with premises in Gloucester Road (the yard at 97a and Westport Granary), the railway yard, Somerford and Tetbury. John passed his share of the company to his eldest son Henry Edward (1864-1892) but after Henry's death Walter became the sole manager of the family owned company.

Samuel Fisher (1851-1924) entered the business in the late 1880s initially by merging with a firm called Harding & Son before trading in his own name. He sold his business which operated from Malmesbury, Hullavington & Somerford to Arthur Lewin Curtis (1898-1968) in 1920. Unfortunately Mr. Curtis went bankrupt in 1932, having relied on loans from his father, turnover dropped from £14,014 in 1927 to just £6,000 in the final year. Dolphins Coal and Coke Co. Ltd. of Malmesbury and Tetbury bought the business from the liquidator for £300. It would seem to have remained unprofitable as on 1 August 1935 Harold Gladwin (1882-1960), who had a baker's at Market Cross, bought it. Mr. Gladwin also purchased the Malmesbury Coal Company from the Alexanders in 1938 and became the sole coal merchant using the town's railway. In 1946 Mr. Gladwin sold to Thomas Silvey Ltd. of Bristol, who traded as the Malmesbury Coal Company using the office at 97a Gloucester Road until about 1964. When the branch line closed in 1962 they moved their depot to Badminton station. It seems their operation closed later in the 1960s.

In 1964 Dolphins Coal & Coke Co. Ltd. returned to Malmesbury by opening an office at 9 Market Cross in conjunction with Tetbury Hand & Steam Laundry Co. Ltd. to take orders and payments. They offered a three day laundry service and also a travel agency! This office moved into the High Street by which time it was just referred to as a travel agency but this closed in 1973. J. Giles ran a small coal business in the Tanyard, Dark Lane in the 1930s which Reg Frayling (1912-1998) took over from the late 1940s until 1972. Small amounts of coal can now be bought in shops such as E & S but local deliveries are made by J. A. Wilson & Sons Ltd. of Hullavington.

E. K. Cole Ltd., Cowbridge House

Towards the end of August 1939 Mr. M.I. Lipman, head of the Electrical Appliances Division of E.K. Cole Ltd., was instructed by the RAF to establish a 'shadow' factory capable of producing radio equipment within a radius of 100 miles to the west of London. Eric Kirkham Cole had started making radio sets in 1924. As the business expanded it moved to a large factory in Southend-on-Sea in 1930. After searching Oxfordshire and South Gloucestershire Mr. Lipman ended up in Malmesbury and the day before war was declared bought Cowbridge House for £6,500 from Sir Philip Hunloke. By Christmas Mr. Lipman had turned the house into a workshop and 20 or so workers were assembling VHF radios. Unfortunately from the start there was much ill feeling between the locals and the newcomers. Many of the young women recruited had previously been in service with the gentry. The Old Bell had a sign saying, "Employees of Messrs. E.K. Cole are not welcome in this bar". A mother with a daughter aged 17 hoped that the daughter would not be paid the minimum wage of £1 per week, as she had only been paid 10s. whilst in service in a local country house. Another young woman attracted by the higher wage was Phyllis Pike (soon to be married to George Elms who had only asked her father for permission to park his bike outside their house!). She earned £1 2s. 6d. per week winding coils and was so good at it she was often the winner of production bonuses.

The summer of 1940 saw the start of radio-location (radar) set production. Robert Watson-Watt had first demonstrated radar in 1936 when his apparatus detected a formation of planes 50 miles away. The Western Development Unit (WDU), which was established in J. E. Ponting's premises in Malmesbury High Street, solved many of the problems of turning designs into workable sets. Some Ekco employees were brought from the parent factory in Southend but as production built up there was a shortage of labour. Other workers, many of them conscripted women, had to be brought in. About 50 women transferred from the Silk Mill when the Ministry of Supply closed that in 1941. With so many women on the staff a day nursery was set up in Swindon Road. Living accommodation had to be provided and the Priory, Halcombe House (off Common Road), Rodbourne House and many other properties in nearby villages were requisitioned. In 1942 twelve prefabricated houses were erected for workers west of Cowbridge House in what would become Cowbridge Crescent. More were built here in 1948. After the war the Borough Council had to continue giving preference to Ekco employees for Council houses. Even into the 1960s there were complaints of 'queue jumping' by Ekco employees over other council tenants as 41 of the 240 council houses were covered by this agreement. The workforce grew to over 1,000 and 22 buses daily brought workers from Bath, Chippenham, Cirencester, Swindon and many local villages.

There was a strong sports and social club. Dances were held in the canteen on Saturday nights and a Ministry of Supply lorry was used to collect some of the women from the hostel in Rodbourne. On one trip Police Inspector Edwards stopped the lorry and although he saw all the correspondence with the Ministry of Aircraft Production authorising this use, a summons was issued for Mr. Lipman to appear before the town's magistrates. The charge was using official petrol for civilian purposes. He was told by his Ministry not to worry about it but the hearing date arrived and he felt it prudent to attend the court. It had not been sorted out so he asked for the case to be adjourned. The magistrate would only allow him until that afternoon so he arranged for a solicitor to be collected from Swindon who was then granted a seven day adjournment! At the following week's hearing the Ministry of Fuel's counsel asked leave to withdraw the charge which was agreed. Mr. Lipman obviously had a dim view of local officials as he maintained the magistrate pronounced he was "guilty but discharged"! During the 1950s & 60s the Social Club provided an annual treat for the children of Malmesbury, the Christmas Party. This was held in Cowbridge House and comprised entertainment including cartoon films, games and much food.

The whole outing including the coach travel each way, being split into groups and the precise timetable was an exciting highlight of the year.

Ekco produced Air Interception radars for the RAF, Air to Surface Vessel sets for Coastal Command and the Fleet Air Arm, adapting these for installation in ships for the Royal Navy (stopping the 100 valves jumping out of their sockets when guns were fired) and Search Light Control sets for the Army. At the end of the war many staff were made redundant, WDU went back to Southend and the factory took on other work, although radar production continued until the mid 1960s, including cloud warning equipment for Comet IV aircraft. Military radios (88 sets) were made and an association with Aldermaston Atomic Energy Establishment began which led to radiation monitoring equipment being produced. This was calibrated by placing a piece of radioactive material on a wooden rule and no doubt these workers received exposure which would now be considered unsafe. The electronic work was transferred to Southend in 1960 but car radios, tape recorders, radiograms and heaters were added to Malmesbury's range of products. 1960 saw Ekco being merged with Pye Ltd. As a result the premises had to be extended in 1963 and again the next year at a cost of £70,000. Electric fires, Thermotube (horticultural heating in 2" steel or aluminium tubes ranging from 1' to 16' in length), night storage radiators and finally gas heaters were also produced at this time. Every day a lorry would take products to the London depot which

Ekco electric fires made at Cowbridge in the 1960s.

was under the seats at Wembley Stadium! All radio production for the group was concentrated at Malmesbury so that the Pye Lowestoft factory could manufacture TVs. From 1968 the factory changed from the Ekco name to TV Manufacturing Ltd., although the factory was still known as the Ekco Works. However this was short-lived and from January 1970 the company became TMC Ltd., standing for Telephone Manufacturing Company.

Telephone exchange equipment in the large workshop at the rear of the site.

The factory now produced telephones and telephone exchange equipment. Contracts flooded in, one for 100,000 push-button phones and 600 staff were employed with up to 20 coaches bringing them to work. Just a year later the company's name changed to Pye TMC and Ekco signs were finally replaced. The research and development department was relocated from Dulwich which resulted in half of the building in front of Cowbridge House being demolished and a modern one put up in 1975. The mid 1970s were a difficult time with 115 out of 400 workers made redundant in 1976. This was despite the arrival of the Company's head office early that year. The following year another 110 were made redundant. In 1980 Philips Telecommunications UK Ltd. took over and the name changed back to TMC Ltd. Research and development of telephone equipment formed an important area of work although manufacturing continued. From 1984 AT & T, an American telephone conglomerate, joined Philips in a joint venture and in that year a new building was built on the east of the site. TMC decided to concentrate manufacture in Glasgow and closed their part of the operation in 1987 leaving just the joint venture, APT-UK, on site. The following year AT & T took full control. In the mid 1990s AT & T were finding it difficult to both operate telephone networks as well as supply equipment to competitors. They split off their manufacturing arm to form a new company, Lucent Technologies. This firm employed more than 700 staff in Malmesbury researching and developing transmission and switching equipment for both mobile and fixed line telephone networks. However job losses quickly began and following the collapse of the technology boom they announced the closure of this site and vacated it in September 2002.

The Minton Group bought the site and sold most of it to Redrow who built 143 houses. The modern office block to the left of the entrance was retained but there are plans to convert this

An aerial view of the Cowbridge site in 1980.

and the old mill into residential accommodation.

Dyson Ltd., Tetbury Hill

James Dyson (b1947) was fascinated and frustrated by devices which failed to work well. To improve the performance of wheelbarrows in soft soil and increase their stability he invented the ballbarrow in 1974. Then he realised that vacuum cleaners were inefficient. As soon as any dust was picked up the pores of the bag became clogged and reduced the suction. He decided a cyclone would allow the circulating air to deposit the dirt in a container without the need for a bag. Having formulated the theory he had to spend more than five years building more than 5,000 prototypes to produce a practical product. He then sought a manufacturer to make it under licence. No British company would take the project on so it was not until 1986 that a Japanese company agreed to produce it for their home market. Using the royalties from this deal he was able to set up his own company in 1993.

Production of the DC-01, an upright cleaner, began at Bumpers Farm, Chippenham but good advertising using the slogan *Say Goodbye to the Bag* and the introduction of the DC-02 cylinder version meant those premises became too small. Dyson found the premises on Tetbury Hill which were empty after Linolite's departure and moved there in 1995. The company became the largest British manufacturer of vacuum cleaners by value (as the product was more expensive) and then by volume. Once again success meant the premises were inadequate but this time a new award winning building was erected to replace the industrial 'shed' in 1999. The workforce grew to 1,400 and another factory was planned but this met with local opposition so was not carried out. However in 2002 production was moved to Malaysia making 800 workers redundant but the number of research and development engineers has since increased. They have been responsible for inventing a washing machine called the ContraRotator which did not prove to be a commercial success; the Airblade, a fast hand drier which has proved popular; and the Air Multiplier, a bladeless fan or heater. Innovation has also improved the design of vacuum cleaners including the introduction of a ball to increase mobility.

The Dyson factory under construction. The car park has never been so empty since.

The company continues to expand and in 2014 announced its intention of constructing a technology park to the north of its present site which has been approved. James Dyson was knighted in the 2007 New Year's honours list.

Edwards and Son, Holloway

Thomas Edwards (1817-1899) was a wheelwright who established a business on Bristol Road, Malmesbury in 1843. His son, John Elford (1843-1916) was working alongside his father by 1861 and they were living in Oxford Street. In May 1870 they took a lease of ground with workshops on the old Bowling Green, Holloway. By 1875 the business, known as Edwards & Son, had progressed to coachbuilding and engaged an apprentice. In 1903 it was John's son Egbert Francis Ethelred (1878-1945) who took over the business. Egbert was a keen Volunteer, serving in the South African

A mobile display of Edwards & Son's products, perhaps for the 1911 Coronation.

War and spent 46 years as a part-time fireman, being the Captain of the Brigade from 1922 to 1942. After Egbert's death the business was bought by Samuel Hoskins (1881-1969), a farmer who had been a customer, for his son Michael (b1920). Michael, who had no previous experience but was able to rely on Bert Paginton an experienced carpenter, rebuilt the business expanding its activities. Fred Willis who had previously been a hurdle maker was established in a wood yard adjacent to 14 Gastons Road, the Gig House in Oxford Street became their office, filling station, store and eventually blacksmith's. The joinery workshop next to 34 Holloway was rebuilt. In 1948 a shop was opened in the High Street followed by others in Chippenham, Corsham, Melksham, Stroud and Trowbridge. The retail arm became a separate company in 1964, still owned by the Hoskins family.

During the 1960s the main business's product lines changed due to greater usage of metal in vehicles and agricultural equipment so more reliance was placed on the building trade. In an effort to bring most of these operations under one roof larger premises were sought and when the railway closed the company intended to bid for the station site. Learning of the Borough Council's interest Mr. Hoskins suggested that he would not compete with them if the Council agreed to build an industrial unit to be let to his company. After the Council bought the site this understanding was forgotten and the units were offered to other companies, so in 1969 the woodworking company moved to Tetbury. By 1971 they were making pinewood kitchen unit furniture and Mr. Hoskins sold the company two years later. The Company was dissolved in 1985.

Hilditch Group Ltd., Gloucester Road Industrial Estate
Mike and Nicky Hilditch formed this auctioneer's in 1990 at this address. It is now the market leader in the resale of medical equipment of all sorts, but also has a large department dealing with catering and hospital goods as well as more general industrial and commercial products. The company has expanded over the years taking over the premises of Ranalagh Gates (which occupied the western half of the large building until going into receivership) and then the Lux unit to the east.

Lux Traffic Controls Ltd., Gloucester Road Industrial Estate
The head office of this company used to occupy the easterly most unit on this site. George Lux (1906-1990), an electrician, came to Tetbury from London during World War II. After the war his family moved to join him and he opened an electrical shop. A customer asked him to make a set of temporary traffic lights and this request gave his son Lawrence the idea for a new business. Lawrence began to manufacture and at first to sell, later to hire out, sets of traffic lights to control traffic around roadworks. The business started in 1967, becoming a private company in 1973. In the beginning things were not very sophisticated, some of the early control units were assembled by Boy Scouts during 'Bob a Job' week! However innovative ideas soon produced new equipment such as the first vehicle actuated system using microwave detectors with specialist trailers to transport the equipment.

Having outgrown the Tetbury shop their head office moved to Malmesbury in 1967 at first in Oxford Street. The moved to Station Yard in 1978 and the company became the world's largest manufacturer and hirer of portable traffic signals. They operated a 24-hour control room able to deliver to site equipment from 49 depots throughout the country. In 1997 BT awarded them a nation-wide contract and they provided training for many organisations including several police forces. However in 2006 the company was taken over by A-Plant who two years later closed this office. They now have a depot at Kemble airfield.

H. & C. Matthews, 7 Burnham Rd
Henry Matthews (1859-1948) served an apprenticeship as a carpentry joiner at Burton Hill House. Being an ambitious young man, at the earliest opportunity he began his own carpentry

Chris Matthews outside the premises in Burnham Road with the old sign advertising their motor hearse, bought after their horses went off to military duties in the First World War. (Malmesbury Chronicles)

business. He rented a workshop and stable in Gastons Lane just outside the Borough boundary about 1880. His brother Charles (1867-1955), a wheelwright and a noted French polisher, was a partner until 1950 but had no children. Henry took on building work and built a number of houses in Minety, thinking nothing of the seven-mile journey each way, pushing his cart. At the beginning of the 20th Century the firm built several elegant houses in Burnham Road and Charles lived at No. 11. Henry's son, (Harry Charles) Stephen (b1884) worked for the business for a while before emigrating to Australia. Stephen's son (Henry) Charles (b1908) worked in the firm all his life and took over on his great-uncle's retirement. In turn Charles' son Christopher returned to Malmesbury after a career in further education to take charge in 1973. The first undertaking was done at the beginning of last century when there were six other carpenters in the town who did such work. In 1973 Chris decided to concentrate solely on being a funeral director until he retired in 2005. The firm was then bought by Cowley & Son of Cirencester and is managed by James Beesley.

Milk Factory, Park Road Industrial Estate
A milk processing factory opened here in February 1919 to take advantage of many local dairy farms. Initially owned by Wiltshire Farmers Ltd. the name changed the following year to Wilts and Somerset Farmers Ltd. Milk was sterilised using a large coal fired boiler and the finished product was despatched to London by rail. At this time churns were carried by a French made De Dion lorry. Wiltshire Creameries Ltd. took the business over and used the first bulk road tanker in Wiltshire which from 1931 was provided by Bulwark Transport of Chippenham. The railway continued to be used by individual farmers but it lost valuable traffic. Cheese was made once a year when there was a surplus of milk, normally in early summer. United Dairies took over the business and as part of their reorganisation closed these premises in 1938. Two of the staff moved to the larger depot at Wootton Bassett which was well placed to supply milk to London

but eventually closed in 2000.

Two Lacre lorries and a Sentinel steam lorry being loaded with milk churns at the factory's loading bay.

Ratcliffe and Son, Foundry Road

Edwin Ratcliffe (1848-1916), the eldest son of a farmer from Bucklebury in Berkshire, opened the Westport Ironworks in 1870. The buildings to the north of the road incorporate some early

Ratcliffe's workshop in the early years of the 20th Century. Most of the machinery is still there today. The three men in front are Otto Sealy, Herbert and Edwin Ratcliffe.

19th Century farm buildings. Edwin had married the daughter of John Hedges who owned an iron foundry in Bucklebury and had presumably been apprenticed to him. Why he moved to Malmesbury is not clear but his brother Norman (1857-1922) owned a chemist's at 19 High Street around the same time. Edwin designed and produced machinery for mills, breweries and factories as well as footbridges and hatches for the river authority. At first his workshop was powered by steam, later by gas until converted to electricity in 1940. Much of the original machinery is still in situ.

Edwin's eldest son, Herbert (1880-1918), ran the business from around 1910 due to his father's infirmity. Unfortunately he was called up late in 1917 and soon afterwards died. After returning from war service the second son, Edwin Norman (1892-1963) returned to the business, which diversified into trades such as plumbing, the repair of steam traction engines and car hire. In its heyday the works employed 15 men. In 1940 Ratcliffe's fitted out the machinery for the Western Development Unit of Ekco when they moved into Ponting's premises in the High Street. The original forge was used in 1981 to make gates that were presented by the town of Tetbury to the Prince of Wales for Highgrove House. The founder's great-grandson Mike now runs the business, which concentrates on the repair and maintenance of garden and farm machinery.

The Plymouth Brethren were allowed to use the first floor of the red brick building on the southern side of Foundry Road before the First World War.

The blacksmith's forge is now operated by the Heritage Blacksmith Partnership of Alex Coode and Simon Doyle who specialise in conservation projects.

A. C. Nurden Ltd., Garden Centre, Cirencester Road
Although there are many local building companies this is chosen as representative due to its wide range of activity. Lawrence Nurden (b1928) was a builder and was followed into the business by his sons Andrew (b1953) and Ian (b1956). Andy's company was incorporated in 1986 although he had been operating for some time prior to that. That same year he opened a building supplies and plant hire depot in an old barn in Park Road, employing 26 full time and a number of part time workers. Unfortunately the site is adjacent to the river and has been flooded several times. In 1998 the premises were expanded and retail customers welcomed. This facility is now run in partnership with Buildbase, a nationwide builders' merchant.

Andy Nurden (left) standing outside his Park Road premises in 1986. (Malmesbury Chronicles)

In 1999 Nurden's took over Addington's Garden Centre on the Cirencester Road. Begun in 1978 by the Earl of Suffolk's brother, Hon. Patrick Howard. Jeremy Addington (who ran the Nursery in Corston next to the Kingway bridge) bought the centre around 1985 obtaining a Royal Warrant from HRH Prince of Wales in 1998. It is now also the base for Nurden's building and plant hire operation.

Sweetnam and Bradley Ltd., Gloucester Road Industrial estate

In 1955 Arthur Bradley and James Sweetnam formed a partnership working on electrical assemblies in the former stables of Westhill House, Bristol Road. They both had an electronics background with Arthur Bradley working for the BBC, where he had been involved with radio and the early days of television and James Sweetnam having worked for Ekco. Three years later the enterprise became a limited company.

In 1970 the company moved to a purpose built facility on the Gloucester Road Industrial Estate, being the first occupants of the new site. In 1972 it was decided to split the business in two with Custom Transformers Ltd. designing and manufacturing transformers in the old Bristol Road premises and Sweetnam & Bradley concentrating on sheet metal work. Custom Transformers expanded their premises until in 2006 they moved to a new factory at White Walls, Easton Grey. Ten houses called The Light have been built on their former site.

Sweetnam & Bradley has moved with the times installing their first Amada CNC computerised punching machine in 1985 with two more added since. An office block was built in 1972 and the production area extended in 1993 and 1996 so the total work area now exceeds 20,000 square feet. The company is now the premier sheet metal work company in Wiltshire.

Willis Brothers, Swindon Road

Frederick Willis (1902-1976) worked as a hurdle maker but moved into factory work. However after the Second World War Frederick and two of his sons Kenneth (b1936) and Brian (b1939) worked for Edwards & Son but in 1958 decided to set up on their own. They used Wynyard Mill (where Frederick's father James (1864-1949) had began his own business at the beginning of the 20th Century). By 1966 Frederick's two other sons, Gerald and Alan (b1945) had joined, moved to new premises at Cowbridge on the Swindon Road. At the same time they took responsibility for building the fences at the Badminton Horse trials. They began constructing event courses overseas in 1980 and have worked at the Barcelona, Atlanta and Sydney Olympic Games as well

The Willis Brothers in the Swindon Road yard, 1986. (Malmesbury Chronicles)

as World Equestrian Games. Although the four brothers are still involved in the business much of the work is now carried out by the next generation.

Wilts and Gloucestershire Standard newspaper

The Wilts & Gloucestershire Standard was founded to further Conservative interests in North Wiltshire and the adjoining part of Gloucestershire. The first edition was published on Saturday, 28 January 1837 and printed at the Standard Printing Works, Oxford Street, Malmesbury. The paper comprised four pages with six columns to the page and cost 5d. (2p), a large sum in those days, but 4d. represented tax, part of the so-called *Taxes on Knowledge*. In July 1840 the paper moved to Cirencester. The Company was taken over in 1852 and lost its political allegiance. A change of owner in 1869 led to it again being an outspoken supporter of the Tories. 1959 saw ownership pass to the Bailey Newspaper Group. They began a Malmesbury and Tetbury edition of the paper in 1984 with an office at 35 Cross Hayes. In 1995 Malmesbury once again had its own edition of the paper, an office at 53 High Street with a resident local reporter. The Bailey family sold the company to Southern Newspapers in 1998 and six months after their take-over they announced that the printing plant at Dursley was to shut with production transferred to Weymouth. Southern Newspapers changed its name to Newscom which was taken over by Newsquest, part of the U.S. publishing Gannett Group, in 2000. Unfortunately by 2013 falling sales had brought an end to the Malmesbury edition and the local office closed.

Xograph Healthcare Ltd.

This company was founded by Charles Staff in 1967. It seems to have been based in Silver Street until it bought a new industrial unit from Malmesbury Town Council on the site of the old market in 1983. For several years it sought larger premises in the town but moved in 1998 to Tetbury. It has expanded further and is now based in Stonehouse. Having begun supplying X-ray equipment the company now supplies all kinds of diagnostic equipment to all types of medical, dental and veterinary institutions.

Their old Malmesbury premises, next to the river in Gloucester Road, now houses the Youth Development Centre. The Youth Club which began during the war, moved in 1951 into its own accommodation in the British Legion premises, Ingram Street. Cyril Cartmell (1918-1978) provided dynamic leadership for almost 30 years including inaugurating the twinning link with Niebull. After Ingram Street became unsafe the new Cartmell Centre in the old school gymnasium attached to Verona House opened in 1985 where it remained until 2008 when it moved to Xograph's old building. An extension to house an indoor skatepark was opened in 2013.

Public Facilities

The Activity Zone Leisure Centre and Swimming Pool, Bremilham Road

Until September 2003 there was an open air swimming pool in Alexander Road. This was planned before the Second World War with Bernard Basevi spearheading the effort to get it built. After the war proceeds from Carnivals helped to raise the funds. It was built at the rear of Alexander Road beside a footpath that led from the Horsefair to allotments at White Lion Park and was finally opened in 1961. The total cost of £12,500 was shared between the Borough Council and public donations. The Chamber of Commerce raised £4,300 from a series of lotteries. Unfortunately

The open air swimming pool in 1964.

gate receipts never matched expenditure and a very substantial subsidy had to be provided from the rates. In 1998 an anonymous donor promised £300,000 towards a new indoor pool with a National Lottery grant providing further finance. It was built next to the Activity Zone in 2005. The first Lottery application was rejected because the plan was thought to be too grandiose and a more modest version was constructed with for example only a small area for spectators to stand. The planning of the Activity Zone was more straightforward and construction began in June 1998. Half of the cost of more than £2.7M was financed by a grant from the National Lottery Awards Panel with North Wiltshire District Council contributing £785,000. Providing facilities for many indoor sports it opened on 19th June 1999.

Market Cross

This area was part of the Abbey precinct and originally a graveyard (an excavation in 1993 discovered human remains from c1020). Over the years the townspeople encroached onto the area until during the 13th Century Abbot Colerne gave it to them. The market area was delineated by St Paul's Church to the north west and the White Lion Inn to the south. The buildings on the north side of Gloucester Street are from a later date.

The Cross is thought to have been erected around 1490, paid for by locals. When John Leland (1506-1552, Henry VIII's antiquary) visited the town in 1542 he described it; *There is a right fair and costly piece of worke in the market-place, made al of stone, and curiusly voultid for poore market folks to stande dry when rayne cummith. There be 8 great pillars and 8 open arches, and the work is 8 square: one great pillar in the middle berith up the voulte.*

It is one of the finest surviving examples. It has been repaired many times, including just before 1800 by the Earl of Suffolk, in 1883 when £140 was raised by public subscription, between 1909 and 1912 by the Borough at a cost of £700 and in 1950 for £909 18s. 7d. The last major work, mainly cleaning, was completed in 1991 at a cost of £53,000, a large part of which was an English Heritage grant and the rest was raised from donations. The donors' names are displayed on an illuminated manuscript held by the Town Council. However the base of central column is still worn away

The Market Cross in 1913 showing the new stone installed during the recent refurbishment. Note Newman's Grocers in the background.

from thousands of bottoms sitting there! In 1995 a large sum, including £109,000 from North Wilts District Council and £5,000 from the County Council was used to re-pave the area around the cross.

During Victorian times the Cross was not treated very well. Richard Jefferies (1848-1887, a journalist and writer) reported in 1867 that: *The cross is now looked upon with very little veneration. Vehicles are run into it for a temporary shelter, and the pillars are covered with printed bills of different colours; men out of work and other idlers have their great rendezvous.* Since then the Cross has been damaged by motor vehicles many times, the most serious being in 1979 when a car transporter demolished five of the tall pinnacles. The stone has deteriorated due to atmospheric pollution much of which comes from exhaust fumes.

Public Conveniences

Councillor Joseph Poole proposed town improvements to include two or three public urinals in 1888 but later dropped the idea. A site within three feet of the Market Cross was chosen in 1895 but this came to naught. Three years later it was agreed to erect a *double circular urinal* costing £18 10s. on the corner of Gloucester Street near the Steeple. This proved to be impractical as a large water tank above was needed for the evenings and Sundays. Further schemes were considered but in 1915 it was decided to wait until the war's end.

In 1923 public conveniences for males and females were built in Oxford Street at the rear of the Town Hall – the doorways can still be seen in the boundary wall. These provided basic facilities (there were no hand basins) but it was not until 1972 that new toilets were built on the corner of Oxford Street and Cross Hayes Lane. These were shortlisted for the South West Loo of the Year in 1989. However by 2003 the public put them on the shortlist for Britain's Worst Toilets! So in 2009 the Town Council decided to close these and allow the public to use the new Town Hall toilets.

St. Aldhelm's Mead

This was supposed to have been given to the Abbey by Queen Mathilda, wife of William the Conqueror, as the site for a fair to be held on St. Aldhelm's feast day, 25th May. In medieval times this extended over a number of days varying from three to eight. With the passage of time the area became privately owned. However in 1933 the Luce family presented it to the town for use as a recreation ground in memory of Charles Luce, the first Mayor and his son Admiral John Luce who had died the previous year. In 1948 a children's play area was erected as the Second World War Memorial. The Town Council later bought the small field between the Mead and the Town Bridge. This is known as Cucking Stool Mead as it is where disorderly women are reputed to have been ducked in the river.

The Mayor, Alderman Reg Young, with Bobbie Vince about to use the slide at the official opening of the play area in August 1950. Ironically this equipment was taken out of use within a short period due to safely fears as there were many hard landings at the bottom!
(Olive Kemp)

Community Organisations

Athelstan Players

There has been a long history of amateur productions in the town. In 1881 the Malmesbury Amateur Dramatic Society under the patronage of the Earl and Countess of Suffolk and Col. Miles performed two farces, *To Paris and Back for Five Pounds* and *Chiselling,* with a musical selection in between to packed houses in the Town Hall. Other performances by this group were reported in the 1890s, 1921 and 1933 with funds being raised for the Cricket and Football Clubs. Also performing in the 1890s were the Malmesbury Amateur Minstrels and a company raised by Mrs. Charrington of Burton Hill House who was the lead actor.

A group of amateur actors in the early years of the 20th Century, including Alfred Rymell on the left in the back row who emigrated to Cleveland, Ohio in 1912 at the age of 21. (Athelstan Museum)

The Athelstan Players first appeared in public at the Town Hall in April 1940 when they performed three one act plays interspersed with variety items. Produced by Mrs. Kathleen Besly, wife of the Midland Bank manager, funds were raised for the Red Cross and the Order of St. John. 11 productions were put on during the war with the proceeds being shared between the Hospital and the National Children's Home. After the war a cot was presented to the Children's Home in memory of Bernard Basevi, one of the group's originators who was killed on active service. After a break of two years Noel Coward's *I'll leave it to you* in 1951 failed to attract the full houses previously enjoyed, but this proved to be unusual. In 1953 Mrs. Besly resigned following her husband's decision to become a priest, having produced all the first twenty productions. There was another 18 month break in 1957/8.

In 1960 two plays were performed in aid of the swimming pool, one of Bernard Basevi's cherished projects. During the 1960s the choice of plays was restricted by a lack of male actors, but a larger auditorium was found at Bremilham School (only available during the holidays) and a clubroom was established above the Old Bell garages. In 1966 the Players established a One Act Play Festival as part of the Carnival and began a series of competitive successes by taking 3rd place in the Wiltshire Drama League. Dr. Hodge who had been President for 26 years, stood down in 1971. The One Act Play Festival was now firmly established and from 1973 was organised independently of the group. In 1977 the Chairman, Megan Mills, warned that the group was in danger of collapse as there were only a dozen active members. But their fortunes completely changed after coming second in the Malmesbury One Act Festival and going on to win the HTV West Drama Award with their entry *Mr. Sampson* being shown on TV. Five years later John O'Brien was awarded Best Actor by HTV West and an extract of *The Laboratory* was shown on TV.

During the 1980s the need for a clubroom and store became more pressing and an appeal for funds was launched to celebrate 50 years in 1987. A site was found on the Flying Monk ground near the football field and Carnival provided a £3,000 grant. Shows continued to alternate between the School and the Town Hall until 2001 when the last performance was held at the Bremilham School before its demolition. The new School does not have a stage. In the new Millennium the group has experience success several times at the Harold Jolliffe One Act Festival in Swindon. In 2010 shows moved from the Town Hall due to higher charges but an alternative venue has been found in St. Marys Hall. Unfortunately the clubroom has been flooded a number of times and it is now proposed to rebuild it with the ground floor set above the height of the highest flood.

1st Malmesbury (King Athelstan) Scout Group, St. Mary's Hall, Westport

This Scout Troop was formed on 8 February 1910 through the munificence of the de Bertodano family of Cowbridge House. Robert Baden-Powell, the defender of Mafeking during the Boer War, began the Boy Scout movement in 1908. The first senior scoutmaster here was Sgt. William G. Perry (1862-1923) who was assisted by Arthur Ponting, and Rev. F. J. Walmsley, Within a year there were five patrols of six scouts each *owing to the number of applicants, probably a new patrol will shortly be created.* Shortly afterwards 'Kangaroo' patrol was formed and there was a total of 55 members. The de Bertodanos bought a big drum and two side drums for the bugle band which took the lead in arranging a collection following the Titanic disaster. During the First World War a patrol with Scouts from Swindon was despatched to Polperro in Cornwall to watch the coast for U-boats. One of the Malmesbury lads concocted a story about an encounter with German spies which was widely reported before he admitted it was a work of imagination. Five former members, including Sgt. Perry's son, were killed during the war.

What must have been one of the first public duties for the Boy Scouts - the proclamation of King George V outside the Hospital at the Market Cross.

In 1922 W. G. Perry was presented with an inscribed pocket case containing £37 10s. on his retirement. Although the de Bertodano family had left the town following Baldemero's death they continued their support until around 1928, paying for annual tea parties and presenting two silver bugles. After it proved impossible to find a suitable Scout-Master the Troop was disbanded in December 1928. Nine months later it was re-formed under Scout-Master J. C. Wade.

In 1931 Mr. Wade resigned due to pressure of work and S. N. Dixon who had been Secretary since formation and Treasurer also had to give up due to ill health. Frank S. Weeks who had been associated with the Scouts for 15 years became the new Scout-Master but he had hesitated in taking over and could *not make his decision until he feels certain of having the support of each of the boys*. During the Second World War the Scouts performed many useful tasks, particularly the collection of pig swill and waste paper before the Councils organised house to house collections. M. C. Ingram, the Boys' School Headmaster, was the leader at this time until he resigned in 1947.

In the 1950s the Troop moved into the Youth Centre in Ingram Street. During the decade there was a shortage of adult helpers and in 1958 this again led to disbandment. Fortunately the Sherston Troop was strong and 12 of the town's Scouts were transported there every week but six members left the movement. Within three months it was temporarily re-formed by Cyril Cartmell, the Youth Leader, but he found he was unable to continue without other helpers and Sherston had to assist again. Despite the lack of a leader for a short period their headquarters was established in the Abbey House squash court with two patrols based there. Although the Primary School headteacher, Gwyn Price, began to rebuild the Troop, the lack of adults continued to restrict activities, the Scouts & Cubs needing 12 in 1967.

The Diamond Jubilee was celebrated in 1970 and eight founder members were able to join the celebrations. There were 30 current members with a waiting list of 17 which grew in the following years. By 1974 money was being raised for a headquarters building and numbers had increased so a 5th patrol was added, the Falcons. It was hoped to meet the need for purpose built accommodation by utilising a site on Bristol Road next to Bremilham Terrace and grant applications were made to raise £20,000 for a new building. But this scheme came to an abrupt halt in 1988 when the Leader and his Assistant both left and the Troop temporarily closed. Once again the boys had to travel to Sherston until 8 months later Gareth Venn, the Borough Arms publican, took over. More disruption followed in 1990 when Mr. Venn moved on and the temporary base of Wiltshire County Council's depot at the junction of Bristol & Bremilham Roads had to be vacated after 18 months. Burton Hill School allowed their old chapel to be utilised. A new scheme for premises in White Lion Park was considered for a long time in the 1990s but an application for Lottery funds failed. In 1997 the collection of waste paper and cans came to an end due to lower prices being received. At the turn of the millennium there was no leader with closure likely once again. However fortunes quickly changed after the arrival of Mike Westmacott who was succeeded by Mrs. Kim Power. In 2002 the acquisition of St. Mary's Hall from the Church of England provided a permanent home, also used by a number of other community groups.

Malmesbury Carnival
This town enjoys celebratory events and the frequency of these increased following the First World War. King Athelstan's Millenary was celebrated in June 1924 with a united church service in the Abbey followed by *the largest and most representative ... procession seen in the old town within living memory.* Participants included many Saxon characters accompanied by Councillors, commoners and other local groups. The procession started at the Secondary School and ended at Burton Hill House where a play was enacted. The following year a Hospital Fete and Old World Fair was held to raise funds for the new Cottage Hospital, organised by Joe Moore and Bill Wheadon. A carnival started the day's proceedings with the procession being marshalled in the Railway

Part of the 1924 procession at the Town Bridge with the Mercians in front! (Athelstan Museum)

Hotel meadow *and it made its way through the profusely decorated streets of the town to the fete grounds* at Burton Hill House. The cavalcade was headed by the Town Band and *was made up of groups and individual "characters," which by reason of their general originality and ingenuity were to provide a sight that was not only pleasing in effect, but was also to give the judges much food for thought later on.* At Burton Hill there were stalls, an auction of farm produce, a 'Gypsy Encampment' for fortune telling, a demonstration by a police-dog, bowling for a pig, folk dancing, side shows, a children's playground, performances of the Royal Wiltshire Yeomanry & Town Bands and a tea tent, finishing with Nicholls' amusement park. More than £400 was raised. In 1926 Mrs. Eleanor Ramsay organised a fancy dress parade and carnival in the hospital grounds. The child competitors then paraded into town. This event took place simultaneously with the hospital Pound Day. On Pound Day 1927 the children in fancy dress assembled in Cross Hayes and led by the Town Band processed via Oxford Street and the High Street to the hospital, collecting money on the way.

In 1928 elaborate arrangements were made for a carnival to raise funds towards restoration of the Abbey. This included a Mile of pennies and a contest for *the prettiest girl in and around Malmesbury*. Events went on for a week ending with a procession. This again started at the Railway Hotel and made its way to Cross Hayes where judging took place before proceeding to Burton Hill House. *All along the route the pavement was lined with pleasure-seeking spectators, all in happy mood. Next to the band came the highly-polished motor fire-engine, fully manned with firemen, under the command of Capt. E. F. E. Edwards. Its close attendant afforded a striking comparison; it was the antique fire-engine of the 16th century. Then followed the 160 competitors in the Carnival, representing characters of all sorts and description – a truly pretty spectacle.* The following year a children's carnival was held in the hospital grounds. The first annual hospital fete was held at Charlton Park in 1930 and comprised a children's fancy dress carnival, stalls and side shows representing each parish, folk dancing and band concerts. This was repeated for the next two years. In July 1933 this relocated to Cowbridge House. During the event Patrick Fry aged two crawled into the marquee where two young lions were loose and the young lad was badly clawed about the neck and face, which required 19 stitches. These fetes raised £217 15s. 10d. in 1930, £241 18s. 11d. in 1931, £302 5s. 4d. in 1932 and £312 in 1933.

Just a month later an "Olde World Fayre" and Carnival was held in the town centre – this is now regarded as being the first Carnival. On the Friday the first Carnival Queen was crowned – the Mayor was handed a large envelope containing the winner's name, however it contained another envelope and another until the innermost was found to reveal that Miss Joan Wilkins had been chosen. After the crowning, two cars took the Queen on a tour of the town before she returned to the Town Hall to start the dance. The following day the procession began in the Railway Hotel's meadow and proceeded to Cross Hayes. *Not for thirty years has Malmesbury seen such crowds as thronged the main streets of this ancient borough last Saturday, the occasion of a carnival held in aid of the Malmesbury and District Hospital and the Royal Agricultural Benevolent Institution. Not that a carnival is any novelty in Malmesbury, such a function having been held for many years in connection with the annual hospital fete and similar ventures.* Prizes were awarded for the best characters in a number of different categories.

The 1934 programme was similar, on Friday the Queen's crowning and a dance, with the procession on Saturday followed by another dance with more than £188 raised. In subsequent years further events were added, the publication of the Carnival handbook, Rogers funfair in Cross Hayes, sports matches, a confetti fight and by 1937 Carnival ran from Monday to Saturday. The 1939 Carnival took place just before the outbreak of war between 11th and 24th August with a wide variety of events including a Flitch Trial (where four couples tried to demonstrate they had lived in harmony for a year), several dances, a baby show, a Tug-of-war contest with teams drawn from a wide area (the winners being Monmouth County Police), Comic sports, Athelstanio (Bernard Basevi) escaping from shackles underwater in the river and a Rag cricket match. There were fairylights in the High Street and floodlighting of the Market Cross, Steeple and Abbey. During the war the Carnival did not take place but many similar events were arranged during war savings weeks.

The Carnival funfair in Cross Hayes, 1937. (Athelstan Museum)

Eilmer on a Carnival float passing Bailey Brothers in the 1960s. A Morris Minor post van can just be seen through the recently widened Post Office entrance. (Athelstan Museum)

In September 1952 the Carnival was revived by a committee chaired by E. A. Hider. A week of events included a Fair, Carnival Queen competition, dances, Grand Sports Day (soap box derby, pram race and conventional sport), cricket match, male voice choir, football match, fencing display, Any Questions, gang show, Youth play, Ball, whist drive, Rogers funfair, confetti battle, with the procession on Saturday. A lorry with 'Jackdaws' toured the villages to advertise the carnival. A record sum of more than £500 was raised with £400 set aside for the swimming pool. Over the following years more innovations were introduced – talent contests, wall of pennies, the programme with tradesmen's adverts in doggerel sold for 6d., six-a-side cricket tournament, an athletic meeting (but it was not until 1956 that Malmesbury had a club to join this competition), shop window dressing and spot the mistake. Candidates for Queen were chosen in each village, often associated with a fund-raising dance.

The Flower Show which had been defunct for 30 years was revived in 1956. American softball teams came from USAF Brize Norton and Fairford and there was a car scavenge hunt. The next year there was a Midsummer Ball at Charlton Park in June. A Crown was bought for the Queen to compete for the title of Wiltshire's Carnival Queen which was held for the first time. Our Queen, Sheelagh Orrit, also won the County title starting the town's enviable record in that contest having three winners and three runners-up over the next eight years. Since the war most of the proceeds had been allocated to the swimming pool fund and £2,500 had been invested in 3½% war stock which unfortunately was not worth the price paid. Even after the pool was opened in 1961 the Carnival continued to provide funds to pay off the loan and then finance a toddlers' pool.

Innovations continued – a barbeque in St. Aldhelm's Mead, a swimming gala, the RAF Royal Tournament team re-enacted Eilmer's flight, Anthony Smith whose flight over Africa was shown on BBC TV, flew from Bremilham School in the only privately owned balloon in UK, a free-fall parachutist (sky diver), a Donkey Derby, model railway exhibition and a scheme to permanently

150

floodlight the Abbey carried out by Linolite. Petticoat Lane started in 1970 but five years later the new vicar, Peter Barton, objected to this being held on Sunday. It was suggested it was in breach of the Shops Act 1950 but after several years it was confirmed the Act did not apply. In 1973 the funfair moved from Cross Hayes to Station Yard. During the 1970s money was donated for children's play equipment, to the Hospital League of Friends for their ambitious projects and for improvements in the Town Hall.

In 1983 £3,112 was raised and the amount steadily increased to £10,360 in 1997. The causes supported included Athelstan Players' clubhouse, Burton Hill School's field studies centre, equipment for the new Cartmell Centre, Christmas lights, new Town Hall lift, Malmesbury Victoria's clubhouse, Marlins swimming club, the hospital's physiotherapy centre, primary school computers, resuscitation equipment for the town's ambulances and the Cartmell minibus. It became difficult to persuade sufficient candidates to enter for the Carnival Queen competition and in 1990 the contest was cancelled although it was revived once five years later. Younger girls competed to become the Carnival Princess instead. In 1994 it was decided to change the funfair operator from the Rogers family who had run it for 60 years to Danters. David Rogers sought an injunction, claiming the fee paid included a deposit for the following year. The injunction was denied but funds were frozen for more than a year until the claim was dropped before it was heard in court.

In the new millennium Carnival continues to proper. Dances no longer feature in the programme but events are scheduled over a month and annual receipts total more than £20,000. Two attempts to set a world record for participants in a pillow fight failed and an ambitious scheme for a Party in the Park lost a very considerable amount. In 2011 Carnival became a charity.

Malmesbury Civic Trust
Malmesbury Civic Trust was formed in July 1963 to fight a proposed development at Daniel's Well. The society promotes Civic Pride, being a guardian of local history and the countryside. Its motto is CONSERVE THE BEST AND IMPROVE THE REST.

A major achievement was to establish the hugely popular Riverwalk, connecting public footpaths with permissive paths in 1972/3. Every year running repairs are performed on stiles, walkways and paths and a major refurbishment of the southern part of the Riverwalk was carried out in 2013. For several years the rivers were cleared. A donation of £3,000 was given to the River Valleys Trust to help buy Conygre Mead. In early years it published the first modern Residents' Guide to services in the town together with leaflets on river and town guided walks. Other books include *Malmesbury Then and Now* for the Millennium, *Our Glorious Dead* (WW1), *Malmesbury versus Hitler* (WW2) and *An Historical Guide to Malmesbury*. The latest publication is *The Walls and Defences of Malmesbury* in conjunction with the Friends of Athelstan Museum. Hundreds of buildings were photographed in 1964 and these are lodged with the English Heritage Archive. A similar set was taken in 2000.

Its conservation principles were promoted by renewing the Town Hall Wesleyan Room windows and repairing the stained-glass window there, refurbishing the Town Hall War Memorials and more recently donating funds towards the United Reformed Church turret repair. By leading the Conservation Area Management Plan team, the society pushed for this to become a Supplementary Planning Document. To improve the town, trees were planted in Corn Gastons and it has twice paid for the planting of trees in Cross Hayes. Members have repainted the railings near St. John's Bridge, various signs and other railings to enhance the appearance of the town. Feeling that the old Railway Station had been forgotten, an information sign was put on the Engine Shed. Every morning volunteers clear the litter from The Jubilee Garden (off Abbey Row) which is maintained for public use. The garden wall was partly destroyed by vandalism in 2012

The bridge over Burntheath stream in 1987. This was replaced for the Millennium using a metal framework taken from Arches Farm's old milking parlour.

and had to be repaired. To promote Malmesbury numerous Town Tours have been undertaken for visitors and residents alike. Annually a new Walk and Talk has been given for Carnival funds. The new Museum was supported by funds in the initial years and now by donating publications for them to sell.

Malmesbury and District Twinning Association
During the early 1950s the Government wanted to encourage youth exchanges with our zone of control in Germany. Wiltshire was linked with Schleswig-Holstein and Malmesbury matched with Niebüll. Cyril Cartmell arranged for a group of 16 children and two adults to be hosted here in July 1954. Mr. Cartmell was brought up in South Shields and suffered a wartime disabling head wound. Whilst working as a typewriter salesman he discovered an aptitude for community work. In 1949 he was appointed as Malmesbury's Youth Officer and founded a Youth Club which met in Westport School until the County Council leased the top two floors of the British Legion Club, Ingram Street in 1951. The Westport Congregational Church also started a club led by Mr. & Mrs. Duke so when a group of 17 young people aged between 14 and 23 visited Niebüll in 1955 they were accompanied by Mr. & Mrs. Cartmell and the Dukes. Peter Kruse, a schoolteacher, was the main organiser in Niebüll. At first there was *some ignorant opposition*, but several of those involved in the early exchanges kept in touch with each other in the following years. Other Wiltshire exchanges have not lasted as long.

After a funding crisis in the early 1970s Malmesbury Town Council proposed a formal twinning agreement between the towns in 1975 and the document was signed the following year in our Town Hall. The search for a French twin found a village called Saint-Molf in southern Brittany. Councillor Ken Silveston discovered in 1988 it is associated with Maildulph. Links continued for around 10 years but Gien in Loiret was chosen instead. An agreement was signed with Gien in 2000 at the Market Cross.

Malmesbury, Cape Province, South Africa was named in honour of the first Lord Malmesbury in 1827. The first official communication between the two towns seems to have been a letter from South Africa in March 1945 requesting a greeting from Wiltshire for presentation to Field Marshal Jan Smuts when he attended the Malmesbury Country Fair near his birthplace. This was duly despatched and a further exchange led to the Freedom being conferred on the Field Marshal that May. Due to his worldwide commitments he was not able to be presented with his scroll in London for another two years. For many years there was infrequent contact – Mayor Herbert Avis sent them congratulations in 1960 when they celebrated the centenary of the establishment of the South African municipality; the two Mayors celebrated a new South African automatic telephone exchange in 1976 by speaking to each other and a few visitors came here. However since Councillor Ray Sanderson visited South Africa in 1997 there have been many exchange visits and a Friendship Agreement was signed in 2006.

Another town, Bad Hersfeld in central Germany, has sought closer ties because St. Lullus, a missionary from Malmesbury, is commemorated there with the Lullusfest every October on the anniversary of his death. The festival has been celebrated since 852.

Malmesbury River Valleys Trust
Conygre Mead, meaning rabbit field, provided a source of meat for the Abbey's monks. In modern times it was used as pasture and wells provided a water supply for the town in the late 19th and early 20th Centuries. Then the Borough used it as a rubbish tip from 1963 to 1967. The Council sold it in 1972 with planning permission for 11 houses which fortunately did not go ahead. In 1992 Malmesbury River Valleys Trust was formed with the intention of purchasing Conygre Mead and preserving it as a public open space. The Trust was able to buy it for £25,000, financed by a £11,700 loan, grants of £10,000 from North Wilts District Council, £3,000 from Malmesbury Civic Trust with contributions from the Preservation Trust, Forrester & Forrester and Jeary & Lewis. The loan was repaid within two years with help from Malmesbury Carnival (£3,500) and many private donations. The actors John Thaw (1942-2002), who lived in Luckington, and James Grout (1927-2012) were Patrons.

Members of the Trust work on the Mead on the first Sunday morning of each month and hold regular Schools Weeks to educate young people about the range of flora and fauna. In 2005 it was designated as a Local Nature Reserve.

Malmesbury and St. Paul Without Residents' Association
This society was formed in 1984 when Linolite announced plans to move from Postern Mill. Letters were sent to the residents of Kingswall, Burnivale, Lower High Street and Bristol Street inviting them to a meeting. Major Reginald Freeman-Thomas was the first Chairman. It was soon decided that membership should be open to the whole town. They opposed residential development at the old Linolite site and extra houses at Reeds Farm in 1994. The Association now involves itself in all aspects of community life, monitoring and commenting on planning applications, highway and safety issues and assisting residents to improve their local amenities.

Malmesbury and Sherston Branch Royal British Legion
The ex-servicemen who returned to Malmesbury after the First World War wanted to improve opportunities for leisure activities and in May 1919 formed the Ivy Branch of the National Federation of Discharged and Demobilised Sailors and Soldiers. The Federation had been founded in April 1917 by the radical Liberal MP, James Hogge who was opposed to the notion that any man capable of civilian work must be fit for military service. Unfortunately it also had a strong anti-officer bias, only being open to other ranks. In Malmesbury the branch initially attracted more than 100 members under the chairmanship of ex-Sergeant Sidney Kite. Within a year membership of the Federation was rapidly declining and a branch of Comrades of the

Some original members of the British Legion branch with a Silver War Badge which was awarded to all servicemen who were discharged due to disability. (Derek Tilney)

Great War was proposed. Although this was open to all ex-servicemen, was non-political and non-sectarian, it had receiving funding from Conservative Party supporters but its main purposes were welfare and remembrance. At the end of June 1920 Charles Gale, who had been a founder of the Federation branch, led the formation of a post of the Comrades. This quickly attracted 69 new members and 38 were transferred from Cirencester. Lt. Col. Morrice was commandant and the committee contained a number of officers but also included ex-Sgt. Maj. W. G. Perry, Sgt. Bunting & Charles Gale. The Comrades supported the Lord Kitchener Memorial Homes in Chatham, Kent for those needing a change of air.

Both of these local organisations closed in anticipation of the formation of the British Legion. The Federation part-funded an outing for members to Cheddar Gorge & Weston super Mare but was wound up in June 1921. The Comrades closed that July, giving £5 to Arthur Pike who was paralysed and £8 3s. to the Cottage Hospital. In November the British Legion branch was formed with Major Holland as Chairman. One of the first social activities arranged was a boxing match in the Town Hall in 1922, a precursor to the formation of the Boxing Club. The Legion decided to form a social club and lease the premises at 9 Ingram Street formerly occupied by Frederick Hughes, a builder. Membership built up slowly until in 1929 36 new members brought the total to 86 ex-servicemen plus 80 honorary members, civilians and women.

In 1930 the branch had its Standard dedicated. Membership continued to rise and from 24 June 1933 a new clubroom was opened in premises lent by Percy Jackson in Cross Hayes behind No. 12 High Street, which it intended to purchase. This move was timely as two years later the old Ingram Street clubhouse collapsed! A wider range of social activities including billiards and skittles was now possible. Welfare became more important and in August 1939 parties of children were sent to a holiday camp in Brislington near Burnham on Sea. The Legion played a part in the preparation for war by encouraging recruitment, particularly for the expanding Territorial Army, and providing members for local defence. Considerable sums were raised during the war by selling refreshments in the club.

At the end of the war Sir Richard Luce offered to buy the Social Centre in Ingram Street for the Legion. 50 new members joined and a Welcome Home Fund was set up. Membership increased to more than 300 and an active social programme began with a Rally in 1947 followed by a week of fundraising around Remembrance Day. The following year the Women's Section was founded led by Mrs. Besly. Major Anthony Turnor became President in 1950. Fetes were held in the grounds of the Grammar School and a children's party was held annually at St. Joseph's School in the early 1950s. However the clubhouse needed repairs and was not well supported. The subscription for using the club rose from 6d. per annum to 3s. in addition to the ordinary membership fee of 3s. Wiltshire County Council's Youth Club was paying rent and contributing to repairs and renewals. But the club continued to lose money so it was closed in 1956 although the other uses carried on. The following year the children were treated to a cinema show instead of a Christmas party.

At the beginning of the 1960s Malmesbury was one of the strongest branches in Wiltshire and this was confirmed by it being awarded the Countess of Suffolk Cup for Efficiency. In 1962 Lady Eva Scott McKirdy presented a Cup for the best Standard bearer in the Malmesbury group of branches. There were also cups awarded for branch players in the Skittles League. Other activities included a Thrift Club which allowed members to save for Christmas, Drumhead services, arranging the County conference here and the planting of a tree in memory of Jack Grimes close to the Memorial Garden. Membership slipped below 300 and by 1974 it was less than 200. In 1972 repairs were required to the Youth Club for which £500 had to be raised. An association was formed with the Wroughton Silver Band which performed a Remembrance concert and this event still continues as a fundraiser.

Derek Tilney became chairman in 1974 and a public bench was placed at Burton Hill. The next year the Women's section had a new Standard and a Field of Remembrance of wooden crosses was laid outside the Abbey for the first time. The Countess of Suffolk Cup was retained. Branches had been formed in villages around the town such as Brinkworth, Crudwell (closed 1978), Great Somerford, Hullavington, Sherston (pre-WW2 & 1946-2008) and Sutton Benger, but many of these had closed. Membership in the 1970s was around 170 but this has slowly decreased to nearer 60. For several years premises were rented from the Town Council at 34 Cross Hayes until around 1980. The Ingram Street premises became unsafe and Wiltshire County Council's lease for the Youth Club expired in 1986. The building was then sold and converted into flats. In 2009 the Sherston branch closed and amalgamated with Malmesbury.

It seems that Malmesbury has always celebrated the Armistice with an afternoon service. In 1920 *Sunday was specially observed as Armistice Sunday, and at the afternoon service in the Abbey about a hundred discharged and demobilised soldiers attended.*

St. Aldhelm Lodge No. 2888, Freemasons, Silver Street

This, one of the largest lodges in Wiltshire, had its origins at an informal meeting at the Bell Hotel in 1900. Henry Hewer, manager of the Capital and Counties Bank, suggested to Joe Moore, the Old Bell's proprietor, that the town should have a Masonic Lodge. Baldemero de Bertodano, a wealthy retired solicitor of Spanish descent who lived at Cowbridge House and already held Grand rank, agreed to help. At the beginning of 1901 a dozen prospective members petitioned for one. After some delay it was consecrated with a service in the Abbey in the summer of 1902. The first Master was Baldemero de Bertodano. Unfortunately Bro. Hewer was transferred to

Spilsby, Lincolnshire before the consecration.

In 1906 the St. Aldhelm Chapter was formed with members from all over Wiltshire. In 1925 the Lodge became the only 'Hall Stone' Lodge in Wiltshire following its donation of £525 towards the new Masonic Hall in London. This was part of the Masonic Million Memorial Fund and was to be the Peace Memorial Hall. This was completed in 1937 but was renamed Freemasons Hall in 1939 after the peace had been shattered. Lodge meetings continued at the Old Bell Hotel for many years until the end of World War II when the Town Hall became a temporary and inconvenient home. In 1958 the Freemasons moved to the Old Independent Chapel in Silver Street where considerable works have been carried out over the years. The Chapel and the cottage next door were purchased in 1974. The Lodge is a very successful charity fundraiser, for example having raised £25,000 in the late 1990s.

Benefit Societies
Before the advent of the Welfare State there were many local societies offering sickness and death benefits (often called Friendly Societies) or simply providing a means of savings, known as Thrift Clubs. There were Friendly Societies associated with public houses including the George Inn, which had 200 members in the 1840s, the Castle Inn and the Three Cups. The Primitive Methodist Society closed in 1929 after experiencing an expensive year and not having admitted any new members since the passage of the National Insurance Act 1911. In 1922 a United Committee was formed of four friendly societies – the Ancient Order of Foresters, the Royal Antediluvian Order of Buffaloes, the Cirencester Conservative Benefit Society and the Church Benefit Society, with the object of raising funds for a friendly society bed in the hospital. A successful fete was held in 1922 but the next two years were dogged by bad weather and the idea was abandoned.

King Athelstan Club
This Benefit Society was founded in 1840 and outlasted most of the other local clubs. On its formation it was hoped *it will not interfere with the old clubs which are so deservedly popular.* Members had to pay contributions which averaged 7s. 6d. per quarter which entitled them to sickness benefit of 10s. per week for six months followed by 5s. for the remainder of the absence from work. There was also a death benefit of £5 although this was funded by a 2s. levy on each member. The National Insurance Act 1911 sounded the death knell for societies of this type as the weekly benefits were very similar but instead of paying approximately 7d. per week to the club, workers had to pay 4d., employers 3d. and 2d. was provided from general taxation. However the King Athelstan Club differed in that every three years the surplus was distributed to members, the last dividend being £2 17s. Another aspect of the club was the annual dinner held at first in the White Lion, then the Bell and finally the George. The club was wound up in 1915.

Court King Athelstan No. 3000, Ancient Order of Foresters (AOF)
This branch was formed on 13 July 1858 in the Kings Arms with Thomas Jones, the publican, Samuel Fowler and Samuel Barkham as founder members. The AOF was founded in 1834 and the King Athelstan Court was part of its Bristol United District. The Court's base moved to the White Lion in the 1860s, the George, the Bell at the start of the 20th Century, the George until 1914 and back to the White Lion about 1918 until closure. The highlight of each year was the annual dinner, attended by a large number of members and distinguished guests. In the 1890s membership peaked at around 280 but declined thereafter. The AOF became an Approved Society to administer National Insurance benefits until 1947 when the state took over.

The Kembro field off Cowage Road was bought as an investment for £400 to be used as allotments but it was sold in 1923 for £205. During the influenza epidemic of 1927 in one month 30 members claimed sick pay of £83 6s. 6d. and three member's wives died making a total benefit paid of £107 6s. 6d., the highest monthly payout. The following year the Court complained about the new scale of Doctors' fees resulting in all four practitioners withdrawing their services. In the 1930s members were able to use convalescence homes free of all expenses, three of which were owned by the AOF. The Court's surplus allowed sick pay to be increased to £1 weekly. The State members were administered from Bristol after 1936 and local membership dropped from around 80 during the Second World War to less than 50 in the 1950s. At the end of 1961 the Court closed with the remaining members transferred to Bristol. The AOF's successor, the Foresters Friendly Society, still operates.

Malmesbury Lodge, Cirencester Conservative Benefit Society

The Cirencester Working Men's Conservative Association Benefit Society was founded in 1890 and the Malmesbury Lodge opened two years later. It was founded on the Holloway principle whereby each member had an individual account which increased through subscription, interest and dividends which at the age of 65 would provide a lump sum. Some elements of insurance were included such as the provision of death benefits for members and their wives. In 1914 the Lodge had 604 members and in the previous year contributions amounted to £423 18s. 11d. and £103 had been disbursed in sick pay, with members' funds totalling £3,531 16s. 10d. In addition a reserve fund of £3,000 was held. A man under 30 could subscribe 7d. per month to insure himself for £10, his wife for £5 and be entitled to 2s. 6d. per week sick pay. The Lodge's meeting place was the Parish Room, Silver Street which held their War Memorial recording the names of 140 members who served their country including 13 who died. This is now displayed in the Town Hall. It is not clear when the Society ceased operating through Lodges (certainly after 1951) and it is now called the Cirencester Friendly Society.

Malmesbury Lodge, G.L.E., No. 3763 and Athelstan Lodge, No. 8333, Royal Antediluvian Order Buffaloes (RAOB)

The RAOB was founded in 1822 by stage hands and theatre technicians in London. It is a charitable rather than a benefit society although it does provide educational grants and convalescent facilities for members and their dependents. This Lodge was inaugurated on 8 August 1921 under the Worthy Primo Brother E. F. E. Edwards, S. N. Dixon, city secretary and F. C. Canham, city

Members of the Royal Ancient Order of Buffaloes about to lay their wreath at the Triangle War Memorial in 1924. The Castle Inn is in the background. (Athelstan Museum)

minstrel. They quickly grew to 80 members who met at the George Hotel. Much fund raising activity, particularly for the hospital, was carried out during the 1930s. However the Lodge closed in 1948.

On 16 May 1951 the movement was revived by the formation of the Athelstan Lodge (Malmesbury) No. 8333 under Primo F. H. Speiser at the Three Cups. During the 1950s they held children's tea parties and Church parades, in 1959 200 brothers wearing their regalia marched behind the Wiltshire Air Training Corps band to the Abbey. Their base moved to the Railway Hotel and in 1962 Bob Arnold who played Tom Forrest in the Archers read the lesson at one of their services in the Congregational Church. The Lodge's 25th anniversary was celebrated in 1976. They finally closed in 2004.

Malmesbury and District Branch of the Hospital Contributory Scheme

Known as the Hospital Savings Association this national society was launched in 1922 and was introduced to Malmesbury in 1930 by Cecil Moore (1889-1945) of 8 St. Mary's Street. Membership grew quickly so that by the end of 1936 there were 1,300 contributors representing every parish in the area. *The purpose of this Contributory Scheme is to provide for our local hospital a steady regular income and at the same time guarantees that any contributor or his dependants requiring hospital treatment shall be provided with the same, without any inquiry as to means, or being subjected to any charges. Should a contributor be treated outside Malmesbury, the charges are met by the Contributory Scheme. Assistance is also given for Ambulance Services, Optical Treatment and Convalescent Homes.* Provided a single man earned less than £4 a week or £5 if married the subscription was just 3d. per week. Contributors would be given a green voucher to show their entitlement and if they attended a 'non-co-operating' hospital had their contributions refunded. The National Health Service brought the main purpose of the scheme to an end so in 1949 members were transferred to the Bristol and West Health Service Fund provided subscriptions were up to date on 5th July 1948. The Hospital Savings Association is now part of Simplyhealth UK, a health insurance company.

Sports Clubs

Malmesbury Amateur Boxing Club

In January 1923 the new Malmesbury Boxing Club held its first competition in the Town Hall which attracted a full house. Charles Jones (1898-1975) was one of the founders as well as being a competitor. He had been sent out to Canada in 1912 and served as a Mountie before he deserted and joined the Canadian Army. When the war ended he returned to his home in Brinkworth, working for Dore Fielder & Company, auctioneers with offices in Swindon and Malmesbury. He competed successfully as a heavy-weight and organised many local tournaments. The club it faded away before World War II but in 1947 Malmesbury Junior Boxing Club was formed at the Social Centre, Ingram Street with Arthur Rogers as trainer. They quickly enrolled 58 active members and at one of their first contests at Devizes won all the bouts. There were senior matches held

Members of the Boxing Club in the late 1940s. Charles Jones is the adult on the right.

in the Town Hall but it was not until 1954 that the adults' club was revived by Arthur Rogers. They were permitted by Linolite to train in the Malting Hall at the Postern Mill, however in 1957 interest waned and the club was wound up. Their trophies were handed to the Youth Club which had a gymnasium in their Ingram Street premises. Attempts were made to re-form the club with training facilities provided by RAF Hullavington in 1961.

In 1977 Fred Wartnaby and Eric Lewis, an ex-boxer, formed the Malmesbury & Brokenborough Boxing Club, although the name was soon shortened. Originally they trained in the primary school gym and the next year held the first contest in the Town Hall. In 1980 their base moved to the newly renamed Cartmell Centre in Ingram Street. Two years later the club had such a good reputation it attracted members from all parts of North Wiltshire and had to close its doors to new senior members. Ranalagh Gates produced a portable ring at cost price, £750 rather than £2,000. However the first and second floors at Ingram Street were closed as a safety measure and in 1986 the club had to move out. After a short period when the boxers had to travel to Swindon for training, the club leased some land at the football field from the Town Council. They built their own gym costing £20,000, which opened in September 1987. The club now has an enviable record and is probably the best in the South West with youngsters getting to the last stages of many national competitions. Just two of the many successes are: Ranje 'Tiger' Singh who became the ABA novice national champion in 1996 but tragically died in 2002; Joe Hughes after winning a series of titles became the ABA light welterweight champion in 2010 and at the time of writing is hoping to re-launch his career. Tony Stannard, the team's coach since 1977, was awarded an MBE in 2006. In 2011 Mrs. S. Winstone, mother of a young boxer, was instrumental in raising £20,000 to make the clubhouse flood proof by rebuilding the floor well above ground level.

Malmesbury Bowls Club

The Malmesbury Bowls Club was formed in 1908 as a spin off from the Cricket Club. It seems early games were played on the cricket outfield following matches. Harry Jones, landlord of the Kings Arms was President, forty 10s. shares were issued to meet capital expenditure and the annual subscription was 7s. 6d. The first ground was on the Kings Arms' meadow, the area to the north of Holloway now occupied by Abbots Gardens. In 1912 the present ground, Little Mead near Wynyard Mill, was leased from Tom Rich for seven years at £6 per annum and improvements costing £12 were paid out of revenue. It was resolved to set aside part as a croquet lawn for ladies with the use of one pavilion and wives of members were invited to join. There were 40 members, B. de Bertodano presented a Challenge Cup and it was proposed to form a League of clubs within a 20/30 mile radius.

After the First World War the number of members varied between 30 and 40 even after the annual subscription increased to 10s 6d. Walter T. Clark renewed the lease although the annual payment doubled to £12. In 1921 the club joined the Swindon group of the Wiltshire County Bowling Association. In 1932 £250 was paid for the renovation of the green using turf from the Marlborough Downs.

Following the Second World War L. W. Besly, the Midland Bank manager, was President but in

The new Bowls Club pavillion in 1964.

1952 was succeeded by Alfred Beuttell, Linolite's founder. In 1958 they entered the national championship of the English Bowling Association (EBA) for the first time and the team included 83 year-old Bill Kaynes (1876-1963). Two years later Mr. Beuttell provided £300 to buy the freehold of the ground. In 1963 Ben Aylward and Raymond Avis become County Pairs Champions, the Club's previous pair of the finalists having been in 1926. In 1964 the new pavilion, costing £300, was opened but flooding led to the ground being unusable two seasons later.

The 1970s was a decade of great success. A full time club steward was appointed and in 1974 part of the river was filled in to construct two new rinks to make a total of six, costing £3,000. An extension was added to the pavilion to provide a larger bar & better toilets. In 1975 the Ladies section was formed and the club had its highest success to date – reaching the County final of the four-rink league, twelve members represented the County and there was good representation in EBA competitions. However the following year this record was surpassed when a team of four men won the National 2-Fours Trophy, being only the second national title to come to Wiltshire and the County 3 rink league was also won. Many other successes have occurred since.

In 1985 an automatic sprinkler system was installed using river water and there were 100 members. The club spearheaded a plan for a large leisure complex on Conygre Mead but this was to be part funded by building three houses on the Baskerville ground. Planning permission was refused and an appeal lost so the plan did not proceed. In 2000 play was interrupted by a streaker and in the new Millennium considerable money has had to be spent repairing damage caused by floods.

Malmesbury Cricket Club
In an early edition of the Wilts and Gloucestershire Standard it reported in 1838 that Malmesbury Cricket Club met for the first time on the Marsh – *The ground is decidedly bad, but we understand another piece will be selected previous to the next meeting.* Another match was played off the Chippenham Road. Other contests took place against a Swindon team, won by Malmesbury and 'married' versus 'singles' teams. Matches were sometimes followed by dinner at the White Lion Inn, at least one of which was hosted by Thomas Luce.

In 1867 the club practised on the Wortheys and Walter Powell MP presented a marquee. In 1880 Malmesbury Amateur Cricket Club had supper at the George Hotel as the season's finale. This event was repeated for the next two years and in 1882 it was reported *The M.C.C., which since the last season has undergone an infusion of new blood and spirit, intends commencing the season ... on the ground of the old club in the "Worthies"* ... The following year the dinner was in the Kings Arms held jointly with Malmesbury Amateur Dramatic Society. Consideration was given to the formation of a club for the working classes, which was not intended to supersede or compete with MCC, to be called the Athelstan Cricket Club but it does not seem to have gone further. Sir Richard Pollen presided at dinners in 1885 and 1886. In 1893 the club restarted under the presidency and patronage of Charles Charrington (1859-1936), who was connected to the brewing family and lived at Burton Hill House. He provided considerable financial support so that in 1895 an unnamed professional player provided coaching; bowling to members on Thursdays & Saturdays between 3pm and 5pm, on Mondays, Tuesdays, Wednesdays & Fridays from 6pm and general coaching on Thursday & Saturday evenings. Thomas Reed, Harry Jones, Arthur Forrester as well as Sir Richard Pollen were amongst the prominent supporters. However by 1899 Charles Charrington had left and as he had previously paid for the groundsman after 1901 no professional was engaged. There was heavy expenditure particularly for fencing and enlarging the ground at the Wortheys. The Suffolk family were great supporters and at a dinner Lady Suffolk said *the fact that our initials, M.C.C., are the same as those of the greatest cricket club there is, ought to be an incentive to rise to fame.* In 1908 the Bowls Club began as an offshoot from the Cricket Club.

However the relationship between the clubs quickly deteriorated, for example it was maintained two sets of Bowls had not been paid for and the Cricket Club demanded them back. However in 1911 the Cricket Club had a dearth of members with only an average of five regular players. It was closed, the proceeds of the sale of stock and effects were kept in a bank account for future use.

It was not until 1932 that the Club was re-formed, the advertisement for the first meeting reading *Non-Members of the Filands Cricket Club, who are interested in cricket, will be welcomed.* The Filands Club played at the Grange on Crudwell Road. Reginald Forrester, a Wiltshire County cricketer, was elected the MCC president and the £30 in the old club's bank account was put to use. The Honourable C. W. S. Douglas of Elm Croft offered a field and the next year entered into a seven year lease – *after a lapse of so many years, it is hoped that the fame of the Malmesbury Club will be revived.* Play seems to have continued throughout the 1930s but at the 1940 Annual General Meeting it was reported the lease had expired, with no possibility of renewal. It was hoped the Secondary School field could be used. However activity seems to have ended for the duration of the war.

In March 1947 a new pitch was established on St. Aldhelm's Mead, previously used for agriculture. However the following year the Club was released from this lease. At the start of the next decade matches were reported on the Wortheys after which Sunday evening services were held there by Rev. Beaghen. In 1951 it was stated it had taken four years to bring the Wortheys ground

The Cricket Team of 1948 - the first post-war year of play on the Wortheys. The two players in the front row on the right are Jack Ellett and Trevor Richards. (Malmesbury Cricket Club)

back from pasture. A tent was used for teas which children damaged by sliding down the sides, leading to four youngsters appearing in the Juvenile Court. In 1954 it was said *no-one – that is during the life of the present club's life of seven seasons – has yet hit a century on Malmesbury Cricket Club ground at the Wortheys. Centuries have been hit by Malmesbury batsmen but always in away matches*. That year there was a Carnival cricket competition which in glorious summer weather attracted the biggest crowds ever. That same year Jack Ellett (1905-1954) died having served as captain for seven years, being the *backbone of cricket in Malmesbury*. Nevertheless the team had a good year winning both the Malmesbury and Tetbury six-a-side knock out trophies. Five years later Trevor Richards (1912-1975), the retiring captain, was lauded for not only having looked after the ground for many years but also being an excellent player. In one match a victory target of 103 was set but Malmesbury were 52 for 4 when Richards came in to face a bowler who had taken 2 for 2. He hit 26 in one over, scoring 47 not out in 12 scoring strokes which included 4 sixes and 4 fours.

The 1960s began with difficulty persuading players to take the captaincy of the three teams, E. A. Hider said *we have a wonderful ground, we have bags of money and yet no one wants to be captain.* However within two years the playing record markedly improved, the 1962 season was said to have been most exceptional – there had been the biggest glut of runs ever known and the North West Wilts Knockout Cup was won for the second year running. Malmesbury was one of six leading clubs in Wiltshire and a licensed bar was wanted in the pavilion. A new clubroom was completed and a new scheme for younger players instituted. £1,700 was spent over 3 years without recourse to loans or grants with most being spent on the clubhouse. 1968 saw the club enter the Wiltshire League for the first time, having only competed in knock out cups previously. This entailed playing against larger towns and ground improvements were needed. Tom Graveney, Worcestershire's captain and Test player came to speak at that year's AGM and followed this up by bringing the full Worcester side to play at the Wortheys against an augmented Malmesbury side. Three test players were on the field that day.

The club was now playing a very high standard of cricket and in 1971 were runners up in the Wiltshire League and joint 4th in the first year of the Western League. The next season they were Champions of the Wiltshire League and winners of Wiltshire Knockout Trophy. Not content with this level of success they went on to win the Western League, a remarkable achievement as they overcame towns such as Cheltenham, Bath, Cardiff and Gloucester, winners again of Knockout Cup and the 2nd team won Wiltshire's Division 2. Richard Cooper, who played for Wiltshire and Somerset, contributed to these triumphs assisted by other talented players like John Scollen who played for the county. In 1975 Trevor Richards died, having been responsible for negotiating the return to the Wortheys after the war and also contributing much to its good state. Three years later the club again topped the Wiltshire League but resigned from it in order to concentrate on the more prestigious Western League.

The club was at its zenith during the 1980s winning the renamed Famous Grouse Western League in 1982 and 1985. At the Festival Week held at the Wortheys in 1983 Malmesbury lost to their more famous namesakes MCC but won against Gloucester Gypsies and a side representing the Western League. By 1990 the League had two divisions with each club having a team in each. Despite a thriving youth section there was a lack of interest in the senior game and the club's fortunes waned. The League has been reorganised into a pyramid structure called the West of England Premier League comprising two Premier Divisions at the top, two intermediate Divisions for the Counties of Bristol & Somerset and Gloucestershire & Wiltshire with lower Divisions in each County. Wiltshire has eight Divisions and Malmesbury's 1st XI play in Division 1 and the 2nd XI in Division 4. There is still a strong emphasis on coaching young players.

Malmesbury and District Darts League
Although darts has been played in public houses for a very long time it seems this league started around 1949. In the early years teams were drawn from the town's pubs such as the Bear, Black Horse, Borough Arms, Duke of York, Rose & Crown, Three Cups along with The Bowls, British

Legion and Gunners clubs. As well as the League championship there was also an individual 1001 competition, a Landlord's Cup and a Wooden Spoon for the team lowest in the league. Starting with around a dozen teams the league reached a zenith in the late 1980s when 29 teams competed in three divisions. Unfortunately in 1990 Tony Clarke, who had been secretary for 20 years, resigned and the league's fortunes began to decline. Skittles was increasingly popular and pubs found it difficult to run teams in both leagues. In 2013/14 only a handful of teams remain and one of these was lost with the closure of the Carpenters Arms, Sherston.

Malmesbury and District Skittles League

In June 1953 the Railway Hotel obtained the first licence for a skittle alley. At the time it was reported there were plenty of players but nowhere to play. The inaugural match was played between Malmesbury N.F.U. and a team from Stroud Brewery. In January the following year an alley opened at the Three Cups, followed quickly by another at the George. However it was not until 1956 that it was decided to form a league with teams from Ekco (A & B), Thomas Silvey & Co., Cricket Club, Three Cups, Young Farmers, Bowls Club, Somerford Show Committee, Railway Hotel and the Rifle Club. Leadership of the League rested with the Railway Hotel which laid on a Knockout competition which attracted teams outside the League. In 1958 20 teams, 14 from Malmesbury and six from Ashton Keynes, Oaksey and Minety competed for the Knockout Cup with only 10 clubs in the League. The League began to attract teams from outside the town – Lea, Minety, Sherston, Great Somerford, Brokenborough and Crudwell being among the first to join. By 1967 there were 23 teams playing in two divisions. The closure of pubs led to clubs having to move, for example the White Lion team went to the Duke of York. By 1985 there were five divisions each of 13 teams. Skittles became even more popular and during the 1990s nearly 100 teams competed in seven divisions. In the 2013/14 season 84 clubs competed in six divisions.

Malmesbury Tennis Club

It seems the Malmesbury Lawn Tennis Club was founded around the start of the 20th Century. In 1908 they played competitive matches against other clubs in Swindon and Chippenham. Courts were rented from Thomas Henry (1860-1949), a farmer who lived at the Gables, Crudwell Road and who had recently arrived in the locality. Clearly the club had some good players as they won more matches than they lost. During the 1920s membership increased and a second team played matches. In 1922 new courts were completed and 78 players entered an 'American' tournament which must have taken a long time as each participant had to play every other. Tournaments were arranged to raise funds for other causes like the hospital and YMCA but in the early 1930s whist drives and dances raised funds for the club. The reason for this was in 1935 £52 was paid for 53 roods and 31 perches of land at Tetbury Hill, the club's present site. The deed was signed by four young members, David Adye, Richard Stuart Travis Cole (known as Ivor), Donald Trevelyan Clark and George Guest, all under 21. Clinker was hauled by cart from the railway station providing the foundation for the new hard courts. In April 1936 the Gazette reported; *We hear that the courts near the cemetery at Tetbury Hill are now ready for play. It will be re-called that the courts of Mr. Henry on the Crudwell road have now been vacated, and games will now be carried on under the control of the Malmesbury Tennis Club.* Play was halted during the Second World War.

At the war's end a lot of hard work enabled the club to get back in action. However in 1952 the three courts at Tetbury Hill had to be resurfaced and members erected concrete posts to form a fence. Unfortunately it was proving difficult to retain members whose numbers halved in the next two years to 40. Sidney Adye retired as Chairman in 1955, having been a member for 54 years, over the years serving as Secretary, Treasurer and Chairman. He was presented with an inscribed clock and elected President. Visitors were able to play on the courts for a fee of 2s. 6d. per game from 1956 in an effort to attract new members, whilst subscriptions were held at 30s. per annum. One side effect of this was that more than half the members played for the club. Serious fundraising began in order to resurface and rewire the courts and in 1958 the courts were relaid with all weather "Red Griselda" on which play began in the following year. Subscriptions had to be increased by 50% and although the refurbishment cost nearly £1,000 it was reported the club had never been so prosperous. In 1960 it was grudgingly agreed to impose the Lawn Tennis Association's (L.T.A.) levy of 1s. per member. A new pavilion, a former builder's hut, which included a dressing room for the first time was provided the following year. Lack of senior members led to the club not enjoying competitive success in the mid 1960s but as the number of members rose successes followed. The Club joined the Chippenham and District League in 1970 and the Ladies team immediately won their league (only one Division) and the men won Division 3. The men were promoted and won Division 2 the next year and in 1974 won Division 1. The number of teams entered into the league has increased over the years and has grown to six or seven.

Junior membership increased and in 1991 they became county champions. The surface of the courts required considerable maintenance and play was limited to the summer months, so the bottom court was changed to a maintenance free surface in 1988. This allowed play all year round and fundraising began in earnest to raise £20,000. Membership of the L.T.A. paid dividends as they provided a substantial loan and grants enabling all three courts to be re-surfaced to the same standard by 1995. Flood lights were provided for the top two courts in 2004, extending still further the potential playing time. In 2012 Toby Rawlings, a professional, was recruited to oversee coaching as part of a major expansion plan. Adjoining land has been bought and planning permission has been obtained to add two junior courts with a new clubhouse.

Malmesbury Victoria Football Club

Football matches were played in the town during the 19th Century, for example a game against Marlborough was reported in 1876 but Malmesbury Town Football Club was formed around 1897. There was a 'grand' entertainment in the Town Hall to raise funds. Various matches were reported, most being played on the Wortheys. However in 1904 strenuous efforts were made to revive the club and play in the Chippenham League. Thomas Reed, the brewer from 32 Cross Hayes, provided financial help and presented a silver cup but there was still a small debt. In 1910 the team were runner up in the Chippenham League and joined the Vale of White Horse (VWH) League but Thomas Reed went to live in Swindon so his support was lost. During the First World War the club was unable to play but after the war's end the Town Football Club restarted. In 1920 they were winners of the VWH Challenge Cup and the following year they won the Chippenham & District League. The Malmesbury & District League was formed in 1923 when teams within nine miles of the Market Cross were invited to join. The Prince of Wales, who often stayed at Easton Grey House, subscribed to pay off the club's debt. The Malmesbury League now invited clubs within 12 miles to join and attracted 11 teams including those from Kington Langley, Tetbury, Avening, Crudwell, Sherston and Chippenham Reserves. They also ran competitions for the Cazalet Cup, Bonwick Shield, Stroud Brewery Cup and Malmesbury Cottage Hospital Cup. Malmesbury Town now played a reasonable standard of football and as a result in 1925 resigned from the Malmesbury League, playing instead in the Chippenham & District and VWH Leagues. In that season they won the VWH League and were finalists in the Cazalet Cup. In the late 1920s finance was again a problem and there was difficulty in finding a suitable pitch. Farmers wanted payment for the use of a field and one was found in Park Road. The decade drew to an end with the shortlived prospect of playing on the Wortheys, J. Mott was elected Captain at season end and the team was still in the VWH League. A new Thursday Football Club was founded to allow shopworkers to play when the shops were closed for their half day.

1930/1 began with the Town Club rejoining the Malmesbury League but their (un-named) ground was under water. W. Rich offered the Kings Wall field which was also used for the Colt Show. Other teams played at Daniels Well. The next season began with no ground, but George Guest offered a field free at Quobwell Farm on Tetbury Road a mile from town which was used for a number of seasons. At the Annual meeting held in the White Lion only 5 attended and it was postponed. The team won the Cazalet Cup, were 4th in the Malmesbury League and 3rd in the Chippenham League. For the following season the senior team joined the Wiltshire League, ending bottom and a Reserve team played in the Malmesbury League. In 1932/3 it was decided not to enter the Malmesbury League and so the team was unable to enter the local cup competitions. As a result the next year they entered the Wiltshire & England Amateur Cup. The Malmesbury League was less popular with only six teams and it seems to have been unable to attract sufficient clubs in 1934/5. The Thursday club was still playing and the Town first team played in Wiltshire Division 2 and the Reserves played in Chippenham's Division 2. Although the Club entered the FA Cup for the first time, at the Annual General Meeting in the White Lion on 9th June 1936 it was reported the club was running at a loss. Attendances were poor, new officers could not be found and the club was wound up. By August there were fowls in the grandstand at the Tetbury Road ground. It seems as though the Club was revived, as in 1939 it was reported to be recovering some of its former prosperity with a balance in hand. The war brought the club's activities to an end but several matches were played by a variety of teams so maintaining interest in the game.

Just after the war's end in September 1945 a match was arranged against Chippenham reserves and Jock Paterson, a prolific goal-scorer, played for the first time. That November a new ground was found at Moochers Lane, Milbourne. The next year Mr. Edmond allowed the Four & Twenty Steps field (behind the Avon Mill and named after the number of steps up to it) to be used for a few months. The Ekco Sports and Social Club had a team called the Colts which was in competition with the Town Football Club for players and a suitable ground. In 1948 both teams played at Corn Gastons. The following season the Town were winners of the VWH Cup for the second year running. The Ekco Colts broke away from the Sports and Social Club, becoming Malmesbury United in 1950. The Town team played in Wiltshire's Division 2 and the VWH Cup whilst United were in the Chippenham & District Youth League. Neither team had a permanent ground, both now playing on another field at Corn Gastons (due to be developed). Towards the end of the 1950/1 season it was agreed the clubs would formally amalgamate for the next season. After amalgamation the first team was in Wiltshire Division 2, the reserves in Chippenham Division 2 and the Colts in Chippenham Youth League. A new ground was found at Backbridge for 1952/3 described as *very good, better than we had before,* an enclosing wall was built and the pitch marked by players. £100 was paid for a dressing room hut. However this ground was only used for one season and a move was made to Bristol Road, near Silveston Way today. However this pitch was poorly drained and was unplayable in bad weather. The Reserve team had to withdraw from the Chippenham League after they had been promoted due to absentees on National Service and players being unfit through injury. The Club had difficulty in raising a single team and the lack of a pitch lowered morale. The Club had played at Milbourne, Burton Hill, St. Aldhelms Mead, Backbridge, Corn Gastons and Bristol Road since the war. However the Chubb family came to the rescue offering a ground at Whiteheath Farm, Corston which was gratefully accepted. The 1956/7 season was the best for 10 years ending runner up in Wiltshire Division 2. The next year three of the Club's players were chosen for the County team, brothers Brian and Kenneth Willis at inside left and right respectively and Don Lacey as centre forward. Wiltshire Division 2 was won and the Reserves moved from the Chippenham League into Wiltshire Division 2.

The 1960s began successfully for the Club. In 1961/2 they won Wiltshire Division 1 and were runners up for the next two seasons. However the state of the Corston pitch prevented entry into the Premier League. The Borough Council announced it was to buy two acres behind the Flying Monk from the brewery but there were restrictive covenants, whereby in the event of redevelopment the brewery would take the land back at agricultural price and no alcoholic drinks could be served on the site. However this land was flooded in December 1967 and again in 1969.

In 1970/1 the move from Corston was eagerly awaited and the Club was renamed Malmesbury United, but this name only lasted for a couple of years. £10 rent a year for 3 seasons was agreed for the Flying Monk but in February 1971 the pitch was *feet under water*. In 1974 a 15 year lease was agreed for £50 a year and in the 1973/4 season the Club teams won Wiltshire Division 1 and Division 2. The next season a new stand and fence were installed at the ground, an Under 12 team and the first team again won Division 1. However the ground was unsuitable for entry to the Wiltshire Combination. Before the 1975/6 season the Club merged with Swindon Victoria, becoming Malmesbury Victoria. In August 1976 David Pictor began an under 15 side and by the end of the decade there were four teams, two senior and two junior. The ground flooded again in December 1979.

The 1980s began with the long held ambition for a clubhouse being realised and teams in Wiltshire County League Divisions 1 and 3. The League comprised four Divisions with 18 teams in each. Problems continued with poor drainage, 23 matches were postponed, games had to be played at Seagry and Bremilham School. The Club spent £450 to improve the ground. Perhaps the pitch difficulties contributed to the first team being relegated to Division 2 and two years later to Division 3. In 1987/8 a new club, initially called the Kings Arms Kestrels, then Malmesbury Kestrels played in the Chippenham & District Sunday League Division 5. Although the Kestrels gained promotion, they seem to have faded away within a few years. Malmesbury Victoria clawed their way back to Division 2 although the second team was in Division 4. At the end of the decade the Malmesbury Youth Football Club (MYFC) started.

The Clubhouse was refurbished in 1991 and finances were helped by sponsorship from Hyam's Autos and Andy Nurden. Within two years an extension was required for the clubhouse and the senior team was runner up in Division 2. In the next season they were second in Division 1 but the League expressed concern about the lack of ground surrounding the pitch which had decreased due to river erosion. In 1999/2000 the club again topped the Wiltshire League and were promoted into the Hellenic League Division 1 West. For nine seasons they remained in that Division until they were runners up in 2008/9. However they only enjoyed a single season in the Premier Division before being relegated. Also the club was not able to provide the facilities demanded by the higher standard although floodlights were installed in 2004. Following severe financial difficulties mainly due to flooding in the winter of 2013/14 the club resigned from the Hellenic League in May 2014.

The Youth Football Club ran into difficulty when the education authority demanded payment for the use of the Primary School's ground so in 1993 they moved to White Lion Park. Within a year they had 150 young players, eight teams and needed more pitches. The planning authority provided a catalyst for change when only permission for 12 months was given for their temporary changing room. Lord Suffolk and Richard Fry of the Red Bull Inn came to their rescue by offering land next to the pub. In June 1996 planning permission was obtained and three full sized and three smaller pitches have been made. Comprehensive changing facilities costing £300,000 were opened in 2009.

Public Houses, Hotels and Beer Houses

From 1869 until 2005 the licensing of premises to sell alcohol was the responsibility of magistrates. This was an era of restrictions which has only recently been eased. The temperance movement developed at the end of the 19th Century and remained a strong force until the 1930s. The Government became concerned about drunkenness which led to the Habitual Drunkards Act of 1879 and a series of Inebriates Acts during the last years of that Century. The 1902 Licensing Act established compensation funds for licensees who were refused renewal of their licence due to the desire to encourage temperance. These were funded by a levy on all licensed premises. Alcohol licence duties were raised considerably in 1909 and again at the start of World War I. In 1915 the Government introduced very restricted opening hours to try to minimise absenteeism from munitions factories. This included a gap during the afternoon when pubs had to shut which remained in force for more than 70 years. It was also forbidden to buy drinks for anyone else. Two years later reductions were ordered in the gravity of beers to reduce their alcoholic strength. Beer consumption had halved by the war's end. The Licensing Act 1921 continued the restricted hours imposed during wartime. Only in 1988 was there a substantial relaxation of licensing hours with opening allowed between 11am and 11pm each weekday, and from noon until 3pm and 7pm to 10.30pm on Sundays. From 2005 the licensing authority became the District or Unitary Council.

Angel Inn, 5 Oxford Street

When acquired by the old Corporation in 1620 this was the Angel Inn but it is unclear when this usage ceased. The rear of these premises was converted into a meeting room by the Warden & Freemen in 1993. Recently this has been rented to commercial tenants.

Athelstan Inn, Cross Hayes

This was a beer house at the rear of 28-30 High Street which seems to have closed during the late 1880s. It was variously known as Athelstan's Head, King Athelstan, Athelstan's Arms and Athelstan Inn.

Barley Mow, 21 St Mary's Street

This operated as the Barley Mow beer house from at least the middle of the 19th Century to 1921. Luce's Brewery owned it from 1871 until the Stroud Brewery took over in 1912. The auction particulars read; *Stone-built, containing: Public Kitchen, Beer Store, Sitting-room, 3 Bedrooms and Attic. Yard in rear with Coalhouse, washing Shed, Stable, Pigstye and underground Cellar.* The Police objected to the renewal of licences at five local pubs in 1921 and the Stroud offered no opposition except for the Barley Mow. It was pointed out *the house accommodated a large number of wayfarers, whom the landlady, who was a war widow with three little children, supplied with food.* Unfortunately the landlady, Mrs. Minnie Salter (1881-1951), *admitted that to get to her stable, horses would have to come through the house.* The Magistrates expressed surprise such arrangements still existed and refused to renew the licence. In 1988 it became a dentists' surgery.

Bath Arms, 40 Horsefair

The Bath Arms opened its doors around 1850 and continued as a pub until publican Charles Emery (1900-1957) died. It was then used as an off licence but in 1995 closed due to business being taken by supermarkets and it became a private house.

Bear Inn, 53 High Street

One of the town's coaching inns, it became the Bear in the late 1830s but closed in 1963. The building dates back to the 18th Century although the pub was established the previous century. It was taken over by the Duck Brewery in 1896. In 1923 William Carter became the landlord having served in 12th Lancers during the First World War. He was very active in the local community and always gave any serviceman a warm welcome. After his death in 1942 his widow Elizabeth (1870-1964) continued to run the pub and lived in the premises after closure until her death. West Country Ales decided to concentrate on fewer, better pubs and felt money was better spent on the Rose & Crown and Three Cups. The frontage is now occupied by the Strakers Estate Agents with a number of other businesses around the courtyard behind.

The Bath Arms Off Licence with Mr. & Mrs. Smith in 1985. Until 1983 Mrs. Smith ran Joy's Store 34 Bristol Street. (Malmesbury Chronicles).

Black Horse Inn, Burton Hill

This pub is known to have existed for at least 150 years before it closed in 1971. This was one of the Duck Brewery pubs. Just before closure the darts team won many trophies being league champions for 18 out of 21 years before transferring to the Borough Arms. The building was bought and demolished by the Rural District Council which had a

The Black Horse Inn, 1964.

depot behind. The whole site was then developed into Barley Close and Orchard Court.

Black Swan, 14 High Street

The history of this pub has been difficult to establish. It seems to have been on the site of part of the Griffin Inn.

The Boot, 34/36 St. Johns Street

The surviving deeds of these cottages go back to 1880. These state *one of which cottages when occupied by William Clark was called the Boot Inn.* No record of this ale house has been found in 19th Century trade directories and although early census show a man of this name, his occupation is given as labourer.

Boulton's Barm & Beershop, 22 Gloucester Street

Barm is the foam on the top of fermented liquor which can be used to form brewer's and baker's yeast. It seems that William Boulton (1846-1906), who was also a breeches maker, opened this establishment around 1895 after coming to the town from Upton-on-Severn. Following his

The Borough Arms in 1964. Young, Sabey & Harris' electrical & radio shop in the foreground and the YMCA beyond.

The Brewery Tap in 1986 with the Bus Waiting Room on the right and Jenny Galbraith's Country Cousins occupying the rest. (Malmesbury Chronicles)

death his widow Ann (1853-1938) carried on the business for several years but she was no longer listed as a beer seller in 1915. Mrs. Boulton moved from these premises about 1933 and Herbert England (1904-1961) opened a turf accountant's here which was carried on by his son Douglas.

Borough Arms, 7 Oxford Street

In 1706 the Guildhall was split into smaller plots and the western part became a pub called the Boar's Head until around 1840 when it was renamed the Borough Arms. Still owned by the Old Corporation it was the only town pub which in the 1930s sold Warne's beer from their Tetbury brewery. In 2014 it closed and was empty at the time of writing.

Brewery Tap, 34 Cross Hayes

This beer house was next door to Cross Hayes brewery and was owned by Esau Duck. Mrs. Ann Garlick is listed as the publican in 1875 and the directories do not record any other keeper until Joseph Garlick (1843-1923) returned to Malmesbury at the start of the 20th Century. He remained in charge until his death when his daughter Maud (1879-1965) took over until closure in 1952. The Borough Council bought it from the Stroud Brewery two years later. It was used by them as a bus shelter on the ground floor with the Royal British Legion and Civil Defence using the upper floors in the 1960s. An oak table made from a tree in Cross Hayes was removed from here to the Town Hall.

Castle Inn, 82 The Triangle

Opened in 1662 as the Weavers Arms, it probably changed its name to the Castle Inn at the beginning of the 19th Century when the Old Bell Hotel no longer used that name. Joseph Moore (1828-1866 & unrelated to the family at the Bell) was a licensee whose obituary read; *At a very early age he entered the army as a cavalry soldier ... and passed through many hardships, and some service during the Crimean war, for which he was rewarded by several medals, and a pension. His honours were, medals for good conduct in the field, the Turkish medal, and the medal and clasps for Inkerman and Balaclava. It was at the latter affair that Mr. Moore lost his right arm, he being one of the gallant 600 who made the dashing charge under Lord Cardigan. We have seen the brave fellow moved to tears*

at the mention of Miss Nightingale, from whom, we believe, he had received special attention while in hospital. The pub was taken over by Luce's Brewery in 1890. In 1912 its accommodation was described as; *Tap-room and pantry adjoining, Bar, Service bar, Parlour Club-room, 5 Bedrooms and Attic, Yard in rear, with Wash-house and Wood-shed, outer Yard with Stabling and Entrance from Burnivale.* It was closed by West Country Brewery in 1961 who stated *with 13 public houses and a population of 2,700, Malmesbury is a town that is "over-pubbed."* Max Woosnam's plans to turn it into a bistro never came about, Charles and Mary White turned it into an art gallery in the 1970s but it is now a private house.

The Castle in the 1930s with a Stroud Brewery lorry (R. Wiles)

The Castle just before closure. In the background is the general store at No. 34 Bristol Street run by M. F. Tidd at this time, later called Joy's Store when Joy Smith was in charge.

Coopers Arms, Tetbury Road
Situated near Sunset Hill about two miles from the town, this was always regarded as a Malmesbury pub. As was usual for these small hostelries, the landlord required another income which in this case was farm manager. In 1955 the licence was transferred to Percy Hazell of Lytchett Matravers, Dorset whose wife was related to a former landlord of the Duke of York. The pub was renowned for the considerable number of brass ornaments on the walls of the bar. Two years after Mr. Hazell took over Police Sergeant Mallard observed through a chink in the curtain six people in the bar at 10.50pm, two of whom were fined £1 each for drinking after hours and Mr. Hazell received a £5 fine for aiding and abetting them. The following year the Stroud Brewery relinquished the licence and sold the property with 25 acres to Mr. Hazell.

Crown
There was a pub of this name in town around 1540 but there is nothing further known about it.

Europa Restaurant (Guildhall), 9 Oxford Street
In 1411 Henry IV gave permission for a merchant guild hall to be built. Monarchs strictly controlled places where large public gatherings could be held. The Europa is probably this building. The oak roof has been dated circa 1420 and there is a rare late medieval pottery finial on the front of the gable end. Originally the hall would have been bigger, probably with seven bays rather than the existing four. It was probably reduced in size around a century later and reconstructed with stone walls instead of oak columns infilled with wattle and daub. The outlines of doors and windows can be seen in the sidewall remaining from when the building was divided into two cottages. Inside there is a fireplace high up the wall. The Old Corporation met here from 1414 to 1542. Refurbished in 1989 and used as the Old Guildhall Restaurant from 1991 to 1994, it then became the Guildhall pub. Unfortunately the customers of this establishment gained a reputation for anti-social behaviour and after the licence was suspended for a time, the pub closed in 2013. The freeholders, the Old Corporation, found a new tenant who converted the premises into a restaurant which opened in February 2014.

The George Veterinary Hospital (George Hotel), 20 High Street
A coaching inn with origins in the 16th Century, the present building dates from 1788. Richard Jefferies in 1867 wrote; *The George Commercial Hotel, where good accommodation can be obtained for man and horse at moderate charges, and where the antiquary may congratulate himself upon residing in a house that has been established nearly two centuries.* The main doorway was originally an open archway allowing coaches through the building and wheel ruts can still be seen. In 1929 the publican, George Gay, during a visit of Chapman's Zoo sat in the lions' cage to drink two bottles of beer. The hotel closed in 1977. Plans to redevelop it into shops and offices or a supermarket failed.

In 1978 Messrs. Oura, Griffin and Bown moved their veterinary practice here. It had started in the 1930s when Major Robert Tindle (1883-1961) began a horse practice working from Quarry House, Corston. Mr. Llewellyn 'Nipper' Constance (1917-1993) who had been invalided out of the Royal Army Veterinary Corps joined him in 1942. Treating cattle and (unusual for the time) small animals, Nipper operated from Rodbourne, moving to Lea and finally in 1949 to Burnham House, Malmesbury. Just after the end of the war Peter Oura joined. When Mr. Constance left the partnership in 1964 to run a horse practice in Didmarton, Peter became the sole partner assisted by Roger Griffin who had joined a couple of years before. Burnham House was sold and the practice continued from 97 Gloucester Road where Mr. Griffin became a partner. Peter Bown became an assistant in 1968 and later the junior partner. The practice was renamed the George Veterinary Hospital after the move and in the 36 years since taking up residence has become a substantial business. There are branch surgeries in Royal Wootton Bassett and Tetbury with an equine clinic at Garsdon.

The George Hotel in 1924 at the time of King Athelstan's Millenary. No. 22 has changed considerably.

Griffin Inn, 12-18 High Street

Part of the building dates back to 1390 but it is mostly of mid 16th Century origin. Aubrey reported that *Hughes of Wootton Bassett saises that the steeple of Malmesbury Abbey was as high as Paul's and that when the steeple fell, the ball of it fell as far as the Griffin.* In other words the Abbey spire was as high as St Paul's Cathedral and the golden orb at its tip ended up here when the tower collapsed. The Griffin was in use as a pub in 1540 and 1751 but it closed before 1765. The 1803 Manorial survey described the building as: *a large messuage or tenement, formerly the Griffin Inn, in the Corn Market of the High Street – the front lately rebuilt with brick with extensive outbuildings and courtyard, in the occupation of Thomas Hill and son, John Hill; having a freehold house of John Player on the North, and the George Inn on the South thereof.* The pub originally straddled Griffin Alley with stables at the rear and there are a number of wooden beams and squat low doorways visible along the Alley.

Kings Arms Hotel, 29 High Street

A late 16th or early 17th Century inn re-named for the restoration of Charles II. The timber bay windows are 18th Century additions. Its yard used to extend to Olivers Lane, where the flying monk Eilmer is said to have landed in 1010. This was a popular farmers' pub where much money changed hands on market days. The yard was the equivalent of a modern car park - horses & coaches were left here whilst their owners went about their business. Even up until the 1920s an ostler was based here. It is said that Sir Ronald Bouchier, a Royalist Cavalier who carried messages between Bristol and Oxford was murdered whilst staying here overnight. His ghost apparently haunts the room above the archway. This rather tall ghost story was recounted in the Daily Mirror of 17th June 1935 and is reproduced in Stan Hudson's book, *A Hilltop Town*.

On 30th May 1831 this was the venue for a dinner for supporters of the Reform Bill. There were 140 guests including the borough-monger, Joseph Pitt. The speakers did not pull their punches – the Chairman, George Powlet Scrope must have made Mr. Pitt uncomfortable with; *The Boroughmonger, Gentlemen, is an animal of unclean habits and vicious propensities. Like the swine, he is fond of wallowing in the mire, and corruption is his natural element. He has the ravenous appetite of the wolf; but he has also many qualities of the ass, so that naturalists are undecided to which of these genera to refer him, partaking as he does of all three.* R. Gordon MP for Cricklade included these words; *Even in the County of Wilts, where there are so many sinks of impurity and corruption, the Borough of Malmesbury stands pre-eminent,* and John Lewis; *This Borough, the rottenest of all other rotten boroughs, must ... be cleansed of the impurity with which it has been so long deluded.*

Harry Jones (1853-1911) took over as the landlord in 1880 after the death of his father Thomas who was the previous licensee. Harry was Mayor in 1885, started the custom of having an annual Civic Church Service, was the first to wear robes of office and presented the Council's emblem of authority, the silver mace. The eulogy delivered at his funeral gives a detailed picture; *For upwards of 30 years Mr. Jones has been one of the most conspicuous figures in the town. He had a distinctive personality. He was one of those rare and isolated individuals who, once seen, are never forgotten. He has been described by the author of a "Travel through Ten Counties" as a veritable John Bull in the flesh, and also as the embodiment of the spirit of Charles Dickens, either of which generalisations fitted him exactly. His portly form and jolly, red face were set off to perfection in the old-world habitaments which he delighted to affect – trousers turned up to the ankles, a long loose-fitting coat of a cut of other days, a white or brightly coloured waistcoat of the Dick Swiveller pattern, and on his head a tall, straight-brimmed white hat of a style which was popular in the middle of the last century, and which was in truth, and in fact, his crowning glory. In winter and summer, in sunshine and shadow, his features wore a perpetual smile, and he was perhaps as well known as any man in England. That had been proved in several ways. On several occasions friends in America, on writing to him, have merely sketched Mr. Jones's familiar lineaments, or adorned the envelope with his portrait, accompanied with the injunction "Find him in Wiltshire," and in every instance the letter reached its destination in safety. In one instance the only instruction to the postal authorities were a few lines scratched in the resemblance of an overturned colander with the accompanying words. "His Hat, Wiltshire," and even this found its*

Mr. & Mrs. Jones outside the King's Arms Hotel. The iron railings were removed for scrap in World War 2.
Tom Rich, fishmonger, ice merchant and game dealer occupied No. 27.

way to Mr. Jones's hands.

In the principal room ... there is a remarkable and, we should say, unique collection of communications in small oak frames. Any event of importance which happened in the lives of the Royal Family called forth Mr. Jones's respectful congratulations or sympathies, and replies to these were received from her late Majesty Queen Victoria, the late King Edward VII, the present King, the German Emperor, the King of Spain, Mr. Asquith, Mr. A. J. Balfour, and Lord Lansdowne, amongst others.

Many famous personalities stayed at the Inn (he disliked the word hotel) and King Edward VII called in whenever he was in the area. The path between the High Street and Kings Wall by the Post Office was to be called King Edward the Seventh's Walk but this was too much of a mouthful and was shortened to King's Walk.

Knoll House Hotel, Swindon Road
For many tears home of the Luce family it became vacant in 1967. After being used as a private house from which the owner unlawfully conducted his engineering business, it became a small hotel with 6 bedrooms in 1979. Five years later new owners obtained permission to open the public to the public not just residents and carried out a £100,000 refit. By 1989 there were 22 bedrooms and permission was granted for a 15 bed extension but the owners put it up for sale. It was bought by a new company from Kingston, Surrey but within five years the company was in receivership. New owners obtained a good reputation being awarded 4 stars by the English Tourist Board and 3 stars & 2 food rosettes by the Michelin Guide. Unfortunately after the closure of nearby Lucent Technologies, the hotel closed in 2003. Permission was granted for a small housing development but during the building the body of a murdered young woman was found on the site. The hotel extension was demolished, the original house turned into 3 dwellings with other new houses built in the grounds.

The Knoll House Hotel in 1985. (Malmesbury Chronicles)

Lamb Inn, 63 Gloucester Road

This is a 17th Century house which was divided into three a century later. At some stage this was a pub but no details are known.

Nags Head, 38 Gloucester Street

This was a beer house with its own brewhouse in the garden. In 1799 it was bought by John Garlick, the High Street butcher who changed its name to the Jolly Butcher. However it reverted to being a dwelling house in 1805. At the end of the 19th Century the house was converted into a Saddler & Harness Maker's shop by James Hobbs. He was born in Porlock and came to Malmesbury in the 1860s, originally living in Gloucester Road, then at the Triangle but at the time of the 1901 census was at No 38. He traded as James Hobbs & Son (his son Robert had worked with him but died in 1897). James' wife Mary died in 1904 and he seems to have moved shortly afterwards. Arthur Watts continued the business and is thought to have added the shopfront. The premises were then taken over by Arthur Tanner in 1922, who followed the same trade but later sold fancy leather goods. Around 1965 it became a Do It Yourself shop called the Kit Box. Eric & Olive Brown owned the shop for 25 years after 1973.

Oddfellows Inn, 49 The Triangle

In 1596 there is mention of a grammar school in the Sheepfair opposite the Three Cups and it was probably here. The master, Robert Latimer, instructed Thomas Hobbes and later taught John Aubrey. The Oddfellows Inn on this site was supposed to have been opened in 1799 and it closed before being sold by the Stroud Brewery to J. H. Wilkins in 1921. About 10 years later it became the premises of a hairdresser and continued as such until 1980. By the early 1990s it had become a private house.

Old Bell Hotel, 13/17 Abbey Row

Bishop Roger of Sarum upgraded the town's defences by building a stone castle on this site very close to the monastery about 1130. The monks disliked the close proximity of soldiers and arranged the demolition at the first opportunity after the King gave permission in 1216. During an excavation when the hotel car park was extended, remains of what was probably the castle keep were found.

The Old Bell in 1910 with the flag at half-mast following the death of King Edward VII.

It is thought that Abbot Walter Loring (Abbot from 1208-1244) had a new building put up on the site of the demolished castle in around 1220 to house his important guests. Although much altered, the stone hooded fireplace in the Great Hall dates from this period. It is because the building has catered for guests continuously from then that the Old Bell claims to be England's oldest hotel. The facade dates from the 18th Century but the rear elevation is older. It has been open as a pub since at least 1703, originally known as the Castle. The name was changed to the Bell in 1798. Just after the turn of the 20th Century, the owner Joseph Moore (1858-1947) is supposed to have found a hoard of gold which enabled him to carry out extensive works. Two cottages adjoining the Bell to the west were demolished leaving only the front wall (which is still there). At the same time he bought Castle House to the east. This together with a large extension to the west was completed in 1908 (see the date stone JM 1908 on the eastern chimney) and it was renamed the Old Bell Hotel. The Moore family sold the hotel in 1930 after nearly a century's ownership.

Castle House was a 17th Century house occupied by two 'little Miss Luces', (Susannah Hollis 1823-1905 & Sarah Grace 1835-1887) before it was incorporated into the Bell. They kept a pony with a four-wheeled carriage and held bible classes for women every Sunday afternoon. After Susannah's death Harry Duck lived here for about a year before Jo Moore bought it.

Plough Inn, 12 Foxley Road

The Plough, built around 1840, was known as the 'last and the first' for Commoners going to work on their allotments on King's Heath. It sold only beer until 1961 when it was granted a full licence. Mrs. Amy Slade was the publican between 1917 and 1946, being succeeded by her son Arthur who carried on until closure in 1970. During the 1950s you might have come across Harold Macmillan (1894-1986) who used to drop in for a pint of beer here during his term as Prime Minister when he visited his daughter then living at Thornhill Farm.

The Plough Inn, 1964. After conversion into a private house a second storey was added in the middle.

Prince and Princess, Market Cross
Situated to the north of the Market Cross this beer house was open through the 19th Century until the late 1880s. It was regarded as a den of iniquity, a resort of thieves and worse, a sheer mockery of its genteel title. Owned by the Luce Brewery it was demolished and the land to the east of it was given by Charles Luce to a panel of

The building on the right was a Reading Room and Sunday School. The Prince and Princess had a narrow frontage but the site wrapped around the Reading Room.

trustees who built the Cottage Hospital here in 1896.

Railway Hotel (Flying Monk), 120 Gloucester Road

The Railway Hotel was built in 1875, shortly before the railway was completed and directly opposite the station. Originally called the Railway Commercial and Farming Hotel and Posting House, its first landlord was Harry Jones who moved to the Kings Arms in 1880. A skittles alley

was added in 1953 and of course there was extra business when the market met in the meadow behind. Following the closure of the railway in 1964 the brewery held a competition for a new name and that chosen was the Flying Monk. The pub acted as headquarters for Malmesbury Victoria Football Club for many years and its successful darts team transferred to the Old Bell. It was demolished in 1984 to make way for the Gateway store, the

Before flood relief measures in the 1980s the Railway Hotel was sometimes cut off although its high floor level saved the interior.

development of which was delayed apparently because the land belonged to British Rail rather than the brewery which had sold it. Probably this was a result of the Wilts and Gloucestershire Railway scheme which came to naught.

Rajah Restaurant (Green Dragon), 6 Market Cross

The Green Dragon at the end of the 19th Century. The gas lamp to the left of the Market Cross was moved after the introduction of motor cars.

Originally an Abbey hospitium (guest house) in the grand days of the 14th Century, this building still contains an original stairway. It seems to have been called the Green Dragon for centuries until 1921. This pub was reputed to sell only pints of beer, no halves! At the time of the sale of the Luce property to Stroud Brewery the accommodation was; *Smoke-room, Serving-bar, Kitchen, Scullery, Pantry, Beer Cellar and 2 Bedrooms. Small yard in rear with Wash-house, &c. Large Cellar in basement.* A proposal to raise funds from the public to purchase the building and pull it down so the Abbey could be better seen was defeated due to its antiquity. The last licensee, Robert Roper (1863-1947) turned the premises into the Abbey Café. It was renamed the Apostle Spoon, after an old spoon found there, in 1977 until closure in 1996. After being unoccupied for a period, the Rajah Indian Restaurant opened in 1998.

Red Bull, Sherston Road

Although in Brokenborough parish, being so close this pub is used by townsfolk. It seems to have been started by William Fry (1843-1906) in the second half of the 19th Century. On his death his son Harry Fry (1879-1953) took over followed by his son, Victor (b1915) who in turn was succeeded by his son Richard (b1949). The family's connection continues. Malmesbury Youth Football Club began using pitches next to the pub and in 2008 £290,000 was spent on clubhouse facilities for them.

Red Lion, 2 High Street

There was a pub called the Red Lion Inn here in the late 18th Century. A lease was granted to Thomas Player in 1783 for the Inn, but another lease referred to *messuages lately built on the ground on which the Red Lion Inn formerly stood*. The further history is explained under High Street shops.

Rose & Crown Inn, 102 High Street

This is an 18th Century building which had this name first as a private house and then as a pub since at least 1830. To the left of the doorway look out for the etched window with the Stroud Brewery's name. This was one of Luce's establishments and the 1912 description was; *Brick-built and rough cast, with a frontage of about 63 feet to Lower High-street, containing: Tap-room, Parlour and Bar adjoining, Sitting-room, Beer Cellar, Wash-house and Scullery, and 5 Bedrooms and Loft, large Yard with 2-stall Stable, Loose Box, Coal and wood Shed, good Garden, 2 Pigstyes and Meal Shed.* Frederick James Woodward (1884-1959) was licensee for over 50 years until his death when his daughter, Edith Castle, took over for another seven years. The pub was shut for

The Rose and Crown in the early 20th Century before the High Street was tarmaced.

six months in 1985 after Bud Barnes shut the doors when he had incurred over £2,000 in parking fines. Having lost a leg in an accident, he found walking difficult but was not granted a disabled parking permit.

Royal Oak Inn, Foxley
This was located on Highfield Farm adjacent to the Common. Although not strictly part of Malmesbury this was an important place for the Commoners who would call in for a drink after new members had been 'turfed and twigged' on New Year's Day. Because of this connection it was known as the Slappy Arms. In 1892 it was rendered unfit for habitation after two walls collapsed causing the roof to fall in. It must have been rebuilt as it closed in 1924 but has since been demolished.

Salutation, Tower House
This inn was part of the northern range of Tower House but it closed before 1803.

Saracens Head, 31 Holloway
There is supposed to have been an inn of this name here.

Shoe Inn, 2 Cross Hayes Lane
This was a beer house known as the Shoe on which a lease was granted in 1792.

Smoking Dog (Greyhound Inn), 62 High Street
The deeds show that the Greyhound Inn opened in 1760 and remained a pub to just after 1875. Henry Long was the owner in the 1870s and ran an omnibus from here to Chippenham until competition from the railway forced him out of that business (he was previously publican of the Green Dragon, Market Cross which had been the pick-up point). At the end of the 19th Century the Greyhound became a cafe and temperance hotel originally run by Charles Wynn. It was a hostel for the Cyclists Touring Club (the name adopted in 1883 by the Bicycle Touring Club of Great Britain which was formed at Harrogate in 1878) where a room could be had for 2s. 6d. Their emblem remains on the outside wall. It remained the Temperance Hotel until the Second World

180

War, later becoming the Avon Cafe until 1986, when it reopened as the Old Greyhound Inn. it was renamed the Smoking Dog in 1989.

Spice Merchant (Duke of York), Holloway

This pub probably dates back to the 18th Century. It used to own land next to the river on Blicks Hill and in 1899 there were complaints about the noise coming from steam round-abouts, a steam organ and screaming siren whistles of a fun fair there. Later the land became a Caravan site. The building was described in 1912: *Stone and Brick built, containing: Tap-room, Smoke-room, and Serving Bar, 2 Sitting-rooms, Kitchen, Lobby and 2 Bedrooms, Dairy adjoining, Range of Stabling, Meal House and Pig Stye, also large Club Room with 2 Bedrooms and Lumber-room over, large Yard in*

The Avon Cafe in 1985, now the Smoking Dog. (Malmesbury Chronicles)

The Duke of York before demolition.

rear, with range of Out-buildings, Cart and Calf Sheds, brick yard, Kitchen Garden and Pigstye.

In 1962 West Country Breweries obtained permission to demolish the pub and replace it with *an even grander* prefabricated building which was expected to be put up in a week. However the plan was amended the next year to provide *a cedar-wood building of the Swedish principle* with a prospective life of 150 years rather than 10-15 years. The new building now well set back from the road included a skittle alley and was opened in October 1963.

Suffolk Arms, Tetbury Hill

Originally a farmhouse, a beer licence was first granted in 1857. It was another 100 years until a full licence was obtained. In 1958 it was enlarged with a new restaurant and kitchen. The landlord sought publicity by inviting ITV to film the Smokers' Club Including the Earl of Suffolk. TV cameras came back in 1967 after the breathalyser was introduced when eight customers arrived on horseback. The following year the pub was listed in the Egon Ronay Guide, gaining their top award in 1987. Unfortunately this good reputation was lost in 1998 when it became part of the Red Rooster chain and there were complaints about its appearance. It was closed in February 2003 after a fight to keep it open. A year later planning permission was given for 19 houses called Minot Close after a former Mayor.

The Suffolk Arms, 1964. In the 1990s the restaurant was very popular.

Travellers Rest Inn, 1 West Street

Early in the 19th Century these premises were used as a pub with a malthouse in the courtyard behind. It was closed sometime later that century. Its yard to the east was later used by the GPO as a garage and afterwards by Cross Hayes Antiques until the modern house at 19 Bristol Road was erected in 2002.

Three Horseshoes, 11 Oxford Street

A spirits licence was granted to the Three Horseshoes in 1867. Behind there was a stable and yard with a blacksmith's shop close to the entry into Cross Hayes. Edward Fry (1852-1925) was the licensee from around 1890 and also a carrier running a service to Cirencester and Kemble railway station on Mondays and Fridays until the First World War. He was still the publican when the licence was surrendered by the brewery in 1921. His widow Lavinia (1856-1937) used the premises as a tobacconist's. On her death the Borough Council bought it with the intention of demolishing it to widen Cross Hayes Lane. This scheme was delayed by the war when the building was used as the town library and by the ARP until it was handed over to the County Council in 1955. Two years later it was knocked down.

Three Cups Inn, 90 Triangle

A pub has been on this site from the 15th Century. The present building dates back to the 17th Century although it has been much altered. The right-hand rear wing was probably extended to include No. 2 St Mary's Street. In the first Elizabethan age cloth buyers and yarn sellers would stay here. The pub was reputed to have been the headquarters of General Waller in March 1643 when he was besieging the town. It also featured in a case heard in the Court of Chancery in 1702. Henry Chapman, a butcher of Westport died in 1699. He was the leaseholder of the Three Cups which was apparently worth £300 and he was 'esteemed to be a very rich man.' However he died owing money to a number of people who sued his brother in law and landlord who were alleged to have taken many of the assets of the estate. They said that Chapman was poor and that the inn was frequented by coal-wainers (carriers of coal) and travellers in summer but had little or no custom in winter. By 1930 the Stroud Brewery had renovated the pub, installed electric light and it was reported that *the old inn looks as if it is coming back into its own again.*

The Three Cups in 1901 with a sign at the entrance to Katifer Lane drawing attention to the Fire Station.

Whitbread Flowers refurbished the pub in 1968 but there was an eight week delay after the Civic Trust objected to the use of inappropriate roof tiles. Now owned by Enterprise Inns it has proved difficult to find a permanent tenant.

Unicorn, 92 High Street

This building has been altered many times over the years. It probably started off in the 14th Century as a house side on to the road. During the 17th Century it was a coaching inn called the Unicorn, note the large upper windows with eyebrow mouldings of that period. A niche on the front elevation may have held a model of a unicorn. There was a large courtyard behind. The house was used by Ekco workers during the Second World War when it was split into 3 separate dwellings. Now restored to one house it is privately occupied and is Grade II* listed.

Volunteer, 133 High Street

An early 17th Century building with the front rebuilt in 1835. From the middle of the 19th Century it became the American Volunteer Inn, later shortened to just the Volunteer but this was closed by the brewery in 1921.

Whatley Manor Hotel

Originally called Twatley Manor and built in 1746 the building was greatly extended by Herbert Cox, President of Canada Life Assurance who lived here between 1925 and 1937. Converted

into an hotel in 1974 with 15 bedrooms it was bought in 2000 by Marco and Alix Landolt who spent three years remodelling it into the height of luxury for its guests.

White Lion, 8 Gloucester Street

This name apparently dates back to the 15th Century when the innkeeper, to demonstrate loyalty, adopted the Royal Crest of King Edward IV as his sign. It is said that the King stayed here before the battle of Tewkesbury. Richard Jefferies said the White Lion was *an inn of very antiquated appearance. The walls are said to be of immense thickness. It is considered to have been an appendage to the abbey, used as an hospitium, or place to entertain travellers, which office it still fulfils.* It probably dates back to the 12th Century. Its frontage would have opened on to the medieval market place with the rear courtyard extending to the

The White Lion before the removal of the bow window.

town walls encompassing the present Gloucester House. This yard was used by a travelling circus during the early 18th Century. Hannah Twynnoy, a maid at the inn, teased the tiger, a very rare attraction at the time, which escaped its shackles and killed her. Her gravestone is in the Abbey grounds, halfway between the Tolsey Gate and the main door. It is curious that a servant not only had a burial with expensive headstone in the Abbey but also a memorial in Hullavington church until renovations were carried out there in the 1870s. Clearly there is more to this story than we know. During the run up to the Reform Act 1832 a banquet was held here for the non-reform party which led to a virtual riot outside. Its bow window was removed in 1964 after frequently being damaged by high vehicles. It was closed in 1970 and the stained glass widow with a white lion and the inscription 'Lord Mercy' was presented to the Athelstan Museum.

White Swan, 41 High Street
During the 18th Century there was a pub here called the White Swan. A timetable of 1773 showed that a coach left for Holborn Bridge, London every Wednesday. The pub closed around 1800 and the building was split into tenements either side of Berry's Entry, so called after the proprietor of the property. Later J. E. Ponting built the Post Office on the site. Since its closure it has been occupied by Mindvision, a graphic design company.

Whole Hog, 8 Market Cross
Charles Luce gave premises previously used as the Prince & Princess pub and the Friendly Sabbath School on the corner (which prior to 1870 also served as a Reading Room) to be converted into the hospital. Re-built in 1896 the hospital outgrew these premises and moved to The Manor House on the Chippenham Road at Burton Hill in 1925. The old building was bought by Jones & Son who extended it towards the Market Cross with a shopfront. Between 1935 and 1969 it was the office for the Gas Company, then a cafe and a restaurant before once again becoming a pub in 1991. It gained worldwide fame when the press descended upon it during the escape of the 'Tamworth Two' pigs in 1998.

XXX, St. Michael's House, 14 Market Cross
This is believed to have been the site of St. Michael's Chapel, an original monastery chapel built by Aldhelm. One of his first miracles is said to have occurred during its construction. Many expensive roof timbers were cut ready for use but one was too short. The craftsmen brought this to Aldhelm's attention and after he prayed it was found to fit! This church was burnt down twice and each time this rafter was the only roof timber to survive the destruction. The present building dates from 1796 and has been used as a school, a malt house and at the beginning of the 20th Century the XXX Inn. It was bought by the Countess of Suffolk in 1921 and presented to the Hospital for a maternity ward but was used as accommodation for nurses prior to the move in 1925. Later used as offices in 2003 it was refurbished, being turned into a townhouse and flat with a cottage at the rear.

Index

Hilditch Ltd. 136
Hill, Ernest 120
Hill, Francis 80
Hinwood family 100/1, 119, 127
Hitchings, Leonard 100
H. J. Knee Ltd. 96/7
Hobbes Close 63
Hobbes, Thomas 15, 176
Hodder family 93-95, 117
Hodge, Dr. Bernulf 40, 60, 146
Holloway 45, 54, 56, 86/7, 160, 180/1
Home Guard 26
Horsefair 20, 49, 126, 168
Hoskins, Michael 135/6
Hospital 22, 41-44, 69, 129, 145, 147-151, 157/8, 164/5, 178, 185
House of Lorraine 118
HSBC 98
Hudson, Stan 39, 111
Hullavington, RAF 27
Hulse, Jackie 20
Hyams Autos 113/4, 167

India Tea Stores 94
Ingram Street 24, 130, 147, 154/5, 159
International Stores 109, 113/4
Ireson, Miss 106

Jackson, Percy 110/1, 155
James, Andy 61
Jeary & Lewis 52, 153
Jefferies, Richard 29, 121, 143, 173
Jones, Charles 159
Jones family 20, 34, 37, 89, 93, 96-98, 107/8, 116, 129
Jones, Florence 108, 111
Jones, Harry 37, 40, 58, 160, 174/5, 178
Jordan 24
Joys Store 169, 171
Jupe, Charles 14, 122

Keene, Sidney 104
Kings Arms Hotel 37, 58, 87, 125, 156, 160/1, 167, 173-175, 178
Kings Church 16-18
Kings Heath 28/9, 130, 177
Kings House 75, 123
Knoll House 76/7, 175
K Shoes 99

Larive, Father 21, 22
Lewis, John 112
Lewis, Michael 43
Lewis, Norman 93/4
Library 117, 181
Linolite Ltd. 55, 58, 65, 68, 123/4, 135, 151, 153, 159, 161

Lloyds Bank 100, 109
Lloyds Chemists 100, 114
Lockstone family 77/8, 118, 126
London Central Meat Co. 107, 112, 120
Luce family 12, 22, 26, 32, 34, 41, 75-77, 87, 100, 102/3, 105/6, 120, 123-125, 144, 155, 161, 171, 175, 177-179, 185
Lullus 9, 153
Lux Traffic Light Controls Ltd. 136
Lyne family 95, 107, 126

Maildulph 7
Maison D'Arcy 118
Maison Let 118
Malmesbury & District Twinning Association 152/3
Malmesbury & St. Paul Without Residents' Assoc 152
Malmesbury Borough Council 18, 22/3, 32-34, 36-38, 45, 48, 50, 52/3, 56, 59, 60, 62-64, 88, 117, 136, 142, 153, 166, 170, 181
Malmesbury Building Supples 111
Malmesbury Civic Trust 58, 64, 71, 151-153, 183
Malmesbury League of Friends 43/4, 150
Malmesbury Rendezvous 115
Malmesbury River Valleys Trust 151, 153
Malmesbury Rocks 95
Malmesbury Rural District Council 34, 37/8, 45, 50, 53, 59, 60, 63/4, 88, 109, 169
Malmesbury Town Council 32-34, 141, 143/4, 152, 155, 160
Malmesbury Vintners 103
Malpass, Stan 103
Maltings 65, 125
Manor House 77/8
Market Cross 26, 28, 33, 36, 41, 62, 131, 142-144, 178/9, 185
Marmont family 98, 125
Maslin, Keith 119
Matthews family 136/7
Mattick, Arthur 103, 110
May, James 107
Messiter, James 107
Methodist Chapel, 19, 20, 23, 122
Midland Bank 98, 145
Miles, Lt. Col. Charles 57, 71, 145
Miles, William 103
Milk factory 137/8
Mistral Clothing 112
Minerva Gallery 95, 119
Moir, Charles 51
Moore, Joseph 42, 68, 147, 155, 176
Moore Stephens 109
Moravian Church 19, 20, 91
Morse, Dennis 98, 100
Mortimer, Jacob 106
Mott, John 83, 128, 129, 165
Mundens 74, 78

St. Johns Bridge 31, 55, 151
St. Johns Street 28, 49, 53, 56, 66
St. Mary's Church 13/4, 16, 30, 54, 146/7
St. Marys Street 14/5, 20, 43, 54, 168
St. Michael's House 7, 42
St. Paul's Church 11, 13, 30, 142
Staines Bridge 54
Stainsbridge House 79, 87/8
Stainsbridge Mill 45, 116
Star Restaurant 111
Stephen, King 24, 49
Stitchcraft 117
Storey family 71
Strakers Estate Agents 105
Strange family 93/4, 106
Stroud Brewery 23, 123-125, 164, 168, 170/1, 176,
    179, 183
Stumpe, William 10/1, 66, 80
Summer Cafe 107
Suffolk family 41/2, 53, 56, 140, 143, 145, 155, 161,
    167, 182, 185
Summers, Francis 99
Sweetnam & Bradley Ltd. 140
Swimming pool 142, 145, 150
Symonds, Ray 111

Tanner, George 114/5
Tarantula 93
Taylor, H. C. 118/9
Teagle & Son 112
Telephone 37, 48/9
Tennis 164/5
That New Shop 108
Thomas, Thomas 119
Thompson, William 111
Thornbury, James 101
Thornbury, William 115
Three Cups Inn 15, 91, 125, 156/7, 161, 164, 169,
    176, 181, 183/4
Threshers 103
Thrush family 99
Tower House 40, 53, 78, 80/1, 180
Town Hall 18, 23, 25, 33/4, 36-39, 50, 127, 130, 144,
    145, 150/1, 159, 165, 170
Town wall 24
Trade Centre 102
Triangle 23, 55, 157, 171, 176, 181
Truckle Bridge 32, 49, 54
Twynnoy, Hannah 185

Unicorn Inn 128, 184
United Reformed Church 14/5, 151

Verona House 69, 82, 141
Vets 69, 70, 111/2, 172
Vizard, Jacob 102

Waite family 103/4
Wakefield family 93/4, 108
Walker, James 116, 120
Walkers Grocers 96
Walker, William 109
Wall, George 107
Walton Design 112
War Memorial 27, 33, 55, 151, 157
Warden & Freemen, 28-32, 64, 67, 73/4, 84, 168, 180
Water 45, 66
Weeks family 105
Wesley, John 19
Wesleyan Methodist Chapel 22/3
West Country Cleaners 95, 117
West Street 64
Westhill House 82/3, 116
Westport House 68
Wheadon, Bill 116, 147
Wheal, Mary 106
Wheeler, Herbert 103
White family 93, 104
White Horse Inn 119
White Lion Inn 25, 58, 142, 156, 161, 164, 166, 184/5
White Lion Park 64, 142, 147, 167
Whiteoak, M. 100
W. H. Smith & Son 116/7
Wild Food Co. 112
Wilkins, Edmond 73/4
Wilkins, Henry 119
William of Malmesbury 9
Willis Brothers 135, 140/1, 166
Willsdons Confectioners 95, 98/9, 112
Wilts & Dorset Bank 20, 100
Wilts & Gloucestershire Standard 105, 141, 161
Wiltshire County Council 38/9, 53, 56, 60, 69, 89, 143
Wiltshire Gazette 34, 116, 119
Wiltshire Regiment 25/6, 73, 123
Wine Rack 103
Witts, Colin 99
Wood & Co. 95
Woodward, Alan, 98
Workbox, the 112/3
Workhouse 32, 42, 62, 64, 68/9, 80/1
Wortheys 32, 161-163, 165
Wright, Howard 103
Wyles Shoes 94
Wynyard Mill 72, 160

Yarnold, Frederick 99
YMCA 22/3, 41/2, 49, 125, 127, 164, 170
Yorkshire Insurance Co. 112
Young Sabey & Harris 170
Youth Centre 26, 141, 152, 155, 159

Xograph Healthcare Ltd. 141
XXX Inn 42, 185